REMARKABLE
ANIMALS

REMARKABLE ANIMALS

A UNIQUE ENCYCLOPAEDIA
OF WILDLIFE WONDERS

GUINNESS BOOKS

REMARKABLE ANIMALS has been
designed and produced by
Johnston & Company, Gothenburg,
Sweden.
Project editor and designer:
Ulla Sundén
Copy editor: David A. Christie
Typography: Lena Gustavsson

Published in Great Britain by
Guinness Superlatives Ltd,
33 London Road, Enfield, Middlesex

Typeset by concept Crayford, Kent,
Great Britain
Lithography by Offset-Kopio, Helsinki,
Finland
Printed and bound in Belgium by
Brepols BV, Turnhout

**British Library Cataloguing in
Publication Data**

Guinness remarkable animals: a unique
encyclopedia of wildlife wonders.
  1. Animals — Dictionaries
  591'.03'21   QL7

ISBN 0-85112-867-X

CONTENTS

MAMMALS

The most recent of all the animal lineages, the mammals evolved from an extinct group of small reptiles some 200 million years ago during the age of the dinosaurs. They differ from other animal groups in bringing forth live young, in feeding these on secretions produced by special glands (the 'mammary glands' from which their name derives), in having hair instead of feathers or scales, in being able to maintain their body temperature at a constant level (a feature shared only by the birds), in having a flexible skin, and in possessing sweat glands as a means of cooling the body when it gets too hot.

There are three main groups of mammals alive today. The primitive egg-laying monotremes, represented today only by the Platypus and the echidnas, share many similarities with the earliest mammal-like reptiles. The more advanced marsupials, now confined mainly to Australia and South America, are the descendants of one of the earliest groups of mammals. They give birth to their young after only a few weeks' gestation, after which the embryo-like young complete their development attached to a teat in the 'marsupial pouch' on the outside of the mother's belly. Though once widespread, the marsupials became extinct in the Old World following the rise of the eutherian (or placental) mammals, the group to which most living mammal species belong. These are characterised by a prolonged period of gestation in the mother's womb, where the unborn infant's nutritional needs are provided for by a special organ, the placenta, that develops during pregnancy.

PLATYPUS

The mammal that looks like a duck

When the first specimen was brought back to Europe in 1798, it was declared a hoax constructed from the head and feet of a duck and the body of an otter.

The Platypus (*Ornithorhynchus anatinus*) is one of only two groups of animals within the order Monotremata, the most primitive group of egg-laying mammals. It is a strong graceful swimmer, using its forelimbs to propel itself and its hindlimbs as both stabilisers and rudder. It can remain underwater for several minutes by wedging itself under stones or logs while it searches the muddy riverbed for crayfish and worms. These it locates by feel alone using its sensitive beak, for its ears and eyes are covered by flaps of skin while it is submerged.

The female lays her eggs in a grass-lined nest chamber at the end of a long winding tunnel burrowed into a river bank. Usually 5–10 m (15–30 ft) long, one tunnel was measured as being 30 m (100 ft). When the eggs hatch, they produce a tiny naked infant barely 18 mm (0.7 in) long, little more than a head and shoulders. By the time it

leaves its mother's pouch at 17 weeks of age, it has grown to a length of 34 cm (13 in).

Because the Platypus lacks proper

teats, the young lick their mother's milk from the fur that surrounds the openings of her mammary glands.

PROFILE

Length: *Male 50–60 cm (20–24 in), female 40–50 cm (16–20 in).*
Weight: *2 kg (4.4 lb).*
Distribution: *Throughout eastern Australia and Tasmania.*
Habitat: *Rivers and lakes from sub-tropical coasts to alpine streams at 1500 m (4900 ft) above sea level.*
Breeding: *1–3 leathery-shelled eggs produced in July–August; incubated for 10–12 days before hatching.*
Diet: *Insect larvae, crayfish, tadpoles, worms.*
Longevity: *10–15 years; one lived to the age of 17 years in captivity.*
Notes: *The young have 10 teeth which are later lost and replaced by horny plates in the adult.*

SPINY ECHIDNA

The toothless mammal

Because it feeds on insects which need no chewing, the Echidna has no teeth. Instead, it has a long sticky tongue with which it catches insects.

The Spiny Echidna or Anteater (*Tachyglossus aculeatus*) is one of only 2 species in the family Tachyglossidae of the order Monotremata. This primitive hedgehog-like mammal lays soft-shelled eggs like a reptile. Although the infant Echidna is only 15 mm (0.6 in) long and weighs a miniscule 0.4 g (0.01 oz) at hatching, it grows very rapidly, achieving a weight of 400 g (14 lb) by the time the mother forces it to leave her marsupial pouch 43 days later.

The Echidna has outsized claws on its feet which it uses to tear open rotten logs and to break into the concrete-hard nests of termites. Unusually for a mammal, the male has poison glands and spurs on its hindlegs which are probably used during combat. When attacked by a predator, the Echidna rolls itself into a ball so that it is protected by the spines along its back. Alternatively, it may wedge itself into a crevice or, in sandy soil, it may dig itself down so quickly that it just seems to sink into the ground.

Like many reptiles, the Echidna hibernates during cold weather and during this period it can easily survive without food for as long as a month.

PROFILE

Length: *35–53 cm (14–21 in)*.
Weight: *2.5–6 kg (5–13 lb)*.
Distribution: *Australia and Tasmania.*
Habitat: *Forest, scrubland and desert.*
Breeding: *A single egg produced in June–September, which is incubated by the female for 10 days.*
Diet: *Termites and ants.*
Longevity: *Up to 15 years; one individual said to have lived for 50 years in a zoo.*
Notes: *Although the female has 2 ovaries like all other animals, only the left one actually produces eggs.*

WATER OPOSSUM

PROFILE

Length: *30 cm (12 in), plus a 40 cm (15 in) naked tail.*
Weight: *300 g (11 oz).*
Distribution: *Central and South America from Mexico down to Argentina.*
Habitat: *Rivers.*
Breeding: *Up to 5 young produced in December–January.*
Diet: *Crayfish, shrimps, fish; some fruit.*

The only aquatic marsupial

The only marsupial to have adopted an aquatic way of life, the Water Opossum has a pouch whose opening can be tightened so as to keep its young dry while it is swimming.

The Water Opossum (*Chironectes minimus*) is the South American equivalent of the Otter. With its webbed hindfeet and dense oiled fur, it is an accomplished swimmer that lives by catching fish in the murky waters of the Amazonian and other big rivers of South America. Nocturnal, it spends the days in nests burrowed out of the river banks.

SWAMP ANTECHINUS

The only mammal that dies after mating

Most mammals breed repeatedly during their lives, but the Swamp Antechinus is unique in that the males die at the end of their first breeding season.

The tiny shrew-like Swamp Antechinus (*Antechinus minimus*) is the second smallest of 10 species of a mouse-sized genus of marsupials. These themselves are the smallest members of the large and diverse family of Dasyuridae, a family that also contains some of the largest marsupials, including the Thylacine. Antechinus forage for insects in the soil and leaf litter, scurrying from one piece of cover to another. They are poor climbers, so usually build their nests in tussocks of sedge. The breeding season is very short and intense. The males devote themselves so completely to mating that they have no time in which to feed. Most die of starvation, though some are caught by predators as they scurry about in search of mates. Although most females also die after weaning their first litter, some manage to survive to breed again the following year.

PROFILE

Length: *11–12 cm (4–5 in), plus an 8 cm (3 in) tail.*
Weight: *Male 65 g (2.2 oz), female 42 g (1.5 oz).*
Distribution: *Tasmania and adjoining southeastern coast of Australia.*
Habitat: *Damp scrub and tussock grassland.*
Breeding: *6–10 young produced during an unusually short breeding season.*
Diet: *Insects and insect larvae.*
Longevity: *1 year for males, 1–2 years for females.*

AMERICAN OPOSSUM

The mammal with the shortest gestation period

With a gestation period of just 8–13 days, this opossum holds the record for being the quickest breeder among the mammals. The young are born weighing barely 2 g (0.01 oz).

The only marsupial in North America, the American or Virginian Opossum (*Didelphus marsupialis*) can produce two litters each year, each one containing up to 25 infants. Born blind, naked and grub-like, the tiny young must find their way unaided from the mother's birth canal to the pouch on her abdomen where they can attach themselves to a teat to continue their development.

More than a third of the infants born die on the arduous journey across the mother's belly. The infants possess sharp claws to help them crawl, but these are lost soon after they reach the safety of the pouch.

The myth that the female gives birth through her nose probably arose from the fact that the mother may sometimes lick a path for the infants across her fur

and may even occasionally carry some of them in her mouth and put them in her pouch.

This cat-sized, rat-like marsupial is famous for its habit of feigning death when surprised on the ground away from the safety of trees. The ploy works because most animals that hunt for a living will eat only meat that they have killed for themselves.

PROFILE

Length: *1 m (3 ft 3 in), almost half of which is tail.*
Weight: *Up to 6.5 kg (14 lb).*
Distribution: *Lower Canada, down through the eastern USA to Mexico.*
Habitat: *Woodlands, usually near water.*
Breeding: *Average 10–12 infants per litter, maximum up to 25 per litter.*
Diet: *Any animal or vegetable matter.*
Longevity: *8 years.*
Notes: *Throat and windpipe separated in the young so that they can drink and breathe at the same time.*

INGRAM'S PLANIGALE

The mammal that rides on grasshoppers

While trying to kill grasshoppers as big as itself, this tiny mammal sometimes gets carried off by a grasshopper as it tries to escape.

Tiny Ingram's Planigale (*Planigale ingrami*) is the smallest living marsupial mammal, those in the Kimberley district of Western Australia being especially small. Yet, despite its diminutive size, the planigale is capable of catching and killing grasshoppers almost as large as itself. Animals in captivity have been found to thrive on six to eight 50-mm (2-in) long grasshoppers a day. The planigale is remarkable for its extremely flat skull, which is barely 6 mm (0.25 in) deep. This enables it to stick its head into the tiniest cracks in search of food.

PROFILE

Length: *50–92 mm (2.3–3.5 in), with a tail of 50–78 mm (2–3 in).*
Weight: *5 g (0.2 oz), males being larger than females.*
Distribution: *Northern and eastern Australia.*
Habitat: *Rocky areas or sandy country with tussock grass.*
Breeding: *Breeds in December–March, with a litter of 4–12 young.*
Diet: *Grasshoppers, occasionally crickets.*

MARSUPIAL MOLE

Life in the fast and slow lanes

The Marsupial Mole alternates without warning between periods of frantic activity and sudden sleep, unexpectedly dropping off to sleep when rushing about, only to wake and continue rushing about many minutes later.

Discovered less than 100 years ago, the Marsupial Mole (*Notoryctes typhlops*) uses its horny nose-shield to burrow its way through the soil in search of insects and worms. It tunnels just 8 cm (3 in) below the surface without creating permanent burrows. Like many small mammals, it eats voraciously, consuming its own weight in food each day.

The tail of the Marsupial Mole is about 2 cm (0.75 in) long and is covered with curious horn-like rings of skin.

PROFILE

Length: *10–20 cm (4–8 in), including tail.*
Weight: *680 g (1.5 lb).*
Distribution: *Occurs widely throughout Central and South Australia.*
Habitat: *Sandy ridges, preferably with salt-bush or acacia scrub.*
Breeding: *One infant each year.*
Diet: *Worms and insects.*

THYLACINE

The kangaroo in wolf's clothing

The only large carnivore among the marsupials, the Thylacine looks like a short-legged dog. What it lacks in speed and cunning it more than makes up for in perseverance.

The Thylacine (*Thylacinus cynocephalus*) was once the largest predator on the Australian continent. But it was unable to compete with the native dog or Dingo when these were first introduced by the early aboriginals some 10,000 years ago. It soon became extinct on the Australian mainland, surviving only in Tasmania. But when sheep were introduced there by the early European settlers, Thylacine preyed on the flocks. The resulting programme of extermination meant that by the end of the nineteenth century it survived only in the most remote parts of the island. Although the last specimen in captivity died in the 1930s, tracks and even occasional individuals have been sighted in the more remote parts of Tasmania.

In 1977, a possible sighting of a group of eight (including a mother with cubs) in northern Victoria renewed speculation about the species' survival on the Australian mainland.

The only carnivorous marsupial capable of bringing down the larger species of kangaroos, the Thylacine may itself hop like a kangaroo when it is being pursued. They are agile animals and have been seen to jump heights of 1.8–2.4 m (6–8 ft).

The Thylacine boasts one of the widest gapes in the animal kingdom: it can open its mouth so wide that its jaws are almost in a straight line. Like most of its close relatives, it is active only at night and spends the day lying up in a rocky lair.

PROFILE

Length: *100–130 cm (40–50 in), including a 50–65 cm (20–25 in) tail.*
Weight: *15–35 kg (33–77 lb).*
Distribution: *Formerly throughout Australia, New Guinea and Tasmania; now confined to the remotest parts of Tasmania.*
Habitat: *Savanna woodland or open forest, associated with rocky outcrops.*
Breeding: *2–4 in a litter, with a long breeding season.*
Diet: *Probably medium-sized wallabies, bandicoots, rodents and birds.*
Notes: *The last confirmed sighting of a Thylacine was in 1961; the species may now be extinct.*

NUMBAT

A dwarf among anteaters

Although termite-eaters are usually large powerful animals, this rat-sized marsupial can nonetheless successfully break into the underground nests of termites to feed on the insects within.

The Numbat has no pouch. The young, as can be seen here, cling instead to the female's nipples.

One of only 2 species in the Myrmecobiidae family, the Banded Anteater or Numbat (*Myrmecobius fasciatus*) is a curiosity among the marsupials in many different respects. As the only marsupial species to subsist wholly on termites and ants, the Numbat and its little-known sister species, the Rusty Numbat, exhibit many of the features characteristic of other anteaters: a long snout, a long cylindrical tongue, a bony palate on which to crush termites, and strong claws for digging ants and termites out of rotten wood or underground nest chambers.

The Numbat is the only wholly diurnal marsupial, being active only during daylight. It has the largest brain for its body size of any living marsupial, a characteristic that may be related to its diurnal way of life, with its greater dependence on vision. It is unique among the marsupials in that it lacks a pouch: the young are carried attached to nipples on the outside of the mother's belly. Finally, it has the largest number of teeth (50 in all) of any marsupial, though these are somewhat primitive and are never used for biting.

Although it once occurred throughout much of southern Australia, the Numbat is now restricted to the open woodlands in the southwestern corner of Western Australia.

PROFILE

Length: *245 mm (9.8 in), with a tail of 180 mm (7.2 in).*
Weight: *Male 495 g (17.5 oz), female 415 g (14.5 oz).*
Distribution: *Southwestern Australia.*
Habitat: *Open forest, woodland.*
Breeding: *Litter of 4 young.*
Diet: *Termites, ants.*

RED KANGAROO

The giant with the long-distance leap

Largest of the kangaroos, this animal is capable of leaps of 8 m (26 ft) and has been known to clear fences 3 m (9 ft) high.

The Red Kangaroo (*Macropus rufus*) is the largest of all the marsupial mammals. Yet, despite its massive size, it produces an infant that weighs no more than 28 g (1 oz) at birth. At that stage, the mother is more than 30,000 times the size of its young. The infant or 'joey' spends a full year in its mother's pouch, but by the end of its second year it is fully mature, though not fully grown. Kangaroos continue to grow throughout life, so that old males can sometimes be very large indeed.

Although it seems to move awkwardly as it hops along on its hindlegs, the Red Kangaroo can achieve speeds of up to 40 km/h (25 mph) when pressed. When travelling at full speed, its massive tail acts as a counterweight to balance its head and shoulders as the animal tilts forwards for maximum speed.

Inhabiting the dry grasslands of Central Australia, the Red Kangaroo breeds opportunistically whenever enough rain has fallen to produce a flush of grass. The female can hold a fertilised egg in her womb in a state of suspended animation for many months, waiting for conditions to improve sufficiently to make it worth her while embarking on a pregnancy.

Red Kangaroos are among the most social of the marsupials, usually being found in small groups ('mobs') of up to a dozen animals. Kangaroos are powerful animals and, when cornered, can deliver a kick with their heavily clawed hindfeet that will put even the toughest adversary out of action. When fighting among themselves, they often box with their 'hands'.

PROFILE

Length: *Male 1.15 m (45 in), female 1.0 m (39 in), with a tail of 0.9 m (33 in).*
Weight: *Male 66 kg (145 lb), female 26.5 kg (58 lb).*
Distribution: *Throughout Australia.*
Habitat: *Open plains and scrub desert.*
Breeding: *Single young born after a gestation period of 33 days.*
Diet: *Grass.*
Longevity: *20 years.*

GREATER GLIDER

The mammal that flies without wings

At Milton in New South Wales, Australia, a Greater Glider was seen to cover 550 m (590 yds) in six consecutive glides, the longest of which was 110 m (120 yds).

The Greater Glider (*Schoinobates volans*) is the largest of 6 species of gliding phalangers or possums. By climbing to the tops of tall trees, this cat-sized marsupial can effortlessly cover distances of 90 m (100 yds) or more by launching itself into a long shallow dive to the ground. Flaps of elastic skin along its flanks can be stretched into a gliding wing by extending its arms and legs.

It is a slow and clumsy mover when it is on the ground, but once in a tree it can easily outstrip a predator by alternately climbing and gliding at extraordinary speed.

Its cry, a shriek ending in a series of strangled gurgles, sounds eerily human at night, the time when the glider is most active.

PROFILE

Length: *130 cm (50 in), including a tail of 55 cm (20 in).*
Weight: *1.4 kg (3 lb).*
Distribution: *Coastal highlands of eastern Australia from Victoria to Queensland.*
Habitat: *Forest and tall woodland.*
Breeding: *Births occur during July–August.*
Diet: *Leaves, leaf tips and blossoms of eucalyptus.*
Notes: *Newborn infant is no bigger than the head of a drawing-pin.*

KOALA

The mammal with the dangerously selective diet

The Koala eats only the leaves of just 12 species of eucalyptus gum tree. Its survival has been seriously threatened by forest clearance for city and farmland developments.

The Koala (*Phascolarctos cinereus*) is the only member of its family, the Phascolarctidae, a distant relative of the Phalangeridae, themselves one of the most abundant and diverse groups of marsupial mammals.

Its cuddly bear-like appearance, together with its flat leathery nose and its big eyes, make it one of the most appealing of all animals. Unfortunately, its long silky fur has contributed to its decline through its appeal to the fur trade. In 1924 alone, more than 2 million Koala skins were exported to the fur markets of Europe and America from Australia.

This curious animal is totally arboreal and almost helpless on the ground because it has four hands with which to grip branches, rather than feet for walking on a flat surface. The Koala is able to oppose both the first and second digits of its hands so that it seems to have two thumbs.

It eats 1.5 kg (3 lb) of eucalyptus leaves each day. To help digest the tough leathery leaves, its caecum (the last part of its intestines) is unusually long, about 2–2.5 m (6.5–8 ft) when fully stretched out. One specimen, however, was found to have a caecum no less than 7 m (23 ft) in length!

PROFILE

Length: *60–85 cm (21–33 in).*
Weight: *4–15 kg (9–33 lb).*
Distribution: *Coastal regions of eastern Australia.*
Habitat: *Dry forest and woodland.*
Breeding: *1 infant born every 2 years in September–October.*
Diet: *Leaves of certain eucalyptus trees only.*
Longevity: *20 years in captivity.*

SHORT-TAILED SHREW

The only mammal with a venomous bite

This shrew is unique among the mammals in having glands in its mouth that produce a powerful nerve poison: a single bite is sufficient to kill a small mammal in a few seconds.

The Short-tailed Shrew (*Blarina brevicauda*) is one of just two species of shrew-like insectivores that are found only in North America. It spends most of its time in subterranean burrows and runways, but, in winter, it may burrow through the surface snow cover as though it were soil. It hunts for its food on the surface and may even climb into bushes in .its search for tasty morsels. One was once observed climbing 1.9 m (6 ft) up a small tree to get at some suet placed in the fork of a branch.

The poison with which this small predator subdues its prey is present in the saliva in its mouth, and seeps into the puncture wounds made by its teeth when it bites its prey. The poison is so powerful that it will leave a bite that is very painful for several days even in an animal as large as a man. To help see it through the winter when food is hard to find, the shrew will sometimes hoard snails, beetles and seeds.

Each individual occupies an area of about 0.12 ha (0.3 acres), where it builds its nest of dry leaves under fallen logs or tree stumps.

PROFILE

Length: *75–105 mm (3–4 in), with a tail of 17–30 mm (0.5–1.2 in).*
Weight: *15–30 g (0.5–1.0 oz).*
Distribution: *Throughout southern Canada and most of the USA.*
Habitat: *All types of terrestrial habitat.*
Breeding: *3–9 young in a litter; births can occur any time from early spring to autumn; females may produce several litters each year.*
Diet: *Invertebrates, small vertebrates and some plant matter.*
Longevity: *2.5 years.*
Notes: *Males can breed as little as 50 days after birth.*

SAVI'S PYGMY SHREW

The smallest non-flying mammal in the world

Barely 35 mm (1.4 in) long and weighing less than 2 g (0.1 oz), the pygmy shrew ranks as the real Tom Thumb of the mammal world.

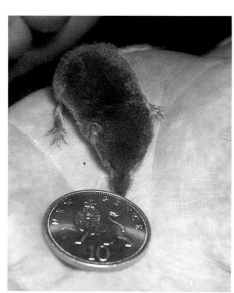

Despite its diminutive size, Savi's Pygmy Shrew (*Suncus etruscus*), also known as the Etruscan Shrew, belongs to the genus that also contains the largest of the true shrews.

Constantly on the go when active, it keeps up a constant shrill chatter the function of which remains obscure. Though usually to be found scurrying about in the grass, it has been known to jump distances of 20 cm (8 in) — more than four times its own body length — to seize grasshoppers and spiders with a rapid snatch.

The pygmy shrew is so small it can even creep into the holes made by earthworms!

PROFILE

Length: *35–48 mm (1.4–2.0 in), with a 25–30 mm (about 1 in) tail.*
Weight: *2 g (0.1 oz).*
Distribution: *Mediterranean area, eastward into Asia as far as Malaya, and southward into Africa as far as the Cape.*
Habitat: *Grasslands.*
Diet: *Insects.*
Breeding: *Unknown.*

COLUGOS

The mammal that wraps itself in a cloak

Like a voluminous cape, the thin flaps of skin between the colugo's extremities have to be tucked up under its arms to avoid being caught on twigs while the animal is climbing in trees.

The two closely related species of colugo or flying lemur (*Cynocephalus volans* and *C. variegatus*) are the only living representatives of their order, the Dermoptera. Their relationship to other mammalian groups has long been a source of mystery, and different authorities have classified them with the true lemurs (in the order Primates) and with the insectivores. They are now generally considered to form a separate primitive order of their own.

Colugos are characterised by the loose flaps of skin that join all their extremities, from the neck, through the wrists and ankles to the tip of the tail. When the animal stretches out its limbs,

these flaps of skin form a taut gliding platform on which it can 'fly'.

Almost helpless on the ground, colugos will try to climb any vertical object near them. Once in a tree, they climb swiftly to the top and launch themselves into the air in a long shallow dive, to land in a tree or bush some distance away. With their large gliding flaps, the colugos are the most efficient of all the gliding mammals and can cover long distances. One was once recorded as covering a horizontal distance of 136 m (147 yds) during which it lost only 10–12 m (32.5–39 ft) in height.

Colugos have an unusual skull that possesses many primitive features. The

teeth are also unique in that some of them are shaped like small combs: their function remains uncertain, though they may be used in grooming or gnawing.

PROFILE

Length: *38–42 cm (15.2–16.8 in), with a tail of 22–27 cm (8.8–10.8 in).*
Weight: *1.0–1.75 kg (2.2–3.9 lb).*
Distribution: *Southeast Asia and adjacent islands of East Indies.*
Habitat: *Forest.*
Breeding: *Single young born in February–March.*
Diet: *Fruit, flowers, leaves.*

RED BAT

The world's hardiest flying mammal

When hibernating in winter, it can withstand its body tissues freezing into ice at temperatures as low as −26°C (−15°F) without suffering any serious ill effects.

One of about a dozen species of red (or 'hoary') bats, the Red Bat (*Lasiurus borealis*) is a member of the most widely distributed group of bats in the New World. Red Bats roost singly or in small groups in trees and shrubs, where they are well disguised against the tree-trunk. Their deep red colour gives them an effective camouflage which functions especially well during the autumn season, when they can easily be mistaken for dead leaves. In fact, when disturbed at roost, they will sway gently from side to side in just the way a dead leaf does.

Red Bats are particularly strong fliers, being able to outfly any other bat. The female will often fly while carrying two or three infants clinging to her fur, a load that can easily exceed her own body weight. Populations living in Canada and the northern USA migrate southwards during the winter, some travelling as much as 2000 km (1250 miles) to spend the winter in northern Mexico.

The Red Bat is, nonetheless, well adapted to cope with the low temperatures that populations in the northern parts of the winter range experience. They are the most heavily furred, have the lowest heart rate at low temperatures, and have the highest red blood-cell count of any bat. When they do go into hibernation, they curl up into a ball so as to minimise the area exposed to the cold.

PROFILE

Length: *50–90 mm (2.0–3.6 in), with a tail of 40–75 mm (1.6–3.0 in).*
Weight: *6–30 g (0.2–1.0 oz).*
Distribution: *Throughout North America and the Caribbean.*
Habitat: *Any well-wooded areas.*
Breeding: *A single litter of 2–4 young produced in May–July*
Diet: *Insects captured in flight.*
Notes: *The only bat to have more than 2 young in a litter.*

VAMPIRE BAT

The only mammal that lives solely on blood

In the 15 minutes it spends feeding on its victim, a Vampire Bat can take in more than its own body weight in blood. It has a substance in its saliva that prevents the victim's blood from clotting.

Contrary to popular belief, the Vampire Bat (*Desmodus rotunda*) does not suck its victim's blood from puncture wounds made by fangs. Instead, it uses its fang-like incisor teeth to remove a thin slice of skin and then licks the blood that oozes out. A bat can drink so much blood at one meal that it is unable to fly until some of it has been digested and the excess liquid excreted.

Vampire Bats are normally active only on dark nights when there is no moon. They fly close to the ground searching for large mammals by using their sense of echo-location (a kind of radar). Once a victim has been found, the bat alights a few feet away and walks across to its victim, using its wrists to support itself.

The bat's feeding is rarely enough to wake the victim, though the bloody mess it makes around the wound may be very distressing afterwards. The bat's saliva contains a substance that prevents blood from clotting, so that blood continues to flow from the wound for some time. A more serious risk is that infected bats will transmit dangerous diseases such as rabies to their unsuspecting victims.

Because blood is easy to digest, the Vampire Bat has little need of teeth. Altogether it has only 20, the smallest number of any bat. These are used in grooming, for Vampires are particularly social animals and take it in turns to clean each other's fur.

Vampires will return night after night to the same victim if it is a particularly convenient one. They may even move their roosts closer to where the victim lives to save themselves the effort of flying a long way home on a full stomach.

PROFILE

Length: *75–90 mm (3.0–3.6 in); no tail.*
Weight: *15–50 g (0.5–1.8 oz).*
Distribution: *South America from Mexico south to Argentina and Chile.*
Habitat: *Most terrestrial habitats.*
Breeding: *Breeds throughout the year; females produce 1–2 litters a year.*
Diet: *Blood of large mammals (including Man).*
Longevity: *12 years.*

MEXICAN FREE-TAILED BAT

The largest bat roost in the world

The Carlsbad Cavern in New Mexico, USA, is home to more than a million bats of this one species every summer. It is the largest concentration of bats in the world.

Almost the entire world population of Mexican Free-tailed Bats (*Tadarida brasiliensis*) concentrates in a series of caves in New Mexico during the summer. The colony in the Carlsbad Cavern is so large that the accumulated guano deposited by the bats over many hundreds of years was used as a major source of nitrates for manufacturing gunpowder during the American Civil War.

A member of the most widely distributed family of bats (the Molossidae), this is one of the few bat species that migrate regularly each year. As winter approaches, the bats disperse to widely distributed breeding areas in Mexico. One bat ringed at the Carlsbad Cavern in November 1952 travelled 1300 km (800 miles) in just 68 days, an average of 19 km (12 miles) per day.

This species also holds the world speed record for bats: one was timed flying at a speed of 100 km/h (62.5 mph).

These bats also exhibit one other unique feature: the communal suckling of infants. It is not known why this happens, but female free-tailed bats seem to be especially tolerant of other individuals' offspring sucking from them.

Although some of the males remain year round in Mexico, the summer colonies in the caves of Texas and New Mexico are the largest bat roosts in the world.

PROFILE

Length: *45–100 mm (1.8–4.0 in)*.
Weight: *10–15 g (0.4–0.5 oz)*.
Distribution: *Southern USA and Mexico.*
Habitat: *Roosts in crevices and cracks in caves.*
Breeding: *Breeds in late winter, with births in June–July.*
Diet: *Mostly moths and beetles.*
Longevity: *15 years.*

AYE-AYE

The primate that looks like a squirrel

With its large, continuously growing incisor teeth and its long bushy tail, this primitive primate bears a striking resemblance to many members of the squirrel family.

One of the most primitive members of the order Primates, the Aye-aye (*Daubentonia madagascariensis*) is the only living member of its family, the Daubentonidae. It has the large eyes of a nocturnal animal and a bushy squirrel-like tail. Unlike squirrels, however, it hops from branch to branch rather than running and jumping.

The Aye-aye commonly feeds on insect larvae, which it finds by tapping on branches with a fingertip rather as a woodpecker does with its bill. Listening carefully with its outsize ears, it can locate the larvae moving about in the wood and then it digs them out using either its long thin fingers or its incisor teeth. Unlike all other primates, it has claws instead of nails on its fingers and toes.

During the day, the Aye-aye sleeps in a large spherical nest about 0.5 m (1.5 ft) in diameter. It constructs its nest out of twigs and leaves in the fork of a tree about 12 m (40 ft) above the ground. Nests may be used continuously over a very long period: one was found to be still in place seven years after it was first discovered — and even then it had not been new.

PROFILE

Length: *360–440 mm (14.5–17.5 in), with a 500–600 mm (20–24 in) tail.*

Weight: *2 kg (4.5 lb).*

Distribution: *Northern and eastern parts of Madagascar.*

Habitat: *Forest, mangrove and bamboo thicket.*

Breeding: *Single infant born in February–March.*

Diet: *Fruit, birds' eggs, insects and insect larvae, bamboo pith.*

Longevity: *9 years in captivity.*

Notes: *Owing to the destruction of the forests in which it lives, the Aye-aye is on the verge of extinction.*

WHITE-THROATED CAPUCHIN

The monkey with the teeth of iron

Their massive molars and immensely powerful jaws allow capuchins to crack open palm nuts that are too hard for any other species of animal to eat.

Sometimes known as the 'organ-grinder's monkey' from its frequent use by travelling entertainers, the White-throated Capuchin (*Cebus capucinus*) is one of 5–6 species in the genus *Cebus* of the Cebidae family of New World monkeys. The most common monkey in South America, its mischievous antics so captivated audiences that it became the commonest monkey in captivity. Rarely, however, do monkeys and apes make good pets, because their large size and boisterous behaviour make them difficult to control.

Capuchins got their names because of their resemblance to capuchin monks, their heads half concealed by a cowl. But, far from being contemplative, capuchin monkeys are highly social animals that live in groups of 15–20. Their movements and social interactions are accompanied by a constant chatter of shrill squeaks and squeals which are strung together in long sequences and phrases.

As with many of the New World monkeys, the White-throated Capuchin's tail is prehensile. It can be used as a fifth hand by the animal, who wraps it around a branch to steady itself as it feeds in the trees high above the ground.

PROFILE

Length: *305–380 mm (12–15 in), with a 380–508 mm (15–20 in) tail.*
Weight: *1.7–4.0 kg (3.7–8.8 lb).*
Distribution: *Central America.*
Habitat: *Forest.*
Breeding: *Single infant born after a gestation period of 6 months.*
Diet: *Fruit, nuts.*
Longevity: *One specimen lived for 32.5 years in captivity.*

JAPANESE MACAQUE

The most inventive animal in the world

In 1957, a young female Japanese Macaque discovered that she could remove the sand from sweet potatoes and wheat grain by washing them in the sea. The habit gradually spread throughout her troop over the next ten years, as the other monkeys copied her, the first documented example of cultural transmission of behaviour in a non-human species. On Honshu, Japan's northernmost island, the monkeys have learned to sit in natural hot springs during the snow-bound winter in order to keep warm.

The Japanese Macaque (*Macaca fuscata*) is one of 13 species of macaque monkeys, an Asian member of the family Cercopithecidae (Old World monkeys). It occurs only on the islands of the Japanese archipelago. Those living on the island of Honshu are the northernmost population of any species of primate other than Man. The Japanese Macaque is a heavily built monkey with a short tail and greyish-brown fur. The male is 20% larger than the female. Like most Old World monkeys, it is an omnivore. Its diet consists of a mixture of the fruits, flowers, and leaves of many different plants, plus fungi, insects, and shellfish.

Mating takes place between December and March but may occur as early as September/October in the far north, where the winter climate is especially severe. A single infant is born after a gestation period of five months. Where food is plentiful (as in captivity), a female can produce an infant every year. But in the wild, most females give birth only once every two or three years.

In some parts of Japan, the monkeys that live in the grounds of temples have been protected for many generations. As a result, some troops have grown to contain as many as a 1000 animals and are the largest groups of any species of non-human primates.

Macaques are among the most sociable of all primates and spend up to 10% of their time engaged in social grooming with their companions. Relationships between close female relatives are particularly close.

PROFILE

Body length: *0.5 m (20 in).*
Weight: *7–10 kg (15–22 lb).*
Distribution: *Japan.*
Habitat: *Forest.*
Diet: *Omnivore with a preference for fruits.*
Group size: *20–200 in wild; up to 1000 when provisioned.*
Longevity: *20–25 years.*
Notes: *Although a good climber, it spends most of its time on the ground, using trees only as places of safety in which to sleep.*

BARBARY MACAQUE

The prop of the British Empire

A legend says that when Barbary Macaques cease to live on the Rock of Gibraltar on the southern coast of Spain, Gibraltar will cease to be part of the British Empire.

Once widespread throughout much of southern Europe and northern Africa, the Barbary Macaque (*Macaca sylvanus*) is the only non-human primate to live in Europe. Long since exterminated from most of its former range, it is found in the wild only in isolated mountain forests in Morocco and Algeria.

The species' only toehold on the European continent today is on the Rock of Gibraltar, where it was re-introduced in the 1740s. Since 1915, the British Army has maintained a free-living colony on the Rock because of the

legend. The monkeys are actually listed on the strength of the British Army, have their own guards and are issued with official rations every day.

In the wild, Barbary Macaques live in small groups of 20–30 animals. When fighting breaks out within the troop, males will engage in a unique behaviour in which the loser will collect a young infant and carry it across to the winner. As the two of them interact over the infant, grooming it and lip-smacking vigorously, tension is reduced and a degree of harmony re-established within the group.

PROBOSCIS MONKEY

The primate with the longest nose

Old males develop long pendulous noses that can be up to 175 mm (7 in) in length. Quite why they do so remains one of Nature's long-standing mysteries.

A member of the large and diverse langur group of the Old World monkey family Cercopithecidae, the Proboscis Monkey (*Nasalis larvatus*) stands apart as being rather odd in many other ways besides its outsized nose.

Unlike most other primates, it readily takes to water and can swim and dive quite well. It is also among the largest of the truly arboreal monkeys. Although the function of the male's nose is still unclear, it may be that it helps in the production of the long drawn-out resonant honking calls that the male monkeys give.

Because Proboscis Monkeys live in dense impenetrable swamp forests in Borneo, they have been little studied and their habits remain something of a mystery.

PROFILE

Length: *Male 660–762 mm (26.5–30.5 in), female 535–610 mm (21.5–24.5 in), with a tail of 560–760 mm (22.5–30.5 in).*
Weight: *Male 11–22.5 kg (24.0–49.5 lb), female 7–11 kg (15.5–24.0 lb).*
Distribution: *Borneo (Asia).*
Habitat: *Low mangrove swamp and other inundated forests.*
Breeding: *A single infant.*
Diet: *Leaves and some fruit.*
Longevity: *Rarely survives more than a few days in captivity.*

PYGMY CHIMPANZEE

Man's closest relative

First identified as a distinct species as recently as 1928 from a single specimen in a museum collection, the Pygmy Chimpanzee is probably the closest living relative to Man.

Although not in fact smaller than other chimpanzees, the Bonobo or Pygmy Chimpanzee (*Pan paniscus*) has an unusually small head. Nonetheless, it is extremely intelligent and is thought by some to be the most intelligent species after Man. Its retiring nature and the fact that it lives in the dense jungles of Central Africa meant that it remained undiscovered until well into the 20th century.

Noisier and more active than Common Chimpanzees, Bonobos live in communities of 50–60 animals that inhabit a particular area of forest. The animals roam the forest in search of food, forming loose groups of 15–20 individuals; the membership of a group is constantly changing as individuals leave and others join. Chimpanzees are long-lived animals whose lifelong relationships with each other are as complex and involved as those in the best soap-operas.

PROFILE

Length: *700–830 mm (28.0–32.8 in), with no external tail; 1.1–1.2 m (44–48 in) when standing erect.*
Weight: *Male 37–61 kg (81.5–134.0 lb), female 27–38 kg (59.5–83.5 lb).*
Distribution: *Congo basin, Africa.*
Habitat: *Forest.*
Breeding: *A single offspring produced every 3–4 years.*
Diet: *Fruits, leaves, insects.*
Longevity: *Probably up to 40 years.*
Notes: *Chimpanzees do not reach physical maturity until they are 10–14 years old.*

HOOLOCK GIBBON

Greatest acrobat in the animal world

Its long slender arms and hooked hands enable the gibbon to swing rapidly from branch to branch. It can cover up to 12 m (39 ft) in a single leap.

One of 7 species of Hylobatidae (lesser apes), the Hoolock Gibbon (*Hylobates hoolock*) is a familiar sight swinging overarm through the treetops in the forests of southeast Asia. Its rapid movements and great agility make it the unequalled 'king of the canopy'. Gibbons live in small family groups, each consisting of a single breeding pair and their offspring.

Every morning, soon after sunrise, the female performs what is one of the most remarkable events in the forest. Her 'great call' — a loud shrill wail that rises to a long drawn-out crescendo — fills the morning air for 15 minutes or more. Each female's call stimulates her neighbours to reply, so that waves of sound float across the treetops of the forest.

One of the most arboreal of the primates, gibbons have four hands rather than two feet and two hands. Nonetheless, they will occasionally descend to the ground, where they usually walk upright on two legs with their long arms outstretched for balance.

Gibbon infants cling to their mother's chest, just as do those of all other higher primates. But, to give her infant extra support while she is swinging through the trees, the mother often draws up her legs to form a kind of cradle.

PROFILE

Length: *456–635 mm (18.0–25.5 in), with no external tail.*
Weight: *5–8 kg (11–17.5 lb).*
Distribution: *Southeastern Asia and associated islands of the Sunda shelf.*
Habitat: *Forest.*
Breeding: *Single infant born after a gestation period of 210 days.*
Diet: *Mainly fruit, some leaves.*
Longevity: *23 years in captivity.*
Notes: *Gibbons take 6–10 years to reach physical maturity.*

THREE-TOED SLOTH

The slowest mammal in the world

Each day, this lazy mammal spends 21½ hours asleep. When active, it takes 6½ hours to cover 1 mile (1.6 km) – more than 26 times slower than a walking man.

The Three-toed Sloth (*Bradypus tridactylus*) adopted a life of almost perpetual sleep in order to make itself less conspicuous to predators. The three great hooked claws on its hands (four on its feet) allow it to hang upside down in the upper branches of the tallest forest trees, where it avoids detection by looking like a bunch of dead leaves. Even when alert, its movements are so methodical and slow that it can actually swim faster than it can walk.

Hanging upside down is such a large part of its life that even its hair grows 'backwards' from the wrist towards the shoulder and from its stomach towards its back.

The sloth's lifestyle is so slow that other creatures have taken to living in its long matted fur. Encouraged by the humid dampness of the tropical climate, algae grow in its fur and provide a food supply for a host of mites, beetles and moths.

In order to reduce the amount of moving it has to do, this vegetarian animal has a massive stomach which it can fill with leaves which can then be digested slowly at its leisure. The stomach and its contents when full account for 30% of the animal's total body weight.

PROFILE

Length: *50 cm (20 in).*
Weight: *About 3.7 kg (8.1 lb).*
Distribution: *South America (Brazil north to Honduras).*
Habitat: *Forest.*
Breeding: *A single infant born after a gestation of 120–180 days.*
Diet: *Eats only the leaves of the cecropia tree.*
Longevity: *11 years.*
Notes: *Has no front teeth; because the cheek teeth have no enamel, these teeth grow continuously throughout life to compensate for the heavy wear incurred by chewing fibrous leaves.*

NINE-BANDED ARMADILLO

The only mammal with armour-plated protection

Hard bony plates cover the armadillo's body as a protection against predators. By flexing these plates and bracing its feet, it can also wedge itself in its burrow so firmly that it cannot be pulled out.

One of more than 20 species in the curious family of Dasypodidae, the Nine-banded Armadillo (*Dasypus novemcinctus*) is one of the few species of South American mammals to have successfully invaded North America. This has been possible only because of its ability to dig deep burrows, which it lines with grass and leaves. These provide the animal with a refuge in which to escape both the burning heat of the day and the intense cold of the desert night.

The armadillo's powerful limbs are used to dig burrows up to 6 m (20 ft) long that can go as deep as 1.5 m (5 ft) below ground. When digging, the fore-limbs scrape and loosen the soil which is passed back to the hindfeet to be ejected from the burrow entrance by powerful kicks. To allow the hindlegs to work freely, the tail is braced on the floor of the tunnel in order to bear the animal's weight, so raising the hindfeet clear of the ground.

Armadillos are excellent swimmers, but to avoid sinking under the weight of their armour they have to swallow air to gain buoyancy. Armadillos are unique in giving birth to identical quadruplets. The four infants are produced from a single fertilised egg that subdivides once development starts.

PROFILE

Length: *Up to 90 cm (3 ft), including a 30 cm (12 in) tail.*
Weight: *5.5–7.7 kg (12–17 lb).*
Distribution: *South America from Argentina north as far as the southern USA.*
Habitat: *Semi-desert or arid grasslands.*
Breeding: *Up to 12 (but normally 4) young born in March–April.*
Diet: *Insects, molluscs, small amphibians, reptiles and carrion.*
Longevity: *11 years in captivity.*
Notes: *Its acute sense of smell allows it to detect insects up to 12 cm (5 in) below ground.*

NAKED MOLE-RAT

The rodent that missed out on fur coats

As the only rodent that lacks any kind of fur, this animal's naked wrinkled appearance makes it look like a half-developed foetus that was born prematurely.

The Naked Mole-rat or Sand Puppy (*Heterocephalus glaber*) is one of the most curious of the rodent family. It spends its entire life underground, never coming to the surface except when its burrows are broken open by predators.

The mole-rat lives in a form of society that is unique among the mammals, being similar to that of the Honey Bee. It lives in colonies of 50–100 animals, dominated by a single matriarch who, like the queen bee, is the only female in the colony that breeds. All the other members of the colony are the one matriarch's offspring, and successive litters form castes of workers that are each responsible for specific tasks within the colony.

The smallest and youngest offspring are responsible for digging the tunnels and for bringing food back to the central nest. Larger ones patrol the tunnel system, checking for intruders and repairing collapsed sections. The largest form a caste of non-workers: these include males who are responsible for mating with the matriarch, and a few large females who become reproductively active only if the matriarch dies or if they themselves leave to found a new colony elsewhere.

The Naked Mole-rat has the most extensive burrow system of any mole-rat, with a typical colony's tunnels — some 3–4 km (2–2.5 miles) in all — covering an area of 12 ha (30 acres).

Because their burrow systems are well insulated by the ground, mole-rats seldom experience any significant variation in temperature. As a result, they have all but lost the ability to maintain body temperature and they now have the poorest capacity for thermoregulation of any mammal.

PROFILE

Length: *60–92 mm (2.4–3.5 in), with a tail 26–44 (1.0–1.5 in) long.*
Weight: *30–80 g (1.3–3.2 oz).*
Distribution: *Eastern Africa.*
Habitat: *Arid semi-desert between 600 m and 1800 m (2000–5800 ft) above sea level.*
Breeding: *The matriarch of a colony can produce up to 4 litters of 5–12 pups each year.*
Diet: *Roots, bulbs, tubers.*
Notes: *The tunnel system is mainly for harvesting food, so tunnels tend to concentrate in areas where preferred roots are found.*

CHINCHILLA

Owner of the warmest fur coat in the world

Living at 3000–6000 m (10,000–20,000 ft) up in the Andes Mountains, the Chinchilla needs a warm coat to survive. Its fur is the softest and densest of any known mammal.

The Chinchilla (*Chinchilla laniger*), the only species of its genus, is one of a number of small South American rodents adapted to life in desert habitats. Living on one of the tallest mountain ranges in the world at altitudes where only the hardiest grasses and herbs will grow, the Chinchilla uses crevices and holes in the bare rocky landscape as its burrows. With little water available in these arid high-altitude deserts, it obtains all the mois-ture that it needs from herbs that store dew.

Its dense coat with its soft silky hair is so attractive that it soon became the most valuable fur for its size and weight. A coat made only from the pelts of wild-caught animals once sold for US $100,000. The demand for their skins became so great that Chinchillas were wiped out from many parts of their range. In one year alone, 200,000 skins were exported from Chile.

PROFILE

Length: *225–380 mm (9–15 in), with a 75–150 mm (3–6 in) tail.*
Weight: *0.5–1.0 kg (1.0–2.2 lb), females larger than males.*
Distribution: *South America from Bolivia to Chile.*
Habitat: *Semi-desert, rocky mountainside above 3000 m (10,000 ft).*
Breeding: *Up to 3 litters a year, each of 1–4 young.*
Diet: *Grasses and herbs.*
Longevity: *Up to 20 years in captivity, but probably 10 years in wild.*
Notes: *Active within an hour of birth.*

BLACK-TAILED PRAIRIE DOG

Builder of the largest towns in the world

In 1901, a prairie dog colony (or 'town') was estimated to cover an area 160 × 380 km (100 × 240 miles). It was thought to contain around 400 million individuals.

The Black-tailed Prairie Dog (*Cynomys ludovicianus*) is one of several members of the squirrel family that live in burrows in the ground. Typical burrows consist of a wide shaft about 0.9 m (3 ft) in diameter tunnelled vertically down into the ground for some 3–5 m (10–16 ft). A number of horizontal tunnels lead from the base to nest and storage chambers. At the head of the shaft, a cone of soil is built up to prevent rainwater entering. This also provides a look-out point from which a sentry can keep watch for approaching predators.

Each colony is divided into a number of sub-divisions, the smallest of which is a 'coterie' (essentially a breeding group). Prairie dogs are very social animals and their complex society with its many different levels of relationships requires a highly developed social sense to make it work. To this end, individuals engage in elaborate 'kissing' rituals with every colony member they meet.

Colonies typically consist of about 1000 individuals. Very much larger colonies existed, however, before the extensive control measures instituted earlier this century when ranchers complained about the amount of damage prairie dogs did to grazing lands. Thirty-two prairie dogs eat as much as one sheep, while 256 can eat as much as a cow. A single large 'town' of a million prairie dogs will thus use up grazing that would have supported nearly 4000 head of cattle or 31,000 sheep.

PROFILE

Length: *300 mm (12 in), with 87 mm (3 in) tail.*
Weight: *0.9–1.4 kg (2–3 lb).*
Distribution: *Western USA and northern Mexico.*
Habitat: *Prairie grassland and open plateau.*
Breeding: *Single litter of 2–10 young produced in March–April.*
Diet: *Grass and herbs.*
Longevity: *8 years.*
Notes: *The young are born naked and blind, weighing just 15 g (0.5 oz).*

AMERICAN BEAVER

Master builder among the mammals

Beaver dams are constructed from stones, tree stems, leaves and mud plastered together in layers to create a formidable structure. One was measured as being over 600 m (650 yds) long.

An entirely novel way of life was evolved by the American Beaver (*Castor canadensis*). To avoid being caught by predators, beavers build 'lodges' in the middle of lakes and rivers. Each lodge, built out of mud, sticks and stones by a single pair and their offspring, is up to 1.8 m (6 ft) high and 12 m (39 ft) in diameter. It contains a central sleeping platform above water level. Every beaver lodge is built with several underwater entrances.

So long as the lodge is surrounded by water, the beavers' main predators, such as Wolves, cannot get at them. In order to make sure that the water level around a lodge is deep enough for the underwater entrances to be below the ice during the winter freeze, the beavers build their famous dams. They also anchor logs under the water where they can be easily reached during the winter when the frozen pond surface traps them in their lodges.

Using their massive incisor teeth as chisels, beavers can fell trees up to 0.5 m (1.5 ft) in diameter. Chopped up into smaller sections, the trunks are brought down to the water's edge by the animals floating them along channels specially dug for the purpose.

Beavers have the ability to store oxygen in their tissues and this helps them to remain submerged for 15 minutes or more. To help them see better while underwater, their eyes are covered by a nictitating membrane similar to that found in birds and reptiles.

PROFILE

Length: *0.7–1.3 m (2.3–4.2 ft), with a 215–300 mm (8.5–12 in) tail.*

Weight: *9–32 kg (20–70 lb), with an average of about 13 kg (29 lb).*

Distribution: *Canada and northern USA; European Beaver may belong to the same species.*

Habitat: *Rivers and lakes in wooded areas.*

Breeding: *Mating in January–February, with a litter of 1–8 young born in April–May.*

Diet: *Bark, leaves and twigs of willow, aspen and birch.*

Longevity: *19–20 years.*

Notes: *The beaver is one of the largest rodents in the world.*

MOUNTAIN BEAVER

PROFILE

Length: *300–460 mm (12–14 in), with a 10–25 mm (0.5–1.0 in) tail.*
Weight: *900–1800 g (2–4 lb).*
Distribution: *Rocky Mountains, northwestern USA.*
Habitat: *Forests and thickets near water, up to 2200 m (7100 ft) above sea level.*
Breeding: *Litters of 2–6 infants born in February–March.*
Diet: *Grass and herbage; bark and leaves of trees.*

Host to the world's largest flea

A flea caught in the nest of a Mountain Beaver at Puyallup, Washington, measured no less than 8 mm (0.3 in) in length — the largest flea ever measured so far.

Despite its common name, the Mountain Beaver or Sewellel (*Aplodontia rufa*) is not a true beaver. In fact, it is something of a zoological mystery. Though clearly a member of the order Rodentia, its ancestry and nearest living relatives are uncertain. It is classed in a family of its own, the Aplodontiidae.

It builds simple burrow systems that lead out towards its food sources from a central nest chamber. It does not hibernate in winter, but relies mainly on a store of dried vegetation and moss that it lays down in the summer. Nonetheless, it may sometimes venture out into the open during winter, when it may

tunnel through the snow in search of food.

A moderately good climber, it can climb up to 7 m (23 ft) above the ground to cut down branches from trees. Very secretive and shy, it often occurs in large numbers even in areas where it is thought locally to be completely absent.

EUROPEAN MOLE-RAT

The world's champion burrower

One of the busiest of the burrowing rodents, this small animal makes extensive burrow systems of nests connected by tunnels up to 36 m (117 ft) long.

Whereas true moles dig with their claws, the European Mole-rat (*Spalax microphthalmus*) uses its outsized incisor teeth to loosen the soil. Along the side of its head from its muzzle to its ears is a line of stiff bristles that allows the upper part of the head to be used like a bulldozer blade to pack the excavated soil into the tunnel sides. Although it has small eyes, these are

covered over by skin and the animal is completely blind. The ultimate in burrowing machines, a mole-rat can literally disappear before your eyes if the surface of the ground is not too hard-packed.

During the mating season, mole-rats build mounds above ground that are up to 2 m (6.5 ft) in diameter and 1 m (3 ft) high. The centre contains a nest cham-

ber some 20 cm (8 in) in diameter, below which is a complex series of tunnels and storage chambers. These breeding mounds are usually surrounded by a number of smaller satellite mounds which are connected to the breeding mound by tunnels. Their function remains unclear, but they may be occupied by individual males during the breeding season.

MULTIMAMMATE RAT

PROFILE

Length: *80–100 mm (3.2–4.0 in), with a tail of similar length.*
Weight: *100–200 g (3.7–7.1 oz).*
Distribution: *Throughout Africa south of the Sahara.*
Habitat: *Prefers cultivated areas up to 2100 m (6800 ft) above sea level.*
Breeding: *3–19 (average 10–12) in a litter, with no marked seasonality except in southern Africa.*
Diet: *Grain, meal, dried fish, insects, even soap; occasionally it is cannibalistic.*
Notes: *The species is a host for human plague.*

The fastest-breeding mammal

Capable of giving birth to a litter of ten pups every month, a female can produce as many as 120 offspring a year under ideal conditions.

An apparently undistinguished rodent, the Multimammate Rat (*Praomys natalensis*) has more teats than any other mammal. Though her 24 teats are rarely all used, a female can reproduce very rapidly under the right conditions, with a resulting explosion in the local rat population.

This is one of the most numerous species of rodents in Africa, perhaps because it generally prefers to live near Man and so invariably has access to plenty of food. The presence of these rats in a forest clearing often indicates that a village once stood there, sometimes as long as 20 years before.

Multimammate Rats are less cautious than any other species of rat or mouse and will boldly appear in broad daylight. As a result, many are caught by predators. They prefer to live in crevices and cracks in the ground, but may burrow under the floors and walls of houses.

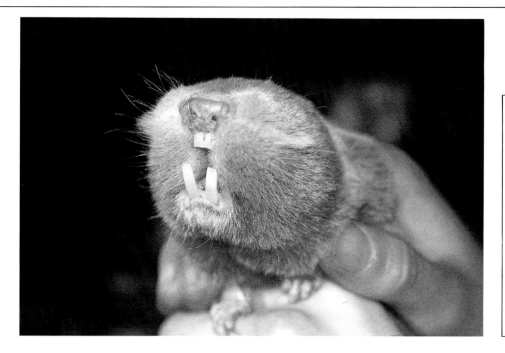

PROFILE

Length: *150–300mm (6–12 in).*
Weight: *133–295 g (4.8–10.5 oz).*
Distribution: *Southern Russia.*
Habitat: *Any habitat with more than 100 mm (4 in) of rainfall a year, up to 2600 m (8500 ft) above sea level.*
Breeding: *Mating in November–January, with a single litter of 2–4 infants born in January–March.*
Diet: *Roots, bulbs of plants.*
Notes: *The fur is reversible, thus allowing the animal to move rapidly backwards or forwards in its tunnel with equal ease.*

EGYPTIAN SPINY MOUSE

PROFILE

Length: *70–125 mm (3–5 in), with a 50–125 mm (2.5–5 in) tail.*
Weight: *50–90 g (1.8–3.2 oz).*
Distribution: *North Africa.*
Habitat: *Rocky areas, but particularly associated with human habitation.*
Breeding: *Litters of 1–5 young born in February to September.*
Diet: *Omnivorous, but prefers plant matter, especially grain.*
Notes: *The gestation period of 42 days is unusually long for mice.*

The only animal to live entirely on bat guano

A colony was once discovered living inside an Egyptian tomb where the only food it had to eat was droppings deposited by bats that used the tomb as a roost.

One of four species of spiny mice, the Egyptian Spiny Mouse (*Acomys cahirinus*) is well protected from predators by a strip of thick spiky hair along its back. Even the domestic cat finds these hedgehog-like animals difficult to deal with. Another feature that helps them to escape from predators is their brittle tail which easily breaks, so leaving the predator with an unappetising morsel while allowing the mouse to get away.

These gregarious mice live in crevices in termite hills or in the abandoned burrows of gerbils and other rodents.

One of their most unusual features is the way in which females who have already given birth act as midwives for other individuals. They will bite through the umbilical cord and lick and clean another female's firstborn infant while the mother delivers the rest of her litter.

Mainly active at night, these mice can climb up the stems of maize plants to eat the corn cob at the top.

GREATER FLYING SQUIRREL

The squirrel that behaves like a bird

Although it glides rather than flies, this mammal's aeronautical abilities allow it to bank and turn while airborne and it will sometimes ride the rising air currents coming up the deep valleys.

One of many species of 'flying' squirrels, the Greater Flying Squirrel (*Petaurista petaurista*) uses the thin flaps of skin between its limbs as a platform on which to glide from tree to tree in search of food. As it lives in very hilly country with deep-sided valleys, it can use the height to undertake very much longer glides than any other species of gliding mammal. The longest recorded glide was one of 450 m (488 yds).

Greater Flying Squirrels are monogamous, each pair apparently remaining together for long periods (possibly even for life). They build a nest in a hollow tree or a cranny in a cliff face, where they spend the day asleep. Active only at night, they travel through the trees by running along branches much as other squirrels do. Only when they encounter a gap between trees that is too large to jump do they launch themselves into the air in a glide.

Because they glide long distances, they have often been able to survive where forests have been cleared providing a few trees are left to provide them with food. When the trees are in bloom, they sometimes gorge themselves so much that they are unable to fly.

STAR-NOSED MOLE

PROFILE

Length: *10–12.7 cm (4–5 in), with a tail of 5.6–8.4 cm (2.2–3.4 in).*
Weight: *40–85 g (1.4–3.0 oz).*
Distribution: *Eastern Canada and northeastern USA.*
Habitat: *Damp soil near permanent water.*
Breeding: *Litters of 2–7 young born in April–June.*
Diet: *Aquatic insects, crustaceans, small fish, earthworms.*
Notes: *Star-nosed Moles can swim and dive well, and frequently swim beneath the ice during winter. All four feet are used in swimming.*

The only aquatic mole

An excellent swimmer, this mole acquires much of its food from the mud at the bottom of streams and ponds, where its curious nose may help it locate prey.

Although a member of the mole family (Talpidae), the Star-nosed Mole (*Condylura cristata*) is unique in several respects, the curious fan of 22 fleshy tentacles around its nose being just the most conspicuous. The exact function of this appendage is uncertain but, when the animal is searching for food, the tentacles are in constant motion. Once it starts to eat, they are drawn up around the nose out of the way.

Unlike most moles, the eyes of the Star-nosed Mole are clearly visible. This is an unusually active species, and can be found busily at work at any time of the day or night and throughout the year. It often comes to the surface to travel in the open, especially when there is deep snow on the ground. This mole's tunnels are quite deep in the ground, so that the surface ridges normally associated with the tunnels of other moles are not normally seen. Many of the tunnels lead directly into water.

PROFILE

Length: *30.5–58.5 cm (12.2–23.4 in), with a tail of 34.5–63.5 cm (13.8–25.4 in).*
Weight: *1.0–2.5 kg (2.2–5.5 lb).*
Distribution: *India to southeast China and adjacent islands of the East Indies.*
Habitat: *Forest in hilly terrain above 900 m (2900 ft).*
Breeding: *Single young born about March–April.*
Diet: *Fruit, nuts, shoots, leaves, insects.*
Longevity: *About 15 years in captivity.*

NORWEGIAN LEMMING

The mammal with its own anti-freeze

Most mammals have to increase heat production to maintain their body temperature when air temperatures fall below freezing (0°C, 32°F), but lemmings do not begin to do so until the temperature reaches −12°C (12°F).

Probably the only aboriginal mammal in Scandinavia, the Norwegian Lemming (*Lemmus lemmus*) is well adapted to life above the Arctic Circle. In order to reduce heat loss as much as possible, it grows a long winter coat that traps a layer of air in the underfur.

Lemmings tunnel under the snow to build burrows and nest chambers that are well protected. In a lemming nest, with a family in residence, 60 cm (2 ft) below the snow surface, the temperature can reach 10°C (50°F) even when the outside temperature is below freezing. Lemmings are so dependent on snow to

keep warm during winter that there are places where there is too little snow for them to live.

Lemmings are famous for their periodic migrations. At intervals that average three to four years, the lemming population reaches such a high density that many thousands of animals migrate in search of new habitats. Their determination is such that they will cross busy roads and pass through large towns without stopping, though the stories of lemmings drowning in large numbers when they reach the sea are untrue.

PROFILE

Length: *80–170 mm (3.5–8.8 in).*
Weight: *40–105 g (1.5–3.8 oz).*
Distribution: *Scandinavia.*
Habitat: *Subalpine tundra and marshy scrubland.*
Breeding: *A female can produce 2 litters of up to 5 pups each during a summer.*
Diet: *Herbs, grass.*
Notes: *Its skin is so loose that it can turn around in its tunnel inside its own skin.*

ARCTIC GROUND SQUIRREL

The rodent that spends nine months of the year in bed

To avoid the rigours of the long arctic winter, this rodent spends most of the year hibernating deep in its burrow, emerging only for the few months of the summer.

The Arctic Ground Squirrel (*Spermophilus undulatus*) is one of some 21 species of ground squirrel that occur throughout Europe, Asia and the New World. As the most northerly of these, it spends most of the summer feeding voraciously. As a result, it grows very fat and often goes into hibernation well before the winter actually sets in. Throughout its long sleep till the following summer, it lives off its stored body fat.

Active throughout the long summer's day, foraging for food, the Arctic Ground Squirrel is sharp-eyed and often rears up on its haunches to keep a lookout for predators. If it spies danger, it vanishes into its burrow.

PROFILE

Length: *332–495 mm (13.3–19.8 in), with a tail of 77–153 mm (3–6 in).*
Weight: *400–500 g (14–18 oz).*
Distribution: *Alaska, northern Canada.*
Habitat: *Tundra, forest.*
Breeding: *Single litter of 2–13 young born each summer.*
Diet: *Seeds, nuts, bulbs, leaves, mice, insects, birds and their eggs.*
Longevity: *2–5 years.*

SHAW'S JIRD

The Casanova of the mammal world

Like all gerbils, male and female jirds form monogamous pairs to raise their young, but the females in fact mate most often with the males in neighbouring territories.

The rat-like Shaw's Jird or Sand-rat (*Meriones shawi*) is one of the commonest inhabitants of the North African deserts. Living in burrows tunnelled under the protective roots of bushes, it forages in runways that fan out across the desert sand towards the best feeding places. Heavily preyed on by jackals and birds of prey, it scampers and sometimes even hops from one thicket to the shelter of another.

PROFILE

Length: *114–130 mm (4.5–5.0 in), with a 90–100 mm (3.5–4.0 in) tail.*
Weight: *60 g (2 oz).*
Distribution: *North Africa (mainly Tunisia).*
Habitat: *Desert.*
Breeding: *Litters of 3–4 young.*
Diet: *Leaves, seeds, bulbs, stems and roots, often stored in burrow.*
Longevity: *5.5 years.*

MANED WOLF

The hunter on stilts

Standing 75 cm (30 in) at the shoulder, the Maned Wolf has by far the longest legs of any carnivore.

With its reddish colour, long ears and pointed features, the Maned Wolf (*Chrysocyon brachyurus*) looks like an overgrown fox. In fact, it is a rather obscure member of the Canidae, the dog family, and is the only species of its genus. Its long legs allow it to travel considerable distances through tall grass at a rapid pace. Yet this itself is puzzling, since none of its abundant normal prey species is particularly fast.

Usually solitary and nocturnal, these odd animals have been little studied and their habits are not well known. They give a weird cry at dusk. Unlike all other canids, they dig with their teeth rather than with their claws.

Certain South American tribes use shavings from the bones of Maned Wolves to make a tea that is supposed to ensure an easy delivery for pregnant women.

PROFILE

Length: *125 cm (50 in), with a tail 30 cm (12 in) long.*
Weight: *23 kg (50.5 lb).*
Distribution: *South America, mainly Brazil, Uruguay, Paraguay and Argentina.*
Habitat: *Pampas grasslands, edge of swamp.*
Breeding: *Litters of 2 pups born in winter.*
Diet: *Small mammals, birds, reptiles, insects, fruit.*

LEAST WEASEL

FENNEC FOX

The fox with the biggest ears

With ears that are the largest of any carnivore relative to its size, the Fennec is said to be able to hear another animal moving up to 1.5 km (1 mile) away.

Smallest and palest of the foxes, the Fennec (*Fennecus zerda*) is a species of the desert. It can survive for long periods without water, and tracks have been found at considerable distances from oases.

Like many desert species, it lives in burrows in the sand. It can dig so rapidly that it seems just to sink into the ground.

For a small canid, the Fennec Fox is unusually agile, being able to spring up to 70 cm (28 in) vertically and about 120 cm (4 ft) horizontally from a standing position.

Fennec Foxes live in groups of up to 10 animals. They are active only at night, when they search for insects and small animals while these are in their nests.

PROFILE

Length: *36–40 cm (14.5–16.0 in), with a tail 20–30 cm (8–12 in) long.*
Weight: *1.5 kg (3.3 lb).*
Distribution: *Arabia, northern Africa.*
Habitat: *Sandy deserts.*
Breeding: *Litters of 2–5 young born in March–April after 50 days' gestation.*
Diet: *Small rodents, birds, eggs, lizards, insects, fruit.*
Longevity: *10–12 years.*

The smallest living carnivore

Barely longer than an adult human's hand, the Least Weasel is by far the smallest carnivore alive today.

Tiniest of all the weasel family, the Least Weasel (*Mustela rixosa*) is nonetheless one of the most widely distributed species in the order. It occurs throughout the northern hemisphere. The North American race is smaller than those found in the Old World.

Like all weasels, it undergoes a colour change into a white winter coat that effectively camouflages it against the snow. Unlike those of other weasels, however, its winter coat fluoresces a bright lavender colour under ultraviolet light.

Least Weasels often appropriate the dens of mice, using the fur of their unfortunate hosts to line the den in order to keep their infants warm during winter. Weasels are tenacious in their pursuit of prey. They can climb and swim quite well when necessary: a member of the larger European race was once observed swimming in the middle of Ullswater in England at a point where the lake was 1.2 km (0.75 miles) wide.

PROFILE

Length: *158–184 mm (6.3–7.4 in), with a 19–23 mm (0.8–0.9 in) tail.*
Weight: *35–70 g (1.3–3.6 oz).*
Distribution: *Europe, northern Asia and North America.*
Habitat: *Woodland, marshy habitats, meadows.*
Breeding: *3–10 young per litter, with up to 3 litters per year.*
Diet: *Small mammals and birds.*

POLAR BEAR

King of the pack ice

An expert diver and swimmer, the Polar Bear commonly hitches rides on ice floes, drifting considerable distances from land. One was once found swimming 320 km (200 miles) from the nearest land.

The largest and most carnivorous of the bears, the Polar Bear (*Thalarctos maritimus*) is also the most nomadic, often wandering widely across the frozen wastes of the northern ice fields.

A Polar Bear can move with surprising speed and agility. It can outrun a Reindeer on land and swim at 4 km/h (2.5 mph) in water. When running flat out on ice, it can achieve speeds of up to 40 km/h (25 mph), leap hummocks of snow up to 2 m (6 ft) high and jump distances of 3.7 m (12 ft).

A small bear can climb a sheer ice wall by digging its claws into the hard-packed ice. Bears have been known to take flying dives of more than 15 m (50 ft) into water from the tops of icebergs when cornered.

Polar Bears hunt by stealth, often lying in wait at blow holes made in the ice by seals until a seal comes up to breathe. Although its creamy-white fur is perfect camouflage in the polar ice fields, its shiny jet-black nose often gives it away. The Polar Bear's sense of smell is, however, acute, and a bear is said to be able to detect seal pups in their calving dens even under 1 m (3 ft) of snow.

PROFILE

Length: *2.2–2.5 m (7.2–8.1 ft); tail 76–127 mm (3–5 in).*
Weight: *Up to 720 kg (1584 lb), though males average about 410 kg (900 lb) and females 320 kg (700 lb).*
Distribution: *Arctic region.*
Habitat: *Ice-bound coasts.*
Breeding: *A female gives birth to 1–4 cubs in March–April, usually in alternate years.*
Diet: *Seals; also fish and seabirds.*
Longevity: *34 years.*
Notes: *Hunted to the verge of extinction, there are now only about 10,000 Polar Bears left in the wild.*

GIANT PANDA

The raccoon in bear's clothing

Despite its bear-like appearance, the panda is, in fact, a member of the raccoon family.

The Giant Panda (*Ailuropoda melano-leuca*) stands apart from the other members of the raccoon family, Procyonidae, in a number of respects. Its diet of bamboo shoots and roots makes it one of the most specialised species in the animal kingdom. In order to crush and pulverise the tough leaves and stems of the bamboo, it has strong jaws and massive jaw muscles, which in turn necessitate a large skull on which to anchor the muscles. Its forefeet are unusual, too, in that they have lobes or pads at the base of the first and second digits that can be used as 'thumbs' for gripping bamboo stems.

Although able to climb into trees when pursued, the panda normally spends its time on the ground. This is partly because its large size and the relatively unnutritious diet necessitates its spending 10–12 hours feeding each day. Pandas sometimes catch fish by flicking them out of the water.

An adult animal consumes up to 20 kg (44 lbs) of bamboo each day. Pandas are said to drink so much on occasions that they become too bloated to move.

Despite their massive size and apparent clumsiness, Giant Pandas are accomplished climbers. Their sharp claws allow them to climb rapidly up vertical tree trunks to escape predators. Unfortunately, they are less skillful at coming down again and often do so head first, sometimes with unfortunate results. Pandas can also swim well. They have been known to paddle across raging torrents when the spring thaw fills the mountain streams with melted snow.

PROFILE

Length: *1.2–1.5 m (3.9–4.9 ft), with a tail of 127 mm (5 in).*
Weight: *75–160 kg (165–352 lb).*
Distribution: *Tibet and western China.*
Habitat: *Bamboo forest in mountains.*
Diet: *Bamboo shoots; occasionally small mammals, birds and fish.*

WOLVERINE

Demon of the forest

This tough bear-like carnivore is said to be prepared to kill almost everything it meets and has even been known to drive bears and pumas from their kills.

With a reputation for aggressiveness and strength, the Wolverine (*Gulo luscus*) is among the most daunting animals to encounter in the forest. It has been known to kill animals as large as Elk and Moose when these have been hampered by the snow. Sometimes also known as the Glutton, it has a voracious appetite and is said to eat more than any other carnivore.

Although not strictly nomadic, Wolverines have immensely large ranges for their size, sometimes as large as 3000 square km (1170 square miles). Their normal gait is a loping gallop and they can climb trees with remarkable speed. Though they lack the speed of cats, they can often outrun deer and other animals on snow surfaces because their large feet prevent them from sinking too deeply.

Among the most playful of the carnivores, the Wolverine's capacity for destructiveness is unbounded. It has been known to destroy completely the contents of huts or tents that it comes across in its wanderings. Wolverines are said to be able to drag carcases that are three times their own weight across rough ground.

PROFILE

Length: *650–870 mm (26–35 in), with a tail of 170–260 mm (6.8–10.4 in).*
Weight: *14.0–27.5 kg (30.8–60.5 lb).*
Distribution: *Throughout arctic and subarctic regions of Europe, Asia and North America.*
Habitat: *Forests.*
Breeding: *Occurs in February–April, with 2–3 young born 2–3 months later.*
Diet: *Any form of meat, but especially carrion.*
Longevity: *16 years in captivity.*
Notes: *Its fur has the remarkable property that it will not freeze even when moist.*

RATEL

An animal that knows no fear

Said to fight with unusual courage and tenacity, the Ratel will take on animals as large as horses and buffalo with a complete lack of fear.

Tough and resilient, the Ratel or Honey Badger (*Mellivora capensis*) has such a thick skin that it is completely impervious to the stings of bees, the quills of porcupines and even the bites of snakes. The Ratel's skin is exceptionally loose on its body, so that when the animal has been caught by the back of the neck it can turn inside its own skin and bite its adversary.

Ratels are quite indefatigable in the pursuit of prey, being prepared to trail their victims at a jog-trot until they have run them into the ground. Nor can small mammals save themselves by retreating down their burrows, for a Ratel can soon dig them out with its powerful claws.

A most remarkable relationship has developed between the Ratel and a small bird known as the Black-throated Honeyguide. When a honeyguide locates a bees' nest, it gives a very characteristic call. Any Ratel nearby is attracted to the calling bird, which then leads the way to the bees' nest. Being completely impervious to bee stings, the Ratel can break open the nest. While it eats the grubs, the honeyguide is free to feed on the wax in the honeycomb which it otherwise would not have been able to get at.

PROFILE

Length: *600–770 mm (24–31 in), with a tail of 200–300 mm (8–12 in).*
Weight: *11.4 kg (25 lb).*
Distribution: *Throughout sub-Saharan Africa; in Asia, from Arabia eastwards as far as Nepal and India.*
Habitat: *Most terrestrial habitats.*
Breeding: *Normal litter size is 2, with 2 litters per year in some areas.*
Diet: *Small mammals, snakes, insects, carrion; also roots, bulbs, fruit and honey.*
Longevity: *24 years in captivity.*

ZORILLA

The smelliest animal on earth

When attacked, the Zorilla squirts a nasty-smelling secretion from its anal glands with great force into the face of its opponent.

Often confused with the spotted skunks of America, the Zorilla or Striped Polecat (*Ictonyx striatus*) is in fact a purely African species. Nocturnal and solitary, it is rarely seen, though it is far from being rare. When it is encountered, it is usually to be seen running along the ground at an easy trot with a rather hunched back. But it can also climb and swim well. The secretions from its anal glands are said to be the most noxious produced by any species. When cornered, it may, after ejecting its anal gland secretions at its attacker, feign death rather like an opossum.

TODDY CAT

The palm civet with a taste for wine

In southeast Asia, palm juice (toddy) is collected in cups fixed to palm trees and allowed to ferment naturally. Toddy Cats often raid these cups to drink the wine.

Besides its liking for palm wine, the Toddy Cat (*Paradoxurus hermaphroditus*) has a particularly close association with Man. It commonly lives in or near human habitation, often taking up residence in the roofs of bungalows.

When cornered by an enemy, the Toddy Cat ejects a nauseous secretion from an anal gland. Unlike that of the African Civet, however, this secretion is not used in the manufacture of perfumes.

The Toddy Cat is primarily a nocturnal animal. The name 'palm civet' derives from its habit of living in the tops of palm trees where the dense mat of prickly leaf-bases provides it with a safe retreat from predators.

SEA OTTER

The mammal that gets tied up at bed time

In order to prevent itself drifting away on the current while asleep, the Sea Otter lies under strands of kelp seaweed. It is said to sleep with its hands over its eyes.

The Sea Otter (*Enhydra lutris*) spends its entire life at sea, though it never strays more than 1 km (0.6 miles) from the coast. But, unlike most marine animals, it lacks a layer of fat to keep it warm in the cold northern waters. Instead, its long dense underfur traps a layer of air that helps to insulate its body.

Sea Otters, which obtain most of their food from the sea bed, can dive to depths of up to 40 m (130 ft). They have voracious appetites, eating as much as a quarter of their own body weight in food each day. Shellfish and molluscs are brought up to the surface to be eaten while the animal swims or floats on its back.

Their teeth are unique, being broad and flat to function as crushing surfaces for breaking the shells of marine molluscs. The animal cracks the tougher shells of mussels by banging them against a stone resting on its chest. When eating sea urchins, it first wraps the animal in a leaf of seaweed so as to break off the poisonous spines that surround the body.

PROFILE

Length: *1.0–1.2 m (39–47 in), with a tail of 25–37 cm (10–15 in).*
Weight: *Male 27–37 kg (59.5–81.5 lb), female 16–29 kg (35–64 lb).*
Distribution: *Pacific coasts of North America across the Bering Strait to the Siberian coast.*
Habitat: *Coastal waters.*
Breeding: *Single pup born every other year.*
Diet: *Shellfish, molluscs, sea urchins, fish.*
Notes: *Pups, which are born in an unusually advanced state of development, are carried on the mother's chest as she swims on her back.*

PUMA

The cat with the greatest geographical range

With a range that extends from Canada to Tierra del Fuego at the tip of South America, the Puma has the greatest north-to-south range of any cat.

Also known as the Cougar, Mountain Lion, Painter and Catamount, the Puma (*Felis concolor*) is one of only two species in the cat family (Felidae) that are not spotted or striped. The largest of the true cats (genus *Felis*), it is also the most widely distributed of all the New World mammals.

Tough and powerful, the Puma is capable of killing prey as large as a Mule Deer. An adult needs to kill about one animal of this size each week. Pumas catch their prey by stalking, rather than running them down like a Cheetah or lying in wait like a Leopard.

Pumas are among the most agile of the cats. When being hunted down, one once jumped 15 m (50 ft) down a cliff face in order to escape. They are excellent tree-climbers and can jump fences more than 2 m (6 ft) high on the run.

PROFILE

Length: *103–197 cm (3.4–6.6 ft), with a 53–82 cm (21–33 in) tail.*
Weight: *35–105 kg (77–320 lb).*
Distribution: *Throughout North and South America.*
Habitat: *Most habitats, but especially mountainous ones.*
Breeding: *Litters typically of 3 cubs, born throughout the year.*
Diet: *Deer, antelope; also rodents and large birds (e.g. rhea).*
Longevity: *20 years.*
Notes: *Cubs are born spotted and with a ringed tail, but lose these markings when they mature.*

SNOW LEOPARD

The cat that lives on top of the world

Rarely seen, the Snow Leopard roams the snow line at around 3700 m (12,000 ft) on Asia's highest mountain ranges.

Probably the most beautiful of all the cats, the Ounce or Snow Leopard (*Panthera uncia*) spends its summers along the snow line at 3700–4000 m (12,000–13,000 ft). But, during the winter, it may come down to altitudes as low as 2000 m (6500 ft), where it has the opportunity of taking goats and other domestic animals in the villages at that level.

Its coat is especially long and the fur dense, making it both warm and unusually attractive. It has one of the longest tails of the cat family in proportion to its size.

Its remote and inaccessible habitat has made the Snow Leopard one of the least encountered species of large cats. Because of this, there has been little research done, and not much is known of its biology.

Like all large cats, the Snow Leopard roars, though it does so only rarely. Presumably, it can hardly afford to give away its position in a habitat where prey are rare and hard enough to find. Like many of the cats, it hunts its prey by stalking them, with a final pounce once the prey is within reach. Snow Leopards have been credited with leaps of up to 16 m (52 ft), though how reliable these claims are remains uncertain.

The Snow Leopard is a solitary animal, although the female is often accompanied by its young, which go along on hunting trips within a couple of birth.

PROFILE

Length: *1.2–1.5 m (3.9–4.9 ft), with a tail of 0.9–1.1 m (2.9–3.6 ft).*
Weight: *23–41 kg (50–90 lb).*
Distribution: *Mountainous areas of Central Asia.*
Habitat: *Rocky habitats along the snow line.*
Breeding: *Litters of 2–4 born in April–June.*
Diet: *Wild sheep, Musk Deer, hares, rodents, goats and domestic stock; occasionally large birds.*

CHEETAH

The finest racing machine in nature

According to an interesting hypothesis, the Cheetah is such a masterpiece of engineering design that an adult specimen without legs would still be able to propel its streamlined body along the ground at 8 km/h (5 mph)—the speed of a fast-walking pedestrian—through sheer muscular contraction.

The Cheetah or Hunting Leopard (*Acinonyx jubatus*) has been described as the 'greyhound of the cats', and in its general conformation, e.g. long slender limbs, narrow chest, supple back and strong hindquarters, and movements, it certainly gives the impression of a coursing dog rather than a big cat. The formation of its claws, rounded and only partially retractile to provide traction, is another idiosyncrasy of the Felidae (35 species), and this carnivore is also unique in the fact that it pursues its victim like a greyhound chasing a hare. Other physical features, however, such as its relatively small head, spotted coat and long powerful tail, point more to a feline connection.

A film sequence of a running Cheetah taken in Kenya in 1959 and very carefully analysed showed that it reached its maximum speed of 90 km/h (56 mph) in 3 seconds from a standing start. At this velocity it completed a singe stride of approximately 7 m (23 ft) in 0.28 seconds. Some imaginative writers have credited this sprinter par excellence with amazing bursts of up to 148 km/h (92 mph), but even when travelling flat out over hard level ground it is extremely doubtful whether it can top 96 km/h (60 mph).

Although this highly specialised cat is the fastest animal on earth, its lightning speed is restricted to short-distance running because it has very little endurance. In the ordinary way a chase of 275–365 m (300–400 yds) is round about its limit, but if it miscalculates the sprinting power of its intended prey and is forced to run an extra 100 m (110 yds) it abandons the chase.

Eight races of Cheetah have been recognised (6 in Africa and 2 in Asia), but most of them are now extinct in the wild state.

PROFILE

Total length: *1.76–2.36 m (5.8–7.7 ft); tail 48–84 cm (19–33 in).*

Shoulder height: *71–84 cm (28–33 in).*

Weight: *42–66 kg (92–147 lb).*

Distribution: *Today its numbers are largely concentrated in eastern Africa.*

Habitat: *Open plains and semi-arid savannas.*

Breeding: *Gestation period 86–95 days: litter size 2–6.*

Diet: *Small and medium sized mammals (mainly gazelles) up to 60 kg (130 lb); also birds, including the Ostrich.*

Longevity: *Oldest captive specimen lived 16+ years.*

Notes: *Despite its reputation as a ruthless hunter, the Cheetah is a shy and inoffensive creature.*

SPOTTED HYAENA

The predator that laughs as it hunts

One of the noisiest of the carnivores, this beast's famous laugh is one of many calls used to co-ordinate the activities of the pack during a hunt.

Half cat and half dog, the Spotted Hyaena (*Crocuta crocuta*) is the largest of the 4 species in the family Hyaenidae. The great scavenger of the African plains, it can also be a formidable hunter in its own right. When several individuals band together, they can take on prey as large as a Zebra or even drive Lions off their kills. Their massive jaws and teeth allow them to crack open the largest bones, so that little remains of a carcase once a Spotted Hyaena takes it over.

A highly social animal, this species lives in groups of 20 or more individuals dominated by a female matriarch. It is renowned for the extraordinary variety of its calls, which serve both to maintain the group's cohesion and to co-ordinate its hunting activities. Hunts are preceded by a ritual of sniffing, licking and scent-marking. Its eerie whoops (given as it hunts) and its uncanny laugh (given on finding food) are among the most unnerving sounds to be heard at night in the African bush, and have given the beast the common name 'Laughing Hyaena'.

Usually active only at night, the Spotted Hyaena spends the day lying up in abandoned Aardvark holes or in its own dens burrowed in sandy soil. In some cases, the inner chamber can be up to 2 m (6 ft) in diameter.

PROFILE

Length: *1.5 m (5 ft), with a 0.5-m (18-in) tail; stands 0.8 m (31 in) at the shoulder.*
Weight: *45–80 kg (100–175 lb).*
Distribution: *Throughout most of sub-Saharan Africa except the Congo basin and the Cape.*
Habitat: *Any type except forest.*
Breeding: *1–2 young per litter.*
Diet: *Any kind of meat or carrion.*
Longevity: *25 years.*

SOUTHERN ELEPHANT SEAL

The most flexible spine in the animal kingdom

Despite its massive size, the Southern Elephant Seal is capable of arching its back over until its head touches its flippers behind.

By far the largest member of the seal family, the Southern Elephant Seal (*Mirounga leonina*) is also one of the most sexually dimorphic of the seals: males weigh nearly four times as much as females. Its name derives from the male's trunk-like nose, which is up to 38 cm (15 in) long. This probably helps in the production of the deep trumpeting sounds made by the males during the breeding season.

Elephant seals breed on beaches around the southern coasts of Argentina and Chile and on the rocky islands off the coast of Antarctica. The males fight ferociously to defend their breeding territories on the beach, slashing at each other with their teeth in battles that,

despite the male's heavily padded neck, often results in heavily bleeding wounds.

Neither males nor females feed much during the breeding season. Females may lose as much as 135 kg (297 lb), some 15% of their body weight, while suckling their young. The animals often eat sand and pebbles from the beach, presumably because they are so hungry. On one occasion, 35 kg (77 lb) of pebbles were removed from a male's stomach.

After the breeding season, Southern Elephant Seals migrate northwards to spend the winter along the pack ice, occasionally even straying up into tropical waters. One young tagged seal

travelled no less than 4800 km (3000 miles) in its first year of life.

PROFILE

Length: *Male 5.0–5.8 m (14.5–21.0 ft), female 2.5–3.0 m (9.8–11.4 ft).*
Weight: *Male 3.5 tonnes (tons), female 0.9 tonnes (tons).*
Distribution: *Subantarctic oceans.*
Habitat: *Open sea; breeds on beaches.*
Breeding: *Single pup produced in February–June every year.*
Diet: *Cuttlefish, fish.*
Longevity: *20 years.*
Notes: *At birth, pups are 1.2 m (3.9 ft) long and weigh 50 kg (110 lb).*

CRABEATER SEAL

The commonest mammal in the world

More than 30 million of these seals are thought to live in the southern oceans around the coast of Antarctica, making this the most abundant mammal in the world.

Despite its name, the Crabeater Seal (*Lobodon carcinophagus*) does not eat crabs. In fact, it lives mostly on krill (a large shrimp that is particularly common in antarctic waters). To help in straining these creatures and other plankton from the sea water, Crabeater Seals have the most complex teeth of any carnivore. Their teeth are elaborately cusped (they have rows of projections on the biting surface) so as to provide a kind of filter.

These seals never come ashore onto dry land. They are associated primarily with the pack ice that jostles the outer edges of Antarctica, but may head north into warmer waters during the southern winter. They breed on small ice floes, usually in isolated monogamous pairs.

Crabeater Seals like to bask in the sun on pack ice, and will even do so within yards of their deadliest enemy, the Leopard Seal. One reason why they are prepared to take this risk is that they are the fastest seal on land. Using powerful thrusts of the hips and vigorous pushes with the flippers, a Crabeater Seal can achieve the quite remarkable speed of 25 km/h (15 mph).

PROFILE

Length: *2.3–2.6 m (7.5–8.5 ft)*.
Weight: *200–225 kg (440–495 lb), females larger than males.*
Distribution: *Southern oceans in antarctic waters.*
Habitat: *Edge of pack ice.*
Breeding: *Breeds September–November; single pup weighing 25 kg (55 lb) born in early spring.*
Diet: *Krill, occasionally small fishes.*
Notes: *Individuals commonly bear scars from attacks by Killer Whales.*

ROSS SEAL

Mystery seal of the Antarctic

Fewer than 50 of these seals had been seen prior to 1945. It is still the least-known member of the seal family.

The rarest of the Southern Ocean seals, the Ross Seal (*Ommatophoca rossi*) has a restricted distribution along the edge of the pack ice off the Atlantic coast of Antarctica. It is usually seen alone, often floating on small ice floes some distance out to sea. The females seem to give birth on ice floes, but the pups — with a length at birth of almost 1m (3 ft) — can swim within a few hours of birth.

The Ross Seal has unusually large eyeballs for its size, suggesting that it dives frequently in the dimly lit water beneath heavy ice. Its preferred diet is squid and octopus taken from the sea bed. Judging by the size of the squid beaks found in one seal's stomach, a Ross Seal can capture squid as large as 2 m (6.5 ft) long.

Its solitary habits and ephemeral habitat on ice floes that are continuously melting away has made the Ross Seal one of the most elusive mammals to study in the wild. So little is known about its natural history that we do not even know how many of them there are.

The Ross Seal has an unusually wide range of vocal sounds, including a variety of trills, coos, chirps and cluckings. In mammals, such versatility in vocal communication is normally associated with an intense social life, so the fact that the Ross Seal is found alone is just another puzzling aspect of its biology.

PROFILE

Length: *Male 1.7–2.1 m (5.5–6.8 ft), female 1.3–2.2 m (4.2–7.2 ft).*
Weight: *Male 129–216 kg (284–475 lb), female 159–204 kg (350–450 lb).*
Distribution: *Coastal waters around Antarctica.*
Habitat: *Edge of pack ice.*
Breeding: *Single pup born in November.*
Diet: *Cephalopods; some fish and krill.*
Longevity: *12 years or more.*

NORTHERN FUR SEAL

Keeper of the largest harem

During the prime of life, a male Northern Fur Seal may hold a harem of up to 40 females on the beaches where they come ashore to give birth and mate.

A fast and skilled swimmer, the Northern Fur Seal (*Callorhinus ursinus*) spends most of the year out at sea scattered over a wide area of the northern Pacific Ocean. But, during the summer, the 1½–2 million animals of this species converge on a small number of breeding grounds on the islands around the Bering Sea.

The month-long breeding season is a hectic time for males. The competition for females is so fierce that harem-holders never feed. By the end of it, they are so thin that they barely have the strength to struggle back down to the sea. After giving birth (and then mating), the females remain ashore to feed their new pups until these are weaned at four months of age. Every few days, the females head out to sea to feed. During these trips, they may head 80–160 km (50–100 miles) out to sea, returning to relocate their own pups from among the thousands left behind in the 'rookery'.

During the autumn and winter, Northern Fur Seals set out on the longest migration of any seal species. During a 10,000-km (6000-mile) round trip, they can travel from the breeding grounds in Alaska to as far as Japan and back.

PROFILE

Length: *Male 1.9–2.1 m (6.2–6.8 ft), female 1.5–1.7 m (4.9–5.5 ft).*
Weight: *Male 180–300 kg (396–660 lb), female 36–68 kg (79–150 lb).*
Distribution: *Northern Pacific Ocean, as far south as Japan and California.*
Habitat: *Open ocean; coastal waters during breeding season.*
Breeding: *Single pup produced in July after 12 months gestation.*
Diet: *Fish, squid, crustaceans.*
Longevity: *21 years.*
Notes: *A female once made 13 dives to depths of 110–140 m (360–455 ft) in 3.6 hours, each dive being about 5 minutes long.*

ROCK HYRAX

The elephant's closest relative

Despite its rodent-like appearance, the hyrax is in fact as closely related to the elephant as to any other species. Hyraxes are the only true hoofed mammals that regularly climb in trees.

The Rock Hyrax (*Procavia capensis*) is one of about 9 species that belong to the Procaviidae, the only living family within the order Hyracoidea. Hyraxes are most closely related to the elephants and to the Perissodactyla order (the odd-toed ungulates). They retain many of the characters of the primitive ungulates from which all modern ungulates are descended, including hoofed toes and the ridged structure of their teeth.

Rock Hyraxes normally live in crevices and burrows in rocky outcrops, but they often climb into trees and bushes to rest or to search for food. Because hoofed toes are not particularly well adapted to climbing on vertical surfaces, the sole of their foot is moist and rubbery and provides considerable traction. To give them even better grip, the centre part of the sole can be pulled inwards by special muscles inside the foot: the vacuum created by this hollow helps the animal to stick to a surface. This grip is so powerful that an animal shot while clinging to a vertical surface may sometimes remain fixed there.

The extinct species of the order Hyracoidea were more varied than the few species alive today. Many of the extinct forms were of considerable size, one of them being about the size of a horse.

PROFILE

Length: *305–380 mm (12–15 in), with no external tail.*
Weight: *0.5–4.5 kg (1–10 lb).*
Distribution: *Throughout Africa.*
Habitat: *Rocky mountainous areas up to 3800 m (12,400 ft) above sea level.*
Breeding: *Litters of 1–6 (typically 3) young born throughout the year.*
Diet: *Leaves, roots and bulbs; some insects (especially locusts).*
Longevity: *About 7 years.*
Notes: *A completely new species of hyrax was discovered as recently as 1974 in the highlands of Ethiopia.*

DUGONG

Mermaid of legend

When the first European mariners brought back tales of mermaids living at sea, they were probably referring to the harmless Dugong of the Indian Ocean.

The strange-looking Dugong (*Dugong dugong*) is one of only 2 species in the family Dugongidae. The other species, Steller's Sea-cow, is now extinct and the gentle Dugong itself is on the verge of following suit.

Dugongs are totally aquatic animals and never come ashore. Their forelimbs are shaped like flippers to give them stability in the water while they swim by lazy thrusts of their flat tails. Of their hindlimbs there is now no trace whatsoever. Even the bones of the pelvis are reduced to a couple of small unattached bones suspended in the muscle wall.

The Dugong's skeleton is unusually dense, probably in order to help it remain submerged while feeding on the marine grasses on the sea bed. Although they have to come to the surface at intervals to breathe, Dugongs can remain submerged for up to 10 minutes.

Dugongs have been hunted almost to extinction both for their meat and for the oil produced from their blubber. An animal weighing 300 kg (660 lb) can yield up to 56 litres (12.5 gallons) of oil.

Dugongs usually live in small family groups of 3–6, but can sometimes assemble in herds of 100 to graze in shallow waters off coastal reefs.

PROFILE

Length: *2.5–3.2 m (8–10.5 ft)*.
Weight: *140–300 kg (310–660 lb)*.
Distribution: *Indian Ocean and western edge of Pacific.*
Habitat: *Coastal waters where suitable vegetation grows.*
Breeding: *Single infant born after a gestation period of 11 months; breeds throughout the year.*
Diet: *Marine grasses.*
Notes: *Front teeth greatly reduced and replaced by horny plates, between which vegetation is pulverised.*

JAVAN RHINO

The world's largest rare animal

As long ago as 1937, there were fewer than 70 Javan Rhinos alive; today, there are only about 50. The species may well be extinct by the end of the 20th century.

Once widespread throughout Indo-China and the neighbouring islands of the Sunda shelf, the Javan Rhino (*Rhinoceros sondaicus*) is now confined to a few remote patches of forest on the island of Java. Its demise is due mainly to intensive hunting for its horn over many centuries. Because the horn was thought to have medicinal properties, the Chinese were prepared to pay half its weight in gold for it.

The horn is not, in fact, true horn, but is composed of hair held together by glue. It is not physically attached to the bones of the skull as true horns usually are, but grows up from the skin. On the rare occasions when this shy gentle animal does attack, it never uses its horn to defend itself, but instead uses the tusk-like incisor teeth that it has on its lower jaw.

These rhinos are solitary animals and spend most of their time hiding in dense forests. They prefer to be near water, and like to wallow in muddy streams or lakes at least once a day.

PROFILE

Length: *3.4 m (11 ft); stands 1.7 m (5.5 ft) at the shoulder.*
Weight: *1 tonne (ton).*
Distribution: *Java (East Indies).*
Habitat: *Jungle.*
Breeding: *Single calf produced after a gestation period of 17 months.*
Diet: *Grass, reeds, twigs.*
Notes: *The horn is only 140 mm (5.7 in) long, the smallest of all the rhinos.*

BABIRUSA

The wild pig with the dental problem

Instead of growing out of the side of the mouth as they do in all other wild pigs, the upper tusks of this species grow up through the top of its muzzle.

Babirusa (*Babyrousa babyrussa*) are unusual pigs for other reasons besides their tusks. They are relatively long-legged for a pig, are the only completely hairless member of the pig family and have the smallest litter size of any pig. They also swim particularly well and have been able to colonise many of the islands scattered along the coast of southeast Asia.

Babirusa live in small herds, foraging in the forests where they root for food on the forest floor. It is said that the males do most of the digging and that the females and young follow behind to eat what the males have dug up.

Legend has it that the Babirusa's tusks are the shape they are so that the animal can hang itself from a branch of a tree in order to have a safe place to sleep at night. The species' name derives from the native name meaning 'pig-deer', the animal being so called because its tusks look more like the antlers of deer rather than the tusks of pigs.

PROFILE

Length: *875–1065 mm (35.0–42.6 in), with a tail of 275–320 mm (11.0–12.8 in).*
Weight: *Up to 90 kg (198 lb).*
Distribution: *Celebes and nearby islands of the East Indies.*
Habitat: *Swampy forests, especially near rivers and lakes.*
Breeding: *Litter size of 2.*
Diet: *Roots, berries, grubs.*
Longevity: *10 years in captivity.*

WHITE-LIPPED PECCARY

An animal not to be tangled with

The most aggressive of the wild pigs, it will attack anything that has wounded another member of its band. An attack by a band of 50–100 is all but unstoppable.

Despite its pig-like appearance, the White-lipped Peccary (*Tayassu pecari*) is not in fact a member of the pig family but a member of a separate family of peccaries, the Tassuidae, which includes only one other species. Peccaries differ in a number of important ways from the true pigs, and are nearly as closely related to the sub-order Ruminantia of the Artiodactyla.

On their backs peccaries have a scent gland which is one of the largest among the mammals. It is 7.5 cm (3 in) in diameter and 1.3 cm (0.5 in) thick. When the animal gets excited, a ridge of hair along its back is erected and the gland emits a musky secretion. The smell seems to function in co-ordinating the behaviour of the herd.

The peccary's sense of smell is parti-cularly well developed. It can detect bulbs of one of its favourite foodplants by their smell even when they are 5–8 cm (2–3 in) below the surface of the ground.

Peccaries are fat and agile, making them formidable animals to attack, especially when in groups. Dogs, Coyotes and Bobcats all give peccaries a wide berth.

VICUÑA

Producer of the world's finest wool

Needed to keep the animal warm high up in the Andes Mountains, the Vicuña's wool is the finest among all wool-bearing animals and is exclusive knitting wool.

The Vicuña (*Vicugna vicugna*) is one of 2 wild species of the camel family (Camelidae) to be found in South America. It roams the high-altitude moorlands at 3500–5757 m (11,400–18,700 ft) in the Andes Mountains. Vicuña are the most graceful of all hoofed mammals, and few sights can be

as enchanting as that of a herd of Vicuña trotting across the stony expanse of an Andes landscape against a back-drop of towering snow-capped crags.

Vicuña have unusual incisor teeth for an ungulate: like those of the rodents, they grow continuously and have ena-mel only on one side. Young Vicuña have

the curious habit of grazing while lying down with their legs tucked under them.

Vicuña are fleet-footed animals that can run at speeds of up to 47 km/h (29 mph), even at altitudes as high as 4500 m (14,600 ft) where the air is too thin to permit most animals to exert themselves.

MUSK DEER

The most fascinating perfume on earth

A single grain of musk will scent more than 50,000 cubic metres (1.7 million cu. ft) of air quite distinctively without losing a significant amount of weight.

Male Musk Deer (*Moschus moschiferus*) are unusual in having a gland on the belly that produces a strongly scented brownish secretion. The musk is stored in a small pouch and is the most powerful natural perfume in the world. About 28 g (1 oz) of this waxy substance can be removed from around a male's gland. Musk was highly prized for use in the manufacture of perfumes and soaps, both in traditional Chinese society and in Europe. The small quantities of musk that were obtained from a single animal meant that it invariably commanded high prices.

Unlike all other deer, Musk Deer lack antlers. They do, however, have a pair of tusk-like canine teeth 75 mm (3 in) in length; these are used in self-defence when the animal is attacked.

PROFILE

Length: *1 m (3.1 ft), with a tail of 38–51 mm (1.5–2.0 in); shoulder height 510–610 mm (20.4–24.4 in).*
Weight: *9–11 kg (20–24 lb).*
Distribution: *Central and north-eastern Asia, from Siberia and Korea to the Himalayas.*
Habitat: *Forest and thicket between 2600 m and 3600 m (8500–11,700 ft).*
Breeding: *Mating in January, with a single infant born in July.*
Diet: *Grasses, mosses and lichen.*

PROFILE

Length: *1.5–1.6 m (4.9–5.2 ft); tail 152 mm (6 in); shoulder height 760–860 mm (30–34 in).*
Weight: *35–65 kg (77–143 lb).*
Distribution: *South America (central Andes Mountains).*
Habitat: *High-altitude moorland above 3500 m (11,400 ft).*
Breeding: *Single young born in February.*
Diet: *Grass.*
Longevity: *Up to 20 years.*

PÈRE DAVID'S DEER

The only mammal never seen in the wild

The last specimens of this deer in the wild died out more than a century ago. But for a pair of animals purchased by the Duke of Bedford in 1898, the species would now be extinct.

Père David's Deer (*Elaphurus davidianus*) is believed to have been an inhabitant of the swampy plains of northern China. The deer became extinct in the wild when its habitat was developed as a rice-growing area several centuries ago. A private herd had, however, been maintained by the Chinese emperors in the Royal Hunting Park outside Peking. In 1865, the French missionary Père Armand David discovered them and bribed the guards to give him two skins, which he sent back to Paris for identification, whereupon the species was named after him.

Later, live specimens were sent to various zoos outside China.

Unfortunately, the few remaining animals of the Chinese herd were killed in 1900 by hungry soldiers during one of China's many civil wars. Only the herd built up by the Duke of Bedford on his English estate thrived well enough to provide specimens for zoos around the world. Since the 1960s, animals from this herd have regularly been sent back to China to re-establish herds in the species' native country. There are now more than 500 individuals in zoos around the world.

MOOSE

The largest living deer

More than three times bigger than any other deer, this is the giant of the deer world; it also boasts the largest and heaviest antlers of any living deer.

Though of massive size, the Moose (*Alces alces*) can walk almost silently through the willow and poplar woods in which it prefers to live. A solitary species by nature, it can often be found standing half submerged in a lake, where it feeds on the aquatic vegetation. Although it occurs only in habitats which are seasonally snow-bound, it will often migrate during winter to areas which have less heavy snow cover. During these migrations, it can move up to 300 km (115 miles).

Moose generally occur at very low densities, typically around one animal per 5 square km (2 square miles). One reason for this is that, being so large, they need a relatively large area to themselves to provide them with enough food. An adult will consume about 19.5 kg (43 lb) of vegetation a day. Although their size protects them from most predators except Man, Moose will retreat into lakes to escape from pack-hunting wolves.

The male's antlers are used mainly for fighting during the breeding season rather than for protection. Their flat shape provides a stable surface on which to push during shoving matches when the males fight over females.

During the last century, Moose were hunted to extinction throughout much of their range in Europe and America. Control measures now ensure that populations remain stable in those areas where they still occur in large numbers, though they are still heavily hunted for their meat. In 1978, 94,000 were killed in Sweden alone, where Moose makes up 2–3% of the total annual meat production.

PROFILE

Length: *2.4–3.1 m (7.8–10.1 ft), with a tail of 5–12 cm (2–5 in); shoulder height 1.4–2.4 m (4.6–7.8 ft).*
Weight: *200–825 kg (440–1815 lb).*
Distribution: *Canada and northern USA, northern Europe as far east as Siberia.*
Habitat: *Well-watered forest.*
Breeding: *1–2 calves born in spring.*
Diet: *Aquatic vegetation, leaves of shrubs and trees.*
Longevity: *27 years.*
Notes: *The maximum recorded antler spread is 2.05 m (80 in).*

GIRAFFE

Skyscraper on the savanna

Old bulls, the tallest living land animals, tower 5.5 m (18 ft) above the ground. Despite their long necks, they have only the same number of neck vertebrae (seven) as all other mammals.

Perhaps the most impressive animal on the African plains, the Giraffe (*Giraffa camelopardalis*) is far from being the ungainly disjointed figure its size might suggest. It can achieve speeds of 47 km/h (29 mph) when running across open ground and it can use its forefeet to very good effect when defending itself. When running, its long neck sways sinuously from side to side.

Giraffes have horns that are quite unlike those of any other species: it has two to five bony protruberances from the top of its skull that are covered in hair. It also has one of the longest and most mobile tongues of any mammal that is not an ant-eater. Its tongue is 456 mm (18.2 in) long.

The Giraffe's legs are so long that, despite its long neck, its head cannot reach the ground. In order to feed from the ground or to drink water, it has to spread its legs wide enough to lower its shoulders. To ensure that blood reaches its head, it has special one-way valves in its arteries.

The Giraffe's height allows it to feed on the leaves of trees that are out of reach of the other herbivores of the African savannas. Its height and good eyesight allow it to detect approaching predators at considerable distances and it probably has the greatest range of vision of any mammal.

There are 9 recognised races of Giraffe (up to 13 have been described), and the distinctions are based on height, colour pattern and the number of horns (up to five). The tallest race is the Masai (*G.c. tippelskirchi*).

ALTITUDE IN THE ANIMAL KINGDOM RECORD HEIGHTS

19'9" 6,02m
11'1,5" 3,39m
7'1" 2,16m
6'2" 2,13m
39,5" 1,00m

PROFILE

Length: *Up to 4 m (13 ft), with a shoulder height of 2.5–3.7 m (8.1–12.0 ft); tail 860 mm (34 in).*

Weight: *550–1800 kg (1210–3960 lb).*

Distribution: *Throughout Africa south of the Sahara, except in the heavily forested areas of West and Central Africa.*

Habitat: *Savanna plains and woodland.*

Breeding: *Mating July–September; single young born 14–15 months later.*

Diet: *Leaves of acacia, mimosa and wild apricot.*

Longevity: *15–20 years; one in captivity lived to be 28.*

ROYAL ANTELOPE

The smallest hoofed mammal in the world

Standing a mere 250–300 mm (10–12 in) at the shoulder, this antelope is much the smallest of all the hoofed mammals.

One of 2 species of pygmy antelope, the Royal Antelope (*Neotragus pygmaeus*) has a reputation in Liberian folklore for cunning and intelligence that is supposed to make up for its diminutive size. Like most other inhabitants of the forest, it is secretive, shy and solitary. When danger threatens, it flees for the safety of thickets, often with long bounds and leaps. It is said to be able to jump distances of 2.8 m (9 ft), about six times its length.

Not only is the Royal Antelope the smallest hoofed mammal, but it also has the shortest horns. Its spike-like weapons (present only in the male) are barely 2.5 cm (1 in) long. It differs from

most of the other small forest antelopes in its diet, being strictly a leaf-eating browser rather than a fruit-eater.

Because of its small size and its habit of walking with its head down, this tiny antelope can often force its way under dense thickets that are impenetrable to larger animals. This ability helps it to escape predators both because it can vanish into a tangle of undergrowth and because predators have difficulty following it.

The species' solitary habits also help by allowing it to escape detection by passing predators. Each Royal Antelope occupies its own territory about 2 ha (4.8 acres) in size. Male territories

are usually a little larger than those of females and often contain the ranges of several females within them.

PROFILE

Length: *45 cm (18 in).*
Weight: *3.1–4.1 kg (7–9 lb).*
Distribution: *West Africa.*
Habitat: *Dense high forest.*
Breeding: *Occurs throughout the year; single offspring per litter.*
Diet: *Leaves.*
Notes: *It often raids cocoa and peanut plantations.*

KLIPSPRINGER

The only animal that habitually walks on tiptoe

Klipspringers differ from all other hoofed mammals in that they walk on the tip rather than the flat of the hoof. This helps to give them better grip on steep cliffs.

The Klipspringer (*Oreotragus oreotragus*) belongs to the Bovidae family of Artiodactyls, which with 215 species is the largest and most diverse family of mammals there is.

The Klipspringer is a small antelope with an unusually thick coat of coarse grizzled fur. The female is slightly larger than the male. Except for one East African race, only the male has horns. These average 10 cm (4 in) in length; the largest ever measured were 15.5 cm (6.2 in) long.

The name of the species comes from the Afrikaans words *klip*, meaning 'rock', and *springer*, meaning 'jumper', and the Klipspringer is, in fact, the only animal south of the Sahara that can compare with the mountain goats and sheep of other continents.

Klipspringers are found on rocky outcrops or steep gorges throughout southern and eastern Africa, at all altitudes from sea level to 4000 m (13,000 ft). They live in pairs on small territories of about 4 ha (2 acres).

Klipspringers feed on the leaves and flowers of various herbs and small shrubs. When these are not available, the animals will stand on their hindlegs in order to reach leaves and fruits that are out of reach. Klipspringers feed at dawn and dusk, but the moon seems to whet their appetite, and they are sometimes seen eating by the light of the full moon.

A single fawn is born each year after a gestation of three months. Births usually occur in April or May. Although capable of reproducing by the age of 12 months, most Klipspringers do not do so until they are two years old.

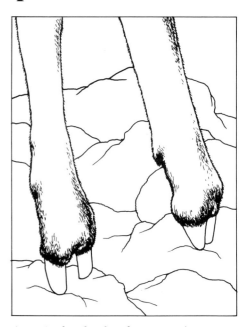

Amazingly, this hoof construction, which is unique to the Klipspringer, makes it possible for the animal to keep its balance on the sharpest ridges and even to climb up practically vertical outcrops.

PROFILE

Shoulder height: *0.5 m (20 in).*
Weight: *15 kg (33 lb).*
Distribution: *Southern and eastern Africa.*
Habitat: *Rocky outcrops and gorges.*
Diet: *Leaves, flowers.*
Group size: *2–3.*
Longevity: *5–7 years.*
Notes: *An exceptional climber, it escapes from predators by bounding up vertical cliff faces.*

SAIGA

The antelope that flees bad weather

During the autumn, large herds of Saiga migrate southwards into warmer climates before the advancing snows of the Russian winter.

The odd-looking Saiga (*Saiga tatarica*) shares a curious feature with the whales: each nostril contains a sac lined with mucous membranes. In fact, its whole nose is greatly enlarged with numerous internal openings lined with hairs and mucous glands, giving it a proboscis-like appearance. This is designed to filter out the dust that the animals would otherwise breathe in when the large herds move across the dry Russian steppe, stirring up the thin soils as they do so.

Although they normally walk with a rather shambling gait, Saiga can produce a remarkable turn of speed when required. Animals have been timed at speeds approaching 60 km/h (38 mph). Because of the way they are built, however, Saiga cannot make sharp turns of direction when trying to escape predators in the way that many other antelopes do.

The horns (which only the males have) were thought to possess medicinal properties by the Chinese, who were willing to pay up to US $250 for a pair. The result was the decimation of the wild population until, in 1920, the species was placed under full protection. Now there are estimated to be over a million Saiga roaming the plains of Central Asia.

SPRINGBOK

The largest migratory herds on record

When Europeans first settled in southern Africa, herds of migrating Springbok contained millions of individuals and often covered the plains as far as the eye could see.

The Springbok (*Antidorcas marsupialis*) is the only gazelle to occur south of the river Zambesi. Its name derives from the stiff-legged bounces (called 'pronking') that it often makes when fleeing from danger. In the process of doing this, the animal leaps 3.0–3.5 m (10–11 ft) into the air, repeating the action five to six times in rapid succession.

Springbok migrate when drought produces a dramatic deterioration in the amount of food available to them. During these migrations, the herds were often so large that they took several days to pass a given point. The vast mass of animals would move across the plain like a giant steamroller, trampling vegetation, crops and even other animals in its path. The destruction caused to crops was so severe that control measures were introduced to reduce the Spingbok population. In the process, however, the species was all but wiped out, and has survived in small numbers only in the most remote parts of its range.

The Springbok has one feature that is unique among the Bovidae (hoofed mammals). Along its back, it has a flap of skin that can be opened out to expose a crest of bristly white hair when it is alarmed.

PROFILE

Length: *1.2–1.4 m (46.8–54.6 in), with a tail of 190–275 mm (7.6–11.0 in); shoulder height 770–845 mm (30–33 in).*
Weight: *32–36 kg (70–79 lb).*
Distribution: *Southern Africa.*
Habitat: *Open dry plains.*
Breeding: *Single infant born in November–December.*
Diet: *Grass, leaves of thorn bushes.*

SITATUNGA

The antelope that hides underwater

This nocturnal antelope spends much of its day hidden in reed swamps. To escape detection, it may even submerge completely until only the tip of its nostrils shows.

Somewhat clumsy on dry land, the Sitatunga (*Tragelaphus spekii*) can move with surprising speed and grace through the marshy swamps in which it lives. This is possible because of the unique structure of its foot: the hooves are long and widely splayed, and the foot joints are so loose that the animal actually walks on these bones. In this way, it gains a large surface area to bear its weight on waterlogged ground where antelopes with the normal small sharp-pointed hooves would sink.

The only aquatic member of the antelope family, this large antelope is generally solitary, though it can occasionally be seen in groups of up to 15 individuals.

PROFILE

Length: *915–1125 mm (36.6–45.0 in) in shoulder height.*
Weight: *45–125 kg (100–275 lb).*
Distribution: *Central and western Africa.*
Habitat: *Swamp and flooded forest.*
Breeding: *Single young born after a gestation period of about 250 days.*
Diet: *Leaves, twigs and fruit of aquatic vegetation.*
Longevity: *20 years.*

CHAMOIS

King of the mountain peaks

Nimble, agile and daring, the Chamois often makes prodigious leaps of up to 7 m (23 ft) when fleeing from danger in the crags of the European Alps.

A distant relative of the goat, the Chamois (*Rupicapra rupicapra*) is the only European member of the widespread group of goat-antelopes, the Rupicaprids. It inhabits the higher reaches of Europe's old mountain chains, from the Alps to the Carpathians. It spends the summers up near the snow line, but descends to lower altitudes during the winter. Even so, when the snow cover becomes too deep for the animals to feed, they have been known to fast for two weeks or more without ill effect.

Chamois are extremely sure-footed, the sole of the hoof being both slightly hollow and rather soft to give it grip on slippery surfaces. When threatened, it invariably retreats to the most inaccessible crags. Its agility on the mountain face is legendary and it can easily jump over obstacles as high as 4 m (13 ft) when being pursued.

The Chamois' skin is particularly soft and was the original source of the 'shammy' leathers that are used for cleaning glass. As a result of the European enthusiasm for hunting, the species was brought to the verge of extinction early in the 20th century.

FOUR-HORNED ANTELOPE

The only wild animal with four horns

Unique among the members of the Bovidae family in having four horns, it also differs from other antelopes in its curious jerky style of running.

The Four-horned Antelope or Chousingha (*Tetraceros quadricornis*) is the smallest of the Asian antelopes. Shy and retiring, it makes a rapid dash for cover at the slightest hint of danger. Unlike most other antelopes, it drinks regularly and therefore seldom strays far from water.

Only the male is horned and, although it characteristically has four horns, the smaller front pair is not always well developed. While the rear pair is typically 12.5 cm (5 in) long, the front pair averages only 2.5 cm (1 in) and never exceeds 6.5 cm (2.5 in) in any individual. In some populations, the two front horns do not develop, but are marked only by two patches of bare black skin.

The Four-horned Antelope also has unusual hooves. These are small and rounded, rather than pointed like those of most other members of the Bovidae family.

YAK

The high-altitude beast of burden

Sure-footed but slow, the Yak's immense powers of endurance have made it the mainstay of the peasant economy of Tibet, for centuries transporting goods and chattels across the mountains.

Massive and lugubrious, the Yak or Grunting Ox (*Bos grunniens*) is a close relative of our own Domestic Cattle, with which it will in fact interbreed. It roams the mountains of the Himalayas and the Tibetan plateau, where it has a marked preference for the moorlands along the snow line. Despite its size, it is surprisingly manoeuvrable on rocks and can climb well. It does poorly at lower altitudes, where it appears to be unable to cope with warmer temperatures.

Docile and easily tamed, the Yak was soon domesticated. It has been used for centuries in Tibet, both for milk and as the main beast of burden. The domestic variety is somewhat smaller than its wild relative.

PROFILE

Length: *3 m (10 ft), standing 2 m (6.5 ft) at the shoulder.*
Weight: *525 kg (1155 lb).*
Distribution: *Tibetan mountains.*
Habitat: *Moorlands up to 6100 m (20,000 ft) in altitude.*
Breeding: *Single calf born in the autumn.*
Diet: *Moorland plants and grasses.*
Longevity: *32 years.*
Notes: *Horns up to 974 mm (38 in) in length.*

PROFILE

Length: *1 m (39 in), standing only 60 cm (24 in) at the shoulder; tail about 126 mm (5 in).*
Weight: *17–21 kg (37.4–46.2 lb).*
Distribution: *India.*
Habitat: *Open forest and woodland.*
Breeding: *Mates during rainy season, with 1–3 young born in January.*
Diet: *Grass.*
Longevity: *One survived for 4 years in a zoo.*

BLUE WHALE

The largest animal the world has ever known

In 1909, a 33.58-m (110.12-ft) long female was brought into the whaling station at Grytviken, South Georgia. No piecemeal weight was recorded for this colossus, but another corpulent female measuring 27.6 m (90.5 ft) caught in the Southern Ocean in 1947 scaled 190 tonnes (187 tons).

The Blue Whale (*Balaenoptera musculus*) belongs to the family of rorquals known as Balaenopteridae (4 species), and is easily identified by its vast size, dark blue-grey mottled coloration and the large number of grooves (up to 94) extending from the throat to the navel. Three races are recognised, including the so-called Pygmy Blue Whale (*B.m. brevicauda*) of the subantarctic waters of the Indian Ocean, which does not exceed 24 m (78.7 ft).

Because of its awesome proportions, statistics on length and weight cannot evoke a true mental picture of the Blue Whale's actual size, but some idea can be gauged by the enormity of some of its internal organs. In the case of the 27.6-m (90.5-ft) female already mentioned, the tongue and heart weighed 4.22 tonnes/tons and 698.5 kg (1540 lb) respectively.

The fact that a Blue Whale calf grows from a barely visible ovum weighing a fraction of a milligramme (0.000035 oz) to a weight of about 26 tonnes/tons in 22¾ months, made up of 10¾ months gestation and the first 12 months of life, is even more remarkable. This is the fastest growth in the Animal Kingdom and equivalent to an increase of 30,000 million-fold.

The Blue Whale attains sexual maturity when it becomes four or five years old.

PROFILE

Length: *20–33 m (65–110 ft); adult male approximately 6% shorter than female.*
Weight: *63–190 tonnes (62–187 tons).*
Distribution: *Formerly worldwide, but now found mainly in polar feeding grounds during summer.*
Habitat: *Open oceans and seas.*
Breeding: *Pairing every 2–3 years; gestation period about 11 months.*
Diet: *Krill (up to 4 tonnes/tons daily) and small fish. Feeds for only 4–5 months annually.*
Longevity: *30–45 years.*
Notes: *Low-frequency pulses made by Blue Whales when communicating with others of their kind measured up to 188 dB, making them the loudest sounds emitted by any living source. They have been detected 850 km (530 miles) away.*

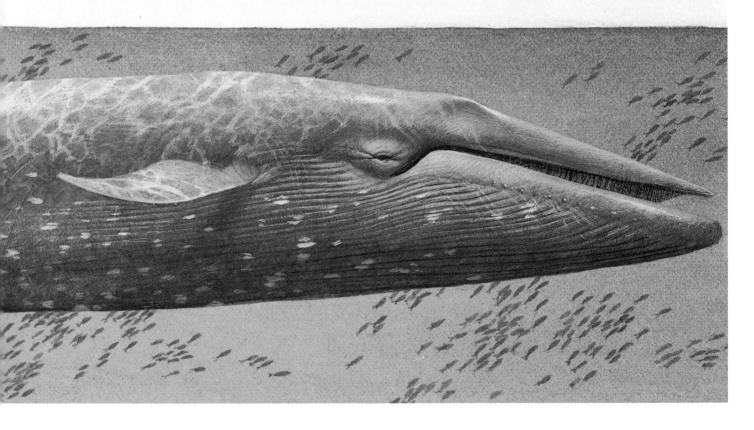

HUMPBACK WHALE

Songster of the seas

The most musical of all the mammals, the Humpback Whale produces 'songs' that have a remarkable haunting quality, especially when many individuals are singing in chorus.

The songs of the Humpback Whale (*Megaptera novaeangliae*) are the most complex sounds to be heard in the natural world. Their function, however, remains uncertain, though their complexity suggests that they serve to identify individuals, both to each other and as members of different communities or populations. They may also help to maintain co-ordination of travel between individuals when, as often happens, they become widely separated out at sea during the great annual migrations to and from their traditional breeding grounds.

Where channels in the water provide particularly good sound-transmission properties, the deep notes may carry for many thousands of kilometres. The notes of the songs change gradually over the course of years, so that completely new song patterns are evolving all the time.

Among the most playful and acrobatic of the whale species, Humpback Whales can leap right out of the water, which is an astonishing feat for an animal of their size. Their flippers are the longest of all the whales, being about 4.3 m (14 ft) in a fully grown individual (about one-third of the length of its body).

Humpback Whales have particularly thick blubber. A 12-m (39-ft) whale can yield as much as 8 tonnes (tons) of whale oil, making this species the richest source of oil for its size.

PROFILE

Length: *11.5–15.0 m (37.4–48.8 ft), average 12.5 m (40.6 ft).*
Weight: *29 tonnes (tons).*
Distribution: *Worldwide.*
Habitat: *Mainly coastal waters.*
Breeding: *Single calf produced in winter after a gestation period of 12 months.*
Diet: *Krill and small fish.*
Notes: *Can remain submerged for 20 minutes.*

SPERM WHALE

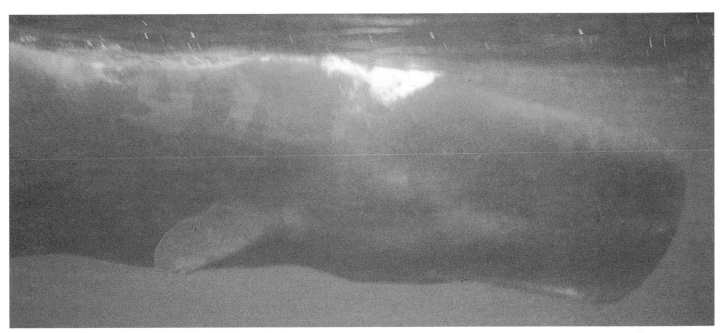

The world's champion diver

The deepest recorded dive was of 2.25 km (1.4 miles) by a whale tracked by sonar, but the stomach contents of another suggested that it had dived to 3.2 km (2 miles).

The bulbous head of the Sperm Whale (*Physeter catodon*) accounts for a quarter of its length. It contains massive organs filled with special waxes (spermaceti oil), the density of which can be varied by the whale in order to alter its buoyancy, thus allowing it to dive effortlessly to great depths. By using this mechanism to maintain neutral buoy-

The spout of each whale species differs in size or shape, making it possible to identify the whale at a distance.

ancy at any depth, it can hang motionless in the water waiting for a suitable prey to appear without using any unnecessary energy or extra oxygen. In a big whale the spermaceti organs can weigh as much as 16 tonnes (tons) — approximately equivalent to the weight of three African Elephants — and account for one-third of the animal's total body weight.

Sperm Whales normally dive to depths of 315–360 m (1025–1170 ft), spending an average of 10.5 minutes below the surface. On deeper dives, however, they can spend up to an hour

underwater, the longest recorded dive being about 90 minutes. When they dive, Sperm Whales descend and rise vertically, so that they re-appear at the surface exactly where they went down.

The Sperm Whale's lower jaw contains 16–30 pairs of large conical teeth, each of which is about 200 mm (8 in) in length: these are the largest teeth in the world. Sperm Whales also possess the largest brain of any living animal species: that of males weighs 7.8 kg (17.2 lb) on average, and some may be as large as 9.2 kg (20.2 lb) — five or six times larger than the brain of Man.

Blue Whale   Sperm Whale   Fin Whale

The Blue Whale's spout is about 15 m (45 ft) high.

Greenland Right Whale   Sei Whale   Humpback Whale   Grey Whale

PROFILE

Length: *Male up to 18.5 m (60 ft), female 11–12 m (36–39 ft).*
Weight: *35–50 tonnes (tons).*
Distribution: *Worldwide.*
Habitat: *Oceanic.*
Breeding: *Single calf produced after a gestation period of 12–16 months.*
Diet: *Squid, cuttlefish; occasionally large fish and sharks.*
Longevity: *32 years.*
Notes: *Individuals are often heavily scarred about the head.*

NARWHAL

Unicorn of the seas

Brought to Europe in early medieval times by Vikings trading from Greenland and Iceland, the long spiralled tusks were at first thought to be those of the mythical unicorn.

The unique tusk of the Narwhal (*Monodon monoceros*) is a greatly elongated tooth. Narwhals possess only two teeth, both of which lie horizontally within the upper jaw bone. In females, they remain embedded within the jaw throughout life. In males, however, the left-hand tooth (exceptionally, the right-hand one as well) grows outwards to pierce the upper lip. Its length (typically 2.8 m, or 9 ft) may be as much as the animal's own body length. The tusk's function is completely unknown, though males have been observed 'fencing' with them, albeit apparently in play. Contrary to popular legend, they are never used to pierce the bottoms of boats, being hollow and too delicate to withstand impact. In fact, broken tusks are quite common.

Narwhals are the most northerly of all the whales, being found well up into Arctic waters where they breed in the sheltered bays and fjords of Norway, Greenland and northern Canada. When the bays freeze up in winter, the Narwhals migrate southwards into warmer waters.

PROFILE

Length: *Males average 4.7 m (15.3 ft), females average 4.0 m (13 ft).*
Weight: *Male 1.6 tonnes/tons, female 0.9 tonnes/tons.*
Distribution: *Arctic Ocean.*
Habitat: *Coastal waters.*
Breeding: *Produces a single calf.*
Diet: *Cuttlefish, crustaceans, fish.*
Notes: *Dives to depths of 370 m (1200 ft).*

KILLER WHALE

Lord of the seas

The stomach of one individual was found to contain the remains of 24 seals, that of another the remains of 13 porpoises and 14 seals.

Despite its reputation for ferocity, the Killer Whale (*Orcinus orca*) is in reality no more aggressive than any other large carnivore. When not hunting, it can even be very gentle, but a hungry individual is a formidable opponent to meet at sea. Its mouth is armed with 40–50 teeth, each of which is 5 cm (2 in) in diameter. Its throat is large enough to swallow a seal or a dolphin with little difficulty.

Killer Whales commonly hunt in packs of up to 50 individuals. Packs are reputed to hunt co-operatively and have been known to tear the large defence-less baleen whales apart while they are still alive. They are particularly fast, often travelling at speeds of 10–13 km/h (6.3–8.1 mph) for long distances. They

frequently indulge in spectacular leaps out of the water, during which they can jump distances of up to 13.6 m (44.2 ft) and reach heights of 1.5 m (4.9 ft) above the surface of the sea.

Other whales and seals become disturbed when a Killer Whale is sighted nearby. A Gray Whale was once reported to have jumped right out of the water and joined a man standing on a rock on the shoreline! When Killer Whales see a seabird or seal on the edge of an ice floe, they are reputed to dive deeply and then rush to the surface to break through ice up to 1 m (39 in) thick, so as to throw the unfortunate animal into the sea where they can get at it.

PROFILE

Length: *Male up to 8.2 m (26.7 ft), female up to 7.0 m (22.8 ft).*
Weight: *A 4-m (13-ft) female weighed 850 kg (1870 lb).*
Distribution: *Worldwide, but mainly arctic and antarctic waters.*
Habitat: *Often coastal waters, but may be found at sea.*
Breeding: *Single calf born after a gestation period of 12 months.*
Diet: *Any large marine animal (especially whales and seals).*
Notes: *Its dorsal fin, particularly conspicuous as it swims just below the surface, is 2 m (6 ft) high.*

COMMON DOLPHIN

The most acute sense of hearing in the world

By emitting series of rapid clicks and listening for the returning echoes, the dolphin can locate individual fish in murky water and even distinguish between a small one and a large one.

The Common Dolphin (*Delphinus delphis*) is one of about 20 species in the family Delphinidae, all of which have a well-developed sense of echo-location. Sounds emitted in the nasal passages are reflected off the frontal bones of the skull to be focused by a mass of fatty tissue (known as the 'melon') situated in its bulbous forehead, so as to form a narrow beam of sound just 9° of arc wide. The returning echoes are 'heard' through a special channel of fatty tissue in the jaw bone and transmitted to the brain independently of the ear.

Common Dolphins may sometimes use this sound beam to stun fish just before they seize them. They can pro-duce a sound wave of about 100 decibels intensity at a distance of 1 m (3 ft) in front of the animal.

The Common Dolphin is the fastest of all the cetaceans, having been timed at speeds of 56 km/h (35 mph). This is possible despite its small size because of special adaptations of body shape, swimming style and skin surface that allow the dolphin to reduce to an absolute minimum the 'drag' on its body caused by turbulence in the water.

Dolphins are particularly social animals and herds of 10,000 or more have been recorded. They are probably one of the commonest species of mammal in the world.

PROFILE

Length: *1.5–2.5 m (4.9–8.1 ft).*
Weight: *Up to 75 kg (165 lb).*
Distribution: *Temperate and tropical seas, worldwide.*
Habitat: *Coastal and offshore waters.*
Breeding: *Single calf, born in summer.*
Diet: *Fish, especially herring and pilchard.*
Longevity: *25–30 years.*
Notes: *Dolphins are extremely intelligent, and may be one of the most intelligent species after Man.*

SUSU

The blind river dolphin

Its eyes are tiny and lack a lens, so that, while they can probably distinguish light from dark, they are certainly unable to recognise objects by sight alone.

Inhabiting the murky rivers of the Indian continent, the Susu or Ganges River Dolphin (*Platanista gangetica*) finds its food in the muddy riverbed partly by feel, using its sensitive snout, and partly by echo-location. It gets its name from the sighing noise it makes when it comes up to the surface for air.

The Susu differs from the oceanic whales and dolphins in being much less streamlined. Unlike these other species, it also has a distinct neck. This is particularly important to the Susu because it enables it to move its head rapidly from side to side while it is searching through the mud of the riverbed for food.

Because of the strong currents in the rivers where it lives, the Susu has to keep swimming in order to avoid being swept downstream. All the while, its sonar ticks continuously away, probing the murky waters for obstacles. It is silent only occasionally, and then for just a few brief seconds at a time as the animal sleeps.

The Susu is unique among the Cetacae in having scalloped tail fins, each clearly showing the five digits of the foot from which it originally evolved. In all other whales and dolphins, this is present only in the embryo but is soon lost as the animal grows and the fin develops into its adult form.

PROFILE

Length: *Males average 1.5 m (4.9 ft), females average 1.7 m (5.6 ft).*
Weight: *Male 35 kg (77 lb), female 44 kg (97 lb).*
Distribution: *Large rivers of northern India.*
Habitat: *Fresh water only.*
Breeding: *Single calf born between April and July.*
Diet: *Fish and other freshwater bottom-dwelling organisms.*
Notes: *The largest individual ever measured was a female 4 m (13 ft) long.*

BIRDS

The one characteristic that distinguishes birds from all other animals is their feathers. These are elaborate structures made of a horny substance called keratin. In some cases, such as the three kiwi species, they are stiff and hair-like, but they are nevertheless of the same basic structure.

The earliest bird existed about 140 million years ago. Nowadays there are around 8600 different species distributed throughout the world from pole to pole. They live in all kinds of habitats, from extreme deserts to freezing pack-ice zones—from sea level to high up in mountains, on land and on water. Birds range in size from the minute insect-sized Bee Hummingbird to the gigantic flightless Ostrich. Many birds cannot fly and these, of course, do not migrate, but countless others do, moving at particular times of the year between two locations; the distances involved in these journeys may be immense—tens of thousands of kilometres—while many seabirds regularly traverse several oceans in search of seasonal sources of food.

All birds lay eggs which hatch out after being heated during incubation. In the vast majority of species this is brought about by the bird sitting on the eggs and using heat from its own body, but a few species use heat from the sun, from volcanic activity or even from rotting vegetation. Some 'lazy' species lay their eggs in other birds' nests and allow them to do all the work.

The huge variation in their appearance and habits is just one reason why birds have fascinated Man for thousands of years and have been the object of incomparable scientific study.

OSTRICH

PROFILE

Height: *2.1–2.7 m (7–9 ft); to shoulder, 1.14–1.45 m (3.75–4.75 ft). Average chick grows 30 cm (12 in) a month during first 5 months of life.*

Weight: *90–156 kg (200–345 lb), adult female much smaller than male.*

Distribution: *Greater part of Africa; introduced to South Australia.*

Habitat: *Grassland and semi-desert.*

Breeding: *6–20 eggs, average weight of egg 1.56 kg (3.44 lb); incubation period 42–48 days.*

Diet: *Omnivorous, eats grass, seeds, insects, small vertebrates.*

Flock size: *5–50.*

Longevity: *30–68 years.*

Notes: *Fastest 2-legged animal on earth: running speed 45–72 km/h (28–45 mph), but inclined to run in wide circles which deprives it of sprint advantage. Good swimmer.*

The world's smallest bird, the Bee Humming Bird, is no larger than the eye of the world's largest bird, the Ostrich.

Dustbin of the avian world

Because the Ostrich has an amazingly elastic throat it can swallow objects up to the size of a small horseshoe, but it sometimes pays the ultimate price for its folly.

The Ostrich (*Struthio camelus*), the largest living bird, regularly swallows stones or quartz pebbles to aid its digestion, and if, when kept in captivity, it cannot find suitable ones it will happily gulp down an amazing variety of articles as substitutes. There is one record of a male bird swallowing two padlocks, with fatal results, and another of these flightless birds met its end after attempting to digest a 90-cm (3-ft) long piece of rope, a spool of film, an alarm-clock key, a bicycle valve, a pencil, a comb, three gloves, a handkerchief, pieces of a gold necklace and two collar studs.

There are now 4 geographical races—the Syrian Ostrich (*S. c. syriacus*) became extinct in 1941—which differ slightly in size, shape and colour. The largest is the Northern Ostrich (*S. c. camelus*) of North Africa, which has been measured at up to 2.7 m (9 ft) in height and can reach a weight of 156 kg (345 lb).

During the mating season the male Ostrich, equipped with huge powerfully-clawed legs, is one of the most dangerous animals on earth; it has been responsible for a number of human fatalities. It is also completely devoid of fear, and there is one story of a vicious old bird rushing on to a railway track and advancing towards an oncoming goods train to do battle: the Ostrich lost!

The classic story that the Ostrich will bury its head in the sand when frightened is based on the manner in which it sits on its nest. By laying its long neck flat on the ground, it looks just like another hillock on the bare scrub-covered veld and is overlooked by its natural enemies.

COMMON KIWI

The bird that sniffs out worms

The long, curved and remarkably sensitive bill, with nostrils near the tip, enables the Common Kiwi to find its food by smell in total darkness.

The Common or Brown Kiwi (*Apteryx australis*) of New Zealand is active only at night (though the race found on Stewart Island may also be out and about in early morning and late evening). It feeds on small insects and berries, but its main diet by far is earthworms which it finds by digging about in the forest floor. The female's bill is longer than the male's, but both sexes have a highly developed sense of smell which is of great importance to them when foraging in the dark for concealed worms. Whereas most bird species have nostrils near the base of the bill, the Common Kiwi's nostrils are near the tip—so that it can snuffle around and literally sniff out its food.

Other unusual characteristics of these weird birds include their odd shape—like that of a pear—and their plumage, which is loose and shaggy and consists of long hair-like feathers more like the fur of a mammal. Kiwis cannot fly because their wings are only about 5 cm (2 in) long; the pectoral (breast) muscles, the muscles which control the wings and allow birds to fly, are undeveloped and this produces the bird's odd pear shape. Their legs and feet are large, thick and powerful, and account for almost one-third of the bird's total weight. For a nocturnal bird, the Common Kiwi has exceptionally small eyes.

Two other, smaller, species of kiwi occur in New Zealand, both sharing the same unique features and nocturnal habits of the Common Kiwi. All three are shy and seldom seen, despite being so famous throughout the world as a symbol of the country of New Zealand itself.

The name 'kiwi' is derived from the shrill whistling call made by the male.

PROFILE

Length: *Male up to about 45 cm (18 in), female up to 55 cm (22 in).*

Weight: *Male about 2.8 kg (6.2 lb), female up to 3.5 kg (7.7 lb) or more.*

Distribution: *Confined to New Zealand, on North and South Islands and Stewart Island.*

Habitat: *Primarily dense forests (kauri etc), occasionally also scrub and grassland.*

Breeding: *1–2 white eggs, each weighing 0.45 kg (1 lb), laid from July to February in burrow; incubation 76–84 days. Chicks hatch fully feathered and active.*

Diet: *Mainly earthworms; also small insects, slugs, snails, woodlice etc, berries and seeds.*

Longevity: *Probably long-lived, perhaps 10 years and more.*

EMPEROR PENGUI

The world's largest and hardiest marine bird

In the depths of the Antarctic, where few other birds survive, a giant penguin spends its entire life, even breeding in 24-hour darkness.

Emperor Penguins (*Aptenodytes forsteri*) stand well over 1 m (3.3 ft) tall, and with a weight of up to 43 kg (95 lb) are almost 40 times heavier than the smallest penguin, the Little Blue (*Eudyptula minor*). They live south of 65°S and rarely venture outside the Antarctic Circle, thus being the most southerly of all birds. To make life more difficult, they even breed in the southern winter — in the harshest climate anywhere in the world: the mean minimum winter temperature is about −20°C (−4°F), winds average 40 km/h (25 mph) but can reach 200 km/h (125 mph), and there is total darkness day and night. To survive in such conditions the Emperor Penguin has two layers of long, dense feathers, and its relatively small bill and flippers also help to reduce heat loss. At colonies, which number from 500 to 25,000 pairs, both adults and young huddle close together to maintain warmth; if they did not do this, they would probably not survive.

After January and February fishing at sea, the birds return to the ice. Following mating, the female lays her single egg in mid-May and goes back to sea; she does not return until after the chick has hatched. The male meanwhile incubates the egg on top of his feet for about two months and, by the time the egg hatches, has fasted for 110–115 days; during this time he lives on fat reserves laid down at sea before the start of breeding, and loses up to 45% of his initial body weight.

These birds are accomplished divers and swimmers, able to spend up to 18 minutes underwater and reaching depths of over 260 m (850 ft).

PROFILE

Height: *Up to 1.15 m (3.8 ft).*
Weight: *20–43 kg (44–95 lb).*
Distribution: *Coasts of Antarctic continent.*
Habitat: *Antarctic oceans; sea ice when breeding.*
Breeding: *1 egg, incubated by male for 62–64 days; chick brooded by female for 40 days. First breeding at 3–6 years of age.*
Diet: *Fish, squid, some crustaceans.*
Colony size: *500–25,000 pairs. World population about 200,000 pairs.*
Longevity: *Average about 20 years. Survival of chicks in first year of life about 19%.*
Notes: *Like all penguins flightless, but uses stunted wings as flippers for powerful swimming.*

WANDERING ALBATROSS

The greatest wingspan of any living bird

In 1957, a male Wandering Albatross was caught in Western Australia which measured 3.6 m (11 ft 10 in) from wingtip to wingtip, and some individuals of this species may have a wingspan of as much as 3.9 m (12 ft 10 in).

It is no coincidence that albatrosses have such long wings. The Wandering Albatross (*Diomedea exulans*) regularly circumnavigates the world, covering anything up to 500 km (270 miles) or more each day (in reality much more, as it soars up and down all the time) and 56,000 km (35,000 miles) every three months. The long, narrow wings of albatrosses are adapted for dynamic soaring over the oceans, using the thermals created by the wave troughs and crests. A large wing area relative to body weight enables them to glide downwind at speed and cover vast distances with minimal effort as they patrol the southern oceans in their search for food. They alight on the sea only to feed or in calm weather.

Albatrosses come ashore only to breed. In the Wanderer this is preceded by highly elaborate dancing displays in which the partners face each other with wings outstretched, bow to each other while vibrating their bills and making groaning sounds, throw back their heads with bills pointing skyward, and fence with their bills.

The breeding cycle is exceptionally long, taking a year to complete: the chicks born in one summer are fed throughout the following winter and are not fully fledged until the next summer. This species therefore breeds only every two years. In addition, the young do not begin breeding until they are five to ten years old. This low productivity, however, is compensated for by the fact that these birds are very long-lived: some may even reach 80 years of age.

PROFILE

Length: *107–135 cm (42–53 in).*
Wingspan: *254–360 cm (8 ft 4 in– 11 ft 10 in).*
Weight: *5.9–12.1 kg (13–26.75 lb).*
Distribution: *Breeds on oceanic islands in southern oceans; at other times wanders the circumpolar area from Antarctica to Tropic of Capricorn.*
Habitat: *Southern oceans.*
Breeding: *Every 2 years: 1 egg, incubation period 2 months or more, fledging period 10–12 months. Young eat up to 1.8 kg (4 lb) of food in one meal.*
Diet: *Cephalopods, fish.*
Longevity: *Normally up to about 40 years, but may often reach 80 years.*
Notes: *Normal cruising speed about 50–90 km/h (30–55 mph).*

GREBES

Birds that eat their own feathers

Over 300 adult feathers were found in the stomach of a Western Grebe chick, but why these birds choose to eat themselves is still not fully understood.

Of the many strange habits in the animal world, one of the weirdest must be that of the grebes (Podicipedidae), which actually pluck and eat their own feathers and even feed them to their young. The young also eat their own feathers, and sometimes pluck them from their parents' bodies. Since there are up to 20,000 feathers on a grebe, it is unlikely that this habit has any detrimental effect on the birds!

Many of the 22 grebe species develop brightly coloured head tufts and plumes in the breeding season, when they are highly territorial and perform elaborate courtship displays on the water. The Great Crested Grebe (_Podiceps cristatus_) exhibits a remarkable sequence of postures, including the 'penguin display', 'cat display', weed-presentation and head-shaking among others. The Western Grebe (_Aechmophorus occidentalis_) also has a spectacular display in which the male and female suddenly rear up and dash across the surface as if on tiptoe.

Grebes build floating nests anchored to waterside vegetation. When the incubating parent leaves its post, it covers the eggs with aquatic vegetation to hide them from predators.

These diving birds eat fish and other aquatic animals and the eating of feathers may assist in the formation of pellets so that the fish bones and other indigestible matter can be ejected; the true reason for this peculiar habit is, however, still debated.

PROFILE

Length: _20–80 cm (8–31 in)._
Weight: _140–1500 g (4.3–33 oz)._
Distribution: _Almost cosmopolitan; most in temperate regions._
Habitat: _Mainly freshwater lakes and rivers; some disperse to coasts after breeding._
Breeding: _Floating nest on water, anchored to vegetation. 2–6 eggs, incubation period 3–4 weeks. Some species colonial._
Diet: _Fish and other aquatic animals, caught underwater._
Longevity: _Little known, probably up to 20 years._
Notes: _The recently discovered Hooded Grebe_ (Podiceps gallardoi) _of southern Patagonia has unique habit of laying 2 eggs but abandoning the second when the first hatches._

SLENDER-BILLED SHEARWATER

Australia's 'fishing sheep'

In southeast Australia and Tasmania these fish- and crustacean-eating seabirds are known as 'mutton-birds' because the flesh of the young has a particularly palatable taste – though not really like that of mutton!

Every year, under strict control, some half a million young Slender-billed Shearwaters (*Puffinus tenuirostris*) weighing about 1 kg (2 lb) each are collected from the nesting burrows to supplement the diet of the local inhabitants. They are canned and sold as 'Tasmanian squab'. Since the breeding colonies are huge, in some cases numbering over 1 million adults, this does

not seem to have affected the total population of the species, which is still a common bird.

The migration of this shearwater is impressive. In May, those that have not been eaten embark on a vast 16,000-km (10,000-mile) journey that takes them right out into the Pacific, then northwest and past Japan up to the Aleutian Islands; the adults return in September,

mainly through the central Pacific, completing a massive figure-of-8 pattern and reaching the Australian coasts in October/November.

A very similar species, the Sooty Shearwater (*P. griseus*), breeds off islands of New Zealand. It, too, is harvested for its tasty flesh.

PROFILE

Length: *41–43 cm (16–17 in).*
Weight: *600–1000 g (1.4–2.2 lb).*
Distribution: *Breeds Tasmania and southeast Australia; at other times pelagic in Pacific Ocean.*
Habitat: *Breeds on offshore islands; open ocean in non-breeding season.*
Breeding: *1 egg laid in burrow; incubation period 45–55 days. Colonial, some colonies numbering over 1 million adults.*
Diet: *Cephalopods, crustaceans, fish.*
Longevity: *Probably 20 years and more.*
Notes: *In Alaska this species is known as the 'whale-bird', from its habit of associating with large cetaceans.*

MAGNIFICENT FRIGATEBIRD

The pirate of the air

With its satanic appearance, long, angular wings, cruelly hooked bill and relentless pursuing of its chosen victim, it is easy to see why this tropical aggressor has also earned itself the name of 'man o' war bird'.

Whether chasing a hapless booby in twisting and turning flight until it disgorges its catch, diving to catch the free meal in mid-air, or gliding and soaring at great height, the aerial ability and manoeuvrability of the Magnificent Frigatebird (*Fregata magnificens*) are unsurpassed. Its piratical habits also extend to stealing eggs and chicks — even of its own species — and picking off newly hatched marine turtles as they make their first, and last, journey to the open sea. It also catches fish, especially flying fish, and scavenges for offal.

Frigatebirds nest in trees in colonies, where the males display by inflating their gaudy red throat sacs until they are as big as a man's head. The colony then appears at a distance as a clump of ripe fruit trees.

This is the largest of the 5 species of frigatebird. All have the same distinctive flight silhouette and are very difficult to tell apart, particularly the females and immatures, the latter taking several years to acquire adult plumage.

Magnificent Frigatebirds sometimes become very tame and will readily associate with Man; they have even been trained to carry messages between islands. This is also one of the few birds capable of riding out a hurricane in flight.

PROFILE

Length: *89–114 cm (35–45 in).*
Wingspan: *2.2–2.4 m (1 ft 3 in – 7 ft 11 in).*
Weight: *1–1.6 kg (2.2–3.5 lb).*
Distribution: *Tropical and subtropical America and Cape Verde Islands.*
Habitat: *Warm coastal waters, coral reefs.*
Breeding: *In colonies in trees, sometimes on ground. 1 egg, incubation period 45–50 days.*
Diet: *Mostly fish, also eggs and young of seabirds, offal and scraps, newly hatched marine turtles.*

AUSTRALIAN BRUSH TURKEY

The bird born with a full set of feathers

Almost all birds are born either naked or with a simple covering of down, but when the Australian Brush Turkey hatches out it is fully fledged and can fly immediately.

Unlike other birds, the chicks of the Australian Brush Turkey (*Alectura lathami*) have no proper egg tooth to help them break out of their shells, so they kick their way out. They already have all their feathers and, once they have wriggled up through the nest mound in which the eggs hatch, they are totally independent of their parents.

Like the Mallee Fowl, the Australian Brush Turkey piles up a big mound of twigs and leaves which acts as an incubator for the eggs. The mound is a little smaller than the Mallee Fowl's, being about 3–4 m (3.3–4.4 ft) wide and 1 m (about 3 ft) high. It is usually built in a shaded area of the rainforest where the damp contributes to the composting

effect of the leaves in the mound, producing a constant warmth to hatch the eggs.

The male tests the temperature of the nest mound by pushing its head into the material, though it probably cannot gauge it so accurately as can the Mallee Fowl.

The Australian Brush Turkey has blackish plumage, with the neck and head bare of feathers. Its dark coloration helps to camouflage it in its dense forest habitat, where it spends much time walking about slowly on the ground. It feeds by raking and scratching at the ground and the leaf litter for insects and their larvae and seeds. Its strong feet are well suited to this

method of feeding. Like other members of its family (Megapodiidae), however, including the Mallee Fowl, it probably eats a wide variety of foods; it certainly takes fruits.

PROFILE

Length: *70 cm (28 in).*
Weight: *1.6 kg (3.5 lb).*
Distribution: *Eastern Australia.*
Habitat: *Mainly rainforests and open wet forests.*
Breeding: *Big nest mound of vegetation. Up to 35 eggs have been laid in captivity.*
Diet: *Seeds, insects and fruit.*
Longevity: *Probably at least 20 years.*

MAGELLAN FLIGHTLESS STEAMER DUCK

The world's fastest surface-swimming bird

In 1985, two observers pursuing one of these ducks in the Chilean fiords reached a speed of 40 km/h (25 mph) in their 40-hp craft, yet were still outpaced by the duck.

The Magellan Flightless Steamer Duck (*Tachyeres pteneres*) has huge feet, the webs of which measure 15 cm (6 in) across when spread. Using these to provide momentum and striking its wings alternately on the water, it thrashes furiously over the surface with head lowered. In this way, it frequently reaches speeds of 15 knots (27 km/h, 17 mph)—and even more when pushed. The foam it creates and the speed of its travel reminded 19th-century sailors of an old-fashioned paddle-steamer, and that is the reason the bird got its strange name.

These are incredibly aggressive ducks. Their territorial fights can be extremely violent. They will not tolerate any other ducks, and when kept in an aviary will immediately kill all other ducks in the same pen. Their large size and formidably aggressive nature are no doubt part of the reason for their success in the wild.

Of the 3 species in the genus *Tachyeres*, the Magellan Flightless Steamer Duck is the largest, some males weighing as much as 6.4 kg (14 lb). All are confined to the southern tip of South America, and only one species, the Flying Steamer Duck (*Tachyeres patachonicus*), can actually fly.

It has recently been discovered that females may possibly be able to fly, but only for a short period during the breeding season.

PROFILE

Length: *73–83 cm (29–33 in).*
Weight: *Male 5.5–6.4 kg (12–14 lb), female about 4.1 kg (9 lb).*
Distribution: *Coasts of southern South America, from Beagle Channel westward and coasts of southern Chile.*
Habitat: *Rocky shores and coastal lakes.*
Breeding: *Well-concealed nest with much down, in tussock grass or kelp near water. 5–8 eggs, incubation period 30–40 days.*
Diet: *Mainly shellfish and other marine organisms, also offal.*
Longevity: *Probably long-lived, 10 years or more.*

TORRENT DUCK

The bird that loves rapids and waterfalls

In the raging waters of the Andean mountain rivers, where ferocious torrents would soon destroy less well-adapted animals, these ducks quite happily spend their entire lives.

The Torrent Duck (*Merganetta armata*) is found along the whole 8000 km (5000 miles) of the Andes Mountains in South America and nowhere else. It occurs from sea level up to 430 m (14,000 ft) and inhabits solely fast-running rivers and streams with hazardous waterfalls and rapids. These ducks have remarkably stiff, almost rigid, tail feathers which help them to steer in the rushing waters and to maintain their balance on treacherous slippery boulders. Without this special adaptation they would inevitably be crushed to death in such an inhospitable habitat.

When feeding, Torrent Ducks stand on boulders, drop into the rapid current and dive; after each dive they return to the same boulder. They also swim nimbly and skilfully on the surface, picking up floating food as it rushes past.

An interesting feature of both sexes is the horny spur up to 13 mm (0.5 in) long which is present on the bend of each wing. The exact purpose of these is not yet understood. Although such spurs which are present on some other birds are often used for fighting, this does not seem to be the case with the Torrent Duck.

MUSK DUCK

The bird that has to starve itself before it can fly

This bizarre-looking duck of Australia is so heavy that it often swims with its body partly submerged, and people once thought that it could not fly at all after a heavy bout of feeding.

This powerful duck is a carnivorous species with a big appetite, often gorging itself on crustaceans, fish and animal food of all kinds. It may easily seem that it is in fact unable to fly because, if disturbed, it normally thrashes across the water's surface in a cloud of spray — as if trying to take off. The Musk Duck (*Biziura lobata*) does, however, fly much more often than is believed, though it lands with a clumsy crash and skids as it hits the water.

This duck is one of the oddest of its family. Its feet are set so far back that it cannot walk properly on land and has to slide along on its belly, while on the water it frequently sinks to the point

that only its eyes and nostrils are visible above the surface. The male possesses a grotesque lobe of skin beneath its bill which, during the breeding season, becomes engorged with blood. When displaying, the male points his head and neck upwards, showing off the lobe, and raises his tail up over the back; he kicks his legs back, and his feet make a loud and characteristic 'ker-plonk' sound as they hit the water, which splashes backwards 2–2.5 m (7–8 ft) behind him.

During the breeding season the oil gland at the base of the Musk Duck's tail produces a very strong, pungent, musky scent — which explains this bird's unusual name.

PROFILE

Length: *Male 60–73 cm (24–28.5 in), female 47–60 cm (18.5–24 in).*

Weight: *Male 2.4 kg (5.28 lb), female 1.55 kg (3.4 lb).*

Distribution: *Southeast and western Australia.*

Habitat: *Well-vegetated swamps, large lakes and bays.*

Breeding: *Nest built in aquatic vegetation or low tree branches. 1–3 eggs, incubation period unknown.*

Diet: *Carnivorous, eats all kinds of animal food, including frogs, fish, crustaceans, birds; also a small amount of vegetable matter.*

Longevity: *Unknown.*

BRAHMINY KITE

The bird that brings luck to warriors

The Moslem name for this bird of prey means 'lucky face', a name given to it after the belief that if a Brahminy Kite appeared in flight above a fighting army then that army would win the battle.

Throughout much of India and southeast Asia to Australia, the Brahminy Kite (*Haliastur indus*) is a very common bird wherever there is water of any kind. It has acquired many names, among them Pondicherry Eagle, Red-backed Sea Eagle, Indian Fish-hawk and Shiva's Kite. The name Brahminy Kite comes from the name of the caste of Indian priests, the Brahmins: it was bestowed upon the bird by Europeans when they learned that this kite was sacred to the Indian god Vishnu.

The reality of this bird's lifestyle is, however, somewhat different. It is a scavenger extraordinaire, even in the heart of cities and around ports, where it becomes very bold and will snatch food from under the very nose of people. It will eat virtually any animal food but is particularly fond of fish, taking individuals of up to 450 g (1 lb) in weight.

The Brahminy Kite is a graceful bird in flight. Among the myths surrounding it is one that it starts fires — though lightning is probably the real culprit.

PROFILE

Length: *About 46 cm (18 in), female larger than male.*

Weight: *Male 400–650 g (0.8–1.4 lb), female 430–900 g (9.7–2.0 lb).*

Distribution: *Southeast Asia from Pakistan to southeast China and south to Sri Lanka, through Indonesia and New Guinea to northern and eastern Australia, and east to Solomon Islands.*

Habitat: *Prefers areas near water (e.g. ricefields) and coasts, but very varied; often lives in towns.*

Breeding: *Builds stick nest at top of tree, often near water. 2–3 eggs, incubation period about 28 days.*

Diet: *Any small animals and animal matter, carrion, refuse; often takes fish.*

Longevity: *Probably up to 7–8 years or more.*

Notes: *This species follows a rather nomadic existence, and is liable to turn up anywhere within its range where prey is abundant.*

LAMMERGEIER

The dropper of bones from the skies

This strange vulture-like bird specialises in eating bones: when these are too large for it to swallow, it carries them 30–80 m (100–260 ft) up in the air and drops them so that they smash into more manageable portions.

Being too slow to compete with other carrion-eaters around a carcase, the Lammergeier or Bearded Vulture (*Gypaetus barbatus*) makes do with the remnants, particularly the bones and their marrow. It has a remarkable capacity for swallowing and can down bones up to 25 cm (10 in) long in one go; it can even gulp down bones 10 cm (4 in) in diameter. If a bone is too large, it carries it in its feet to heights of up to 80 m (260 ft) and then drops it on to flat rocks below; if necessary, it will repeat this procedure up to 50 times until the bone breaks. Special areas of rock slabs may be used regularly, and these are known as 'ossuaries'. Lammergeiers will also pick up and drop tortoises in the same way until the hard shell cracks open and they can get at the animal inside.

There are stories telling how these huge birds even attack large mammals—including human beings—standing on the edge of cliff precipices and try to force them off, but no clear evidence of this grisly habit has yet been presented. Lammergeiers do occasionally kill mammals and birds, but normally the victim is a very old or sick individual. They have been known to kill young goats and lambs; interestingly, Lammergeier means 'lamb-vulture' in German.

In the air, this magnificent bird resembles an enormous cross. It is capable of gliding at up to 130 km/h (80 mph) as it patrols the rugged mountainsides of its natural habitat.

Despite its great size—including a 2.8-m (9-ft) wingspan—it is a master of aerial acrobatics and is capable of incredible flying manoeuvres for so large a bird.

PROFILE

Length: *100–117 cm (39–46 in).*
Wingspan: *Up to 280 cm (9ft).*
Weight: *4.0–7.1 kg (8.8–15.6 lb).*
Distribution: *Eurasia, from southern Europe through Middle East to Mongolia and Central China; also North, East and South Africa.*
Habitat: *High mountain ranges, occurring at up to 4500 m (14,760 ft) in Himalayas; in Israel, below sea level in canyons of Judean Desert.*
Breeding: *Builds a nest of dead sticks, usually in a cave or on an overhung recess on cliff crag. 1–2 eggs, incubation period about 55–60 days.*
Diet: *Bones, carrion, refuse; occasionally kills live animals.*
Longevity: *Up to 40 years in captivity.*
Notes: *This is Europe's rarest bird of prey, with at most only 90 or so breeding pairs remaining.*

HARPY EAGLE

The world's most formidable bird of prey

This most powerful of all eagles is capable of killing and carrying away prey the size of monkeys and sloths.

The huge and magnificent Harpy Eagle (*Harpia harpyja*) inhabits the tropical rainforests of South America. It manoeuvres through the dense forest with astounding agility for so large a bird, moving at speeds of as much as 60–80 km/h (37–50 mph) and snatching monkeys or sloths from the branches. It also takes birds, and may occasionally grab animals from the ground.

The female, which is larger than the male, has long, very powerful talons and the most powerful legs of any bird of prey.

The Harpy Eagle nests in massive trees growing out above the canopy. The nest itself is sometimes as high as 50 m (162 ft) or more up.

PROFILE

Length: *100 cm (39 in) or more.*
Weight: *Male about 4.4 kg (9.7 lb), female up to 6.0 kg (13.2 lb).*
Distribution: *From southern Mexico south to eastern Bolivia and Argentina.*
Habitat: *Tropical rainforest.*
Breeding: *Massive stick nest at top of very tall tree. 2 eggs, incubation period probably about 50 days. Probably nests only every other year.*
Diet: *Monkeys and sloths, also other mammals (large and small) and occasionally birds.*
Longevity: *Unknown, probably long-lived.*
Notes: *Both this species and another huge eagle that feeds on similar food—the extremely rare Monkey-eating Eagle (Pithecophaga jefferyi) of the Philippines—are threatened by destruction of their rainforest habitat.*

SECRETARY BIRD

PROFILE

Length: *125–150 cm (49–59 in);*
height about 1.3 m (4.3 ft).
Weight: *3.4–4 kg (7.5–8.8 lb).*
Distribution: *Africa south of the*
Sahara; absent from forest areas.
Habitat: *Open savanna and grass-*
land, steppe and semi-desert;
prefers vegetation less than 0.5 m
(20 in) high.
Breeding: *Builds platform of sticks*
and grass on top of bush or tree.
Up to 3 eggs, incubation period 45
days.
Diet: *Mainly insects and small mam-*
mals, also reptiles and amphibians;
occasionally eggs and young of
ground-nesting birds.
Longevity: *Probably long-lived, 10*
years or more.
Notes: *The only member of its family*
(Sagittariidae), the Secretary Bird's
true relationships to other birds are
uncertain: it may be close to the
bustards, cranes and seriemas
(order Gruiformes).

The world's most proficient snake-killer

By stamping or kicking with its exceptionally long legs and using its
wings to balance, this peculiar-looking bird of prey is able to kill and
eat even the most venomous of snakes in its African grassland habitat.

The Secretary Bird (*Sagittarius serpen-
tarius*) stalks its prey by walking with
long, measured steps—at about 120
paces per minute or 2.5–3 km/h (1.5–2
mph)—its head and neck jerking backwards and forwards like a domestic
chicken. From time to time it makes
rapid stamping movements or short
darting runs with raised wings to disturb
prey. When it discovers a large snake, it
quickly kicks at it or stamps hard on it,
covering the snake with its wings to stop
it defending itself. In this way it can
easily deal with such dangerous species
as cobras or puff adders, although it
may need to stamp several times on

these before they become immobilised.
If this does not work, it carries the snake
up in the air and drops it.

Most of this bird's food, however, is
made up of small insects, especially
grasshoppers, and small rodents, sup-
plemented by reptiles and amphibians.
These it usually kills with its bill.

A pair of Secretary Birds will cover a
territory that can be anything from 20
square km (7.7 square miles) to 200
square km (77 square miles). The bird
gets its name from the long, black-
tipped, quill-like feathers on its nape,
which could be said to resemble the
quill pen of a secretary of olden times.

PEREGRINE

Nature's fastest-moving creature

When rocketing down on to its prey high in the air, this spectacular falcon has been estimated to reach the incredible speed of 240 km/h (150 mph) and more.

The Peregrine (*Falco peregrinus*) catches most of its food in the air. Like all falcons, its capacity for determining objects at a distance is far greater than Man's—probably about three times greater. The Peregrine spots its intended victim from a distance; it then proceeds to a position diagonally above the prey and, with wings folded, makes a spectacular long, steep dive (known as a 'stoop'), hitting the back of its victim's head with its rear talon.

Various estimates of the speeds reached by Peregrines during these stoops range from 160 km/h (100 mph) to a staggering 440 km/h (275 mph). Although it is probable that they do not normally exceed 180 km/h (112 mph), a speed of 240 km/h (150 mph) is quite feasible. The Peregrine is thus Nature's fastest animal. Perhaps 80–90% of stoops miss their target, but it

seems likely that many of them are made just 'in play'. In normal level flight, the Peregrine barely attains 95 km/h (60 mph).

The main food of this falcon is birds, both small and large. The female Peregrine, which is bigger than the male, is capable of carrying away birds weighing up to 1.8 kg (4 lb), more than her own body weight.

After the Second World War, the sudden rapid increase in the use of pesticides caused a drastic reduction in the numbers of Peregrines in the northern hemisphere. In some areas this bird of prey became extinct, while in many others it was almost exterminated. Following major restrictions on the use of pesticides after the 1960s, a gradual recovery took place, but in parts of its range this remains an extremely rare bird.

PROFILE

Length: *36–48 cm (14–19 in), female 15% larger than male.*
Weight: *Male 330–750 g (0.73–1.7 lb), female up to 1600 g (3.5 lb).*
Distribution: *Cosmopolitan but discontinuous: Eurasia, northern and southwestern North America, extreme southern South America, western and southern Africa, India and southeast Asia to Australia.*
Habitat: *Open country, particularly undisturbed terrain, sea cliffs, inland crags etc.*
Breeding: *Nest usually an earth scrape or an old nest of another bird, on cliff ledge; in some areas, on buildings, tree or on ground. 3–4 eggs, incubation period 28–32 days.*
Diet: *Almost exclusively birds up to size of heron and goose, caught in flight; also small to medium-sized mammals, reptiles, insects.*
Longevity: *Some reach 14 years.*

MALLEE FOWL

The weather-forecasting bird with the built-in thermometer

In order to maintain the correct conditions of temperature in its huge incubator-like nest mound, this extraordinary Australian bird regularly tests the soil temperature and corrects it to within 1°.

In the autumn, Mallee Fowls or Lowans (*Leipoa ocellata*) dig a hole up to 5 m (over 16 ft) wide and about 1 m (3.3 ft) deep. During the winter, they pile into it twigs and leaves collected from a radius of about 45 m (50 yds). When all this material has been wetted by the rains, they cover the lot with sandy soil to a depth of about 50 cm (20 in), making a mound up to 1.5 m (5 ft) high. This nest site may contain up to 299 cubic metres (391 cubic yards) of material, weighing 304 tonnes (299 tons). In spring the rotting vegetation generates heat, so the bird piles extra soil on top to prevent the sun's rays penetrating too quickly; when it gets colder, in autumn, the mound is opened during the warmest hours of the day to allow maximum sun to penetrate. The birds regularly probe the soil of the mound with their bills, and it seems that they are able to judge temperature accurately with their tongue or the inside of their mouth. However they measure it, they always keep the temperature of the incubating mound at within 1° of 34°C (92°F).

The eggs are laid on decaying leaf litter in the centre of the mound. The male checks that conditions are correct before allowing the female to enter and lay, and then closes up the hole again once the female has come out. The eggs, laid over a period of several months, are thus incubated solely by heat from the nest mound. When the chicks hatch, they dig their own way out.

Interestingly, the Mallee Fowl seems able to predict changes in the weather: it sometimes makes the correct alterations to the mound some hours before the weather suddenly changes.

PROFILE

Length: *60 cm (24 in).*
Weight: *Averages 1.7 kg (3.9 lb).*
Distribution: *Southwestern Australia.*
Habitat: *Arid inland scrub, particularly mallee scrub with dwarf eucalyptus trees.*
Breeding: *Huge nest mound of vegetation, with nest chamber in centre. 5–35 (average 15–24) eggs laid at intervals of several days over several months; incubation, by heat from rotting vegetation and sun, about 8 weeks.*
Diet: *Mainly seeds and flowers, also insects and small lizards.*
Longevity: *Up to 25 years in captivity.*
Notes: *Mallee Fowls never see their parents, since the young, once they have dug themselves out of the mound, disappear into the scrub and then move off.*

WHOOPER SWAN

PROFILE

Length: *145–160 cm (57–63 in), of which neck accounts for about half; male averages larger than female.*

Weight: *8–14 kg (17.6–30.8 lb), occasionally up to 16 kg (35 lb).*

Distribution: *Northern Europe and Asia, from Iceland east to Bering Sea; in winter, most move south to temperate regions.*

Habitat: *Breeds on shallow lakes and ponds, sometimes estuaries; in winter found on large lakes, coasts and floodlands.*

Breeding: *Nest is a large mound of vegetation. 2–7 eggs, incubation period averages 35 days.*

Diet: *Aquatic vegetation, occasionally also berries and small aquatic animals.*

Longevity: *Oldest ringed bird 7.5 years, but some probably live to over 20 years.*

Rider of the jet-stream

On 9th December 1967, a flock of 30 swans was detected on a radar screen and then seen by an aircraft pilot at just over 8200 m (27,000 ft) over the Hebrides off western Scotland.

Whooper Swans (*Cygnus cygnus*) breed only in wild regions of tundra and swampland in northern Europe and Asia. They regularly migrate south for the winter, frequently travelling at enormous heights and descending to lower levels when nearing their winter quarters – in temperate regions across the Old World. At 8200 m (27,000 ft), which is just beneath the jet-stream where winds often blow at over 180 km/h (112 mph), the air density and oxygen concentration are only 40% of what they are at the earth's surface. Man cannot survive in such conditions, and the fact that some birds can even fly at such heights shows just how superior their respiratory system is to that of Man.

Spectacular in flight, these big white birds—with a wingspan of up to 240 cm (nearly 8 ft)—are truly wild and often difficult to approach closely, unlike the familiar Mute Swan (*Cygnus olor*) that graces the rivers and lakes of Europe. The Whooper Swan's loud and far-carrying call sounds like a triple blast on a bugle and is among the most evocative sounds in Nature's wide repertoire. Flocks on the water may call in unison and the result gives the impression of singing; for this reason this beautiful bird is called 'Singing Swan' in several languages.

HOATZIN

The enigma of the avian world

With a mixture of primitive and highly specialised characteristics, this extraordinary and unique bird is a mystery to modern ornithologists and was once thought to be the 'missing link' between reptiles and birds.

The adult Hoatzin (*Opisthocomus hoazin*) has the most peculiar shape, with a long, scraggy neck and a ridiculously small, bristle-crested head, big but weak wings, a long and broad tail, and stout but not strong legs and feet. It has a massive crop situated in front of the upper part of the breastbone, the bottom part of which has a large 'keel' covered in leathery skin. When perched, the bird often rests on this keel. Whereas the crop of other birds acts as a kind of storage larder, in the Hoatzin it performs the job normally done by the stomach – that of grinding up food so that it can be properly digested. Another characteristic of the bird is its musky odour.

The chicks of the Hoatzin are even more strange. When born, they have a sparse covering of down and on the 'thumb' and 'first finger' of each wing there are two large claws up to about 2 cm (0.8 in) long similar to those found in the oldest known fossil bird, the Archaeopteryx. The young chicks soon acquire another, warmer down and when only a few days old use their wing claws, bill and feet to clamber about in the dense mangrove and riverside vegetation of their Amazon home. They can swim at this age, and when danger threatens will even drop into the water and swim underwater out of harm's way. Interestingly, they lose both the wing claws and the ability to swim once they become adults.

Hoatzins seldom fly, and when they do it is only for up to 40–50 m (about 45 yds).

PROFILE

Length: *60 cm (23–24 in).*
Weight: *810 g (1.8 lb).*
Distribution: *Amazon basin and surrounding areas, South America.*
Habitat: *Flooded forests and mangroves along overgrown river shores.*
Breeding: *Flat nest of dry twigs built 2–6 m (6.5–19.5 ft) above water. 2–4 eggs, incubation period about 4 weeks.*
Diet: *Leaves, flowers and shoots, also crabs, fish and other small animals.*
Flock size: *10–20.*
Longevity: *Unknown.*
Notes: *Also called 'Stinking Bird' because of its strong smell of musk; natives tend not to kill it for food, as they believe that its flesh stinks and therefore tastes unpleasant.*

REEVES'S PHEASANT

The bird with a unique escape brake

A fast flyer, this pheasant is able to spread its exceptionally long tail feathers and lower them quickly, thus enabling it to stop in flight and to drop into cover and out of danger.

The beautiful male Reeves's Pheasant (*Syrmaticus reevesii*) has one of the longest tails of all birds. Its tail may grow to 150 cm (nearly 5 ft), almost four times the length of its body. In enclosed areas of vegetation this may be a hindrance, but in flight the tail helps the bird to move at speed and probably also acts as a stabiliser. If the pheasant needs to stop suddenly in flight, it simply spreads and lowers its tail, which then becomes a very effective brake.

When displaying on the ground to the shorter-tailed female, the male Reeves's Pheasant fluffs up his neck feathers and spreads wide his tail, thereby showing to advantage the handsome black, white and gold colours.

The natural range of this beautiful bird is in Central China, where it inhabits the open mixed forests of pine and oak on rocky hillsides. It is able to walk long distances in this terrain, and has no trouble in climbing up steep slopes; it can even run uphill at a fair speed, thanks to its long legs.

The male Reeves's Pheasant defends a territory in which there may be more than one female. In winter families keep together, and at times several families may even join together to form small flocks.

The long tail feathers of the male are used as ornaments in Chinese operas. Worn on the cap, they denote that the wearer is a military person.

PROFILE

Length: *Male 150–190 cm (4.9–6.3 ft), including tail of up to 150 cm (4.9 ft); female smaller.*
Weight: *Averages 1300 g (2.87 lb).*
Distribution: *Central China; introduced into parts of North America and Britain and Europe.*
Habitat: *Mixed, open mountain forests from 300 m (1000 ft) up to about 1830 m (6000 ft).*
Breeding: *Nest a shallow depression on ground. 6–8 (occasionally up to 14) eggs.*
Diet: *Seeds, acorns, plant matter, fruits, insects and small invertebrates.*
Longevity: *Probably about 10 years; longer in captivity.*

NORTHERN JACANA

The bird that walks on water

With their outrageously long toes, these inhabitants of tropical freshwater marshes and streams are able to walk on floating vegetation, looking for all the world as if they are walking on water.

With high-stepping gait and a jerk of the tail between each step, the Northern Jacana (*Jacana spinosa*) walks nimbly across the leaves of water lilies and other aquatic vegetation and picks insects, small molluscs and other animal food from the surface of the plants. Its spread toes with their elongated claws cover an amazing area of 12 × 14 cm (4.7 × 5.5 in): its weight is therefore dispersed over a wide area, so it is in no danger of sinking. This bird also has a long, sharp, yellow spur up to 16 mm (0.63 in) long on each wing which it uses in aggressive encounters with others of its species. It utters rasping and chattering calls and a clacking sound like the noise from a typewriter.

Northern Jacanas are polyandrous: each female mates with up to four males, and the roles of the sexes are reversed. Females are much larger than

males and about 77% heavier; they defend territories which average 0.35 ha (0.86 acres), as opposed to an average of 0.15 ha (0.37 acres) for males. The males do virtually all the incubation of the eggs—by sitting on their own wings and holding two eggs between the breast and each wing—and care for the chicks. The young, although active as soon as they hatch, develop slowly and are dependent on the male for a further three to four months.

Outside the breeding season, Northern Jacanas form flocks, sometimes of as many as 200–300 individuals. At this time they may also be seen in irrigated fields or flooded meadows.

Seven other species of jacana occur in South America, Africa, southeast Asia and Australia. One in Africa is known as Lily-trotter and the Australian species goes under the name of Lotus Bird.

COMMON SNIPE

The long-billed bog-dweller with a voice like a sheep

With its cryptic coloration the Common Snipe is well camouflaged among the tussocks of its marshy habitat, but when it displays in spring, the bleating sound it produces as it dives in flight makes it a most distinctive bird.

This widespread bird spends much of its time probing for food with its long 7-cm (2.8-in) bill in soft marshy or boggy ground. Because of its brown, black, buff and white plumage it is not easy to see among the grasses and sedges of this habitat; if approached to within 10–15 m (11–16 yds), however, it suddenly flies up as if catapulted and shoots off on a zigzag course, climbing high and circling before coming down 50 m (55 yds) or more away. Yet, when spring comes, the Common Snipe (*Gallinago gallinago*) has a remarkable and conspicuous display. It circles high in the air and then dives steeply at an angle of 40–45°

towards the ground, producing a loud bleating noise as it plunges earthwards.

The sound produced by a displaying Common Snipe is often called 'drumming'. It is caused by the air rushing over the outer tail feathers, which are held out at right angles to the bird's body as it dives. it usually lasts for about 1½–2 seconds and can be heard up to 1 km (0.6 miles) away. The display is performed especially in the evening and after dark, and in Europe can be seen mainly from March to June.

Snipes locate their food in the ground through the sensitive nerve endings at the tip of the bill.

PROFILE

Length: *25–27 cm (10.0–10.5 in), including a bill of 6–7 cm (2.4–2.8 in).*
Weight: *90–170 g (3.2–6.0 oz).*
Distribution: *Europe and northern Asia, North America, South America and South and East Africa. In winter most migrate south from the northerly parts of the breeding range.*
Habitat: *Wet and marshy ground with plenty of covering vegetation.*
Breeding: *Nest a shallow scrape on ground. 1–6 (usually 4) eggs, incubation period 18–20 days.*
Diet: *Mainly earthworms and other invertebrates.*
Longevity: *Oldest ringed bird 12.3 years.*

ARCTIC TERN

The world's most travelled bird

Every year, some Arctic Terns migrate from their breeding grounds within the Arctic Circle all the way to Antarctic waters and then back again, which for some means a round trip of 35,000 km (21,750 miles).

Arctic Terns (*Sterna paradisaea*) breed in the northern hemisphere, mostly within the Arctic Circle as far north as 84°N, yet they spend the winter in the southern hemisphere, most of them in the Antarctic pack-ice zone. They have even been seen as far south as 78°S. This trip to enjoy the benefits of a second, southern, summer, with its plentiful supply of food, would normally entail a flight of some 13,000 km (8100 miles). In order to exploit following winds, however, the majority of birds, including those from North America, converge on route off the western coasts of Europe and Africa and then cross the South Atlantic to South America, from where they continue on down to the pack ice. In March they return north, again using the route with the best winds. When we consider that some

Arctic Terns live to 30 and more years of age, this means that they have travelled over 1 million km (over 650,000 miles) in their lifetime – and this by a bird only 35 cm (14 in) long and weighing around 100 g (3.5 oz). Not surprisingly, perhaps, not many Arctic Terns reach such an advanced age. Although the speed of flight varies, a bird ringed in Greenland travelled 18,000 km (11,250 miles) in less than three months.

Arctic Terns breed in colonies numbering hundreds or sometimes thousands of pairs. These are generally very noisy places, but every so often all the birds suddenly go completely quiet and then fly up together and out to sea. This odd behaviour is called a 'dread', but the reasons for it are by no means understood.

PROFILE

Length: *35 cm (14 in).*
Weight: *80–145 g (2.8–5.0 oz).*
Distribution: *Circumpolar in northern hemisphere, extending south to Britain and northeast USA. Winters mainly in Antarctica.*
Habitat: *Coasts, river shores, tundra and lakes. In winter, marine.*
Breeding: *Colonial; nest a shallow scrape on ground. 1–3 eggs, incubation period 20–24 days.*
Diet: *Fish, caught by plunge-diving from 1–6 m (3–20 ft); also crustaceans and insects.*
Longevity: *Oldest ringed bird lived to 34 years of age.*
Notes: *Like most terns, this species can cause a fright to intruders at its breeding colonies: all the terns rise up and dive at the intruder, some pulling out only at the very last second.*

SANDGROUSE

Desert dwellers that transport water in flight

In the steppe and desert lands where these birds live, water is hard to come by, so every day they fly long distances to waterholes, soak their belly feathers in water and then fly back with this moisture to their young.

Sandgrouse (family Pteroclididae) are related to the pigeons and doves and are somewhat similar to them in shape. Their habits, however, are very different. Most of the 16 species of sandgrouse live in arid or semi-arid areas of Asia, Africa and southern Europe. As the food they eat is dry (mostly seeds) they need to drink every day, and this they do regularly every morning or evening at a particular 'favourite' pool. Large flocks of sandgrouse, often numbering thousands and sometimes including several different species, gather to drink; once they have had their fill, the males soak their belly feathers in the water and fly back to their young, which leave the nest as soon as they hatch and then shelter under nearby shrubs or rocks. When the parent returns, he stands upright and the chicks drink the water from his belly feathers.

During the nesting season sandgrouse may carry water for 30 km (19 miles). At other times they fly up to 80 km (50 miles) to a waterhole and then back again, travelling at speeds of around 70 km/h (44 mph) and uttering loud, distinctive calls all the way.

One species from the steppes of Central Asia, Pallas's Sandgrouse (*Syrrhaptes paradoxus*), very occasionally performs spectacular migrations known as 'eruptions'. What happens is that large numbers of these birds leave their natural homeland and fly tens of thousands of kilometres to the east and west. In western Europe hundreds of Pallas's Sandgrouse turned up unexpectedly in 1863, 1872, 1876, 1888 and 1908, and many pairs even stayed to breed in Europe in 1888–89. Smaller numbers have made the journey in a few other years.

PROFILE

Length: *25–48 cm (10–19 in).*

Weight: *170–650 g (6.0–22.9 oz); most species around 200–300 g (7.1–10.6 oz).*

Distribution: *Central and southern Asia, Middle East, Africa and southern Europe.*

Habitat: *Arid and semi-arid desert and steppe; one species in mountains of Tibet.*

Breeding: *Nest a shallow scrape on ground lined with a few stones or pieces of dry vegetation. 3 eggs, incubation period 21–31 days.*

Diet: *Mainly seeds; occasionally berries, shoots, leaves and insects.*

Notes: *The belly feathers of sandgrouse have a specialised structure of minute filaments on the side nearest the body; this enables them to hold water and also stops it from evaporating.*

BLUE-CROWNED HANGING PARROT

The bird that sleeps upside down

When resting by day or roosting at night, these small parrots hang upside down from branches, looking just like leaves.

Although bright green in colour with a scarlet throat and rump, gold nape and flanks and a bright blue crown, the Blue-crowned Hanging Parrot (*Loriculus galgulus*) is exceedingly difficult to observe.

It is only about 13 cm (5 in) long—the size of a sparrow—and it feeds in flocks in the tops of tall deciduous trees, where it blends superbly into the green of the foliage.

At night it adopts a most amazing roosting posture: it grasps a branch firmly in its feet, which are held close together, presses its tail hard against the branch, and hangs with its body arched backwards and its head hanging down-

wards like a bat! In this position, too, the parrot is extremely hard to detect; it is presumed that the birds sleep this way in order to make themselves as inconspicuous as possible to nocturnal predators.

While climbing about in the treetops, the Blue-crowned Hanging Parrot uses its beak as an 'extra hand'. It takes huge steps of about 15 cm (6 in)—greater than its own length—and swings in a complete half circle as it moves along the branch.

The Blue-crowned Hanging Parrot is easily tamed. When it is in captivity, it will eat honey, sugarcane and rice, as well as some kinds of fruit.

PROFILE

Length: *About 13 cm (5 in).*
Weight: *Up to around 20 g (0.7 oz).*
Distribution: *Malaysia, Borneo, Sumatra.*
Habitat: *Treetops of deciduous forests.*
Breeding: *Nests in hole in tree, often (unusual for parrots) with some grass as lining. 3–4 eggs, incubation period probably about 16–18 days.*
Diet: *Fruit, berries and nuts, nectar and pollen.*
Longevity: *Insufficient information; most parrots are, however, long-lived.*

KAKAPO

The heavyweight parrot that cannot fly

This rare New Zealand parrot has fairly well-developed wings, but it is so heavy that it is incapable of true flight.

Of all the 332 species of parrot in the world, the extraordinary Kakapo or Owl Parrot (*Strigops habroptilus*) is the most unusual. It is very secretive, has abnormally soft plumage for a parrot, and is a nocturnal bird that lives on the ground; during the day it sleeps in holes under trees or rocks. It is also the heaviest parrot, males weighing up to 2.5 kg (5.5 lb), but its flight muscles account for only 3–4% of its total weight and are therefore insufficient to give power for flight. It has a thick layer of fat under its skin which can form as much as 40% of its body weight.

The Kakapo, although it cannot fly, is said to be able to glide downwards from one point to a lower spot up to 80 m (90 yds) away. Its plumage is marvellously camouflaged, the upperside being a moss-green colour with much brown, black and yellow barring; this makes it almost invisible among the ferns and other ground vegetation in its forest habitat.

A further peculiarity of this parrot concerns the powerful booming calls of the males. The males gather in a restricted area and proceed to boom for 45 seconds, uttering one boom every 3 seconds; they then fall silent for 45 seconds before starting up again.

Previously, the Kakapo was to be found all over New Zealand, but the introduction of rats and stoats from Europe, and the ease with which these as well as the many native predators could kill these slow-moving flightless birds, has, together with the broadscale land clearance that has taken place in the past century, reduced the population to the point of extinction. The Kakapo is now rigorously protected, and efforts are being made to establish the bird on islands off the coast of New Zealand where there are no predators.

PROFILE

Length: *Male 56–64 cm (22–25 in), female 45–56 cm (18–22 in).*
Weight: *Male up to 2.5 kg (5.5 lb), female up to 1.5 kg (3.3 lb).*
Distribution: *New Zealand.*
Habitat: *On ground in mountain forest, occasionally on alpine pasture above tree line.*
Breeding: *Nests in burrow at base of tree, usually between rocks and with several entrances. 2–4 eggs, incubation period uncertain.*
Diet: *Grass, leaves, fern fronds; occasionally lizards.*
Longevity: *Long-lived but precise details unknown; at least 25 years.*
Notes: *A highly endangered species, the Kakapo has recently been discovered in small numbers on Stewart Island off southern New Zealand; this population, if properly protected, may help it to avoid extinction.*

ROADRUNNER

The fastest-running flying bird

Although capable of flying, the Roadrunner prefers to go on foot and is typically seen dashing across a road at speed, with head and tail lowered, before disappearing into the scrub.

It is perhaps not generally realised that the Roadrunner (*Geococcyx californina*) is a species of cuckoo. Its narrow tail up to 25 cm (10 in) long, its 5-cm (2-in) bill with a slight downward curve, and the arrangement of its toes (two pointing forwards and two backwards) are all characteristics of the cuckoo family (Cuculidae). Most cuckoos have loose plumage, but the Roadrunner's is so loose that the bird looks as if it is suffering the after-effects of a nasty shock!

The classic image of the Roadrunner is that of a long-tailed brown bird sprinting at incredible speed along a roadway. In truth its running speed is more of an illusion: although it can reach about 29 km/h (18 mph), it normally moves rather more slowly—at up to 24 km/h (15 mph)—and usually makes short, fast dashes rather than long-distance runs. It is extremely manoeuvrable and can make sharp-angled turns with a skill to rival a hare or rabbit. On the rare occasions that it does fly, this is usually just to reach a nearby perch from where it can display.

Roadrunners feed on any small live animal prey, but particularly on lizards. One of their many local names is 'Lizard Bird'. The Roadrunner rushes along for a few metres, stops suddenly with tail cocked and crown feathers erect, looks around, and then repeats the procedure; when it sees any potential food, it immediately hurtles after it and grabs it with its bill.

A smaller species, the Lesser Roadrunner (*Geococcyx velox*), occurs only in South America. It differs in the colour and pattern of its plumage, but otherwise is similar in general habits to the Roadrunner.

PROFILE

Length: *58 cm (23 in), including tail of 25 cm (10 in).*
Weight: *Up to about 200 g (7 oz).*
Distribution: *Northern California east to Missouri, USA, and south to Central Mexico.*
Habitat: *Scrubby desert and semi-desert.*
Breeding: *Nest a twig platform lined with snake skins, old bones etc, usually 1–5 m (3–16 ft) up in cactus. 3–7 eggs, incubation period about 19 days.*
Diet: *Mainly lizards; also small snakes (including venomous ones), grasshoppers, insects, beetles, mice, occasionally small birds.*
Longevity: *Insufficient information.*
Notes: *Among the numerous stories surrounding this bird is one that it kills rattlesnakes by ramming a piece of cactus down the serpent's throat as it strikes. This has not been shown to be true!*

GREAT HORNED OWL

The smallest range of eye movement of any animal

Most birds can move their eyes within the sockets to a limited extent, but owls have to turn their whole head to look at something even minutely outside their immediate field of view.

Owls have their eyes situated in the front of their face, rather than at the sides of the head as in most birds. This provides them with binocular vision, so that they can see with both eyes at the same time an object within an arc of 60–70° in front of them. This ability helps them to judge exactly how far away the object is and to gauge its correct dimensions.

The eyes of the Great Horned Owl (*Bubo virginianus*) are huge, but the eye sockets are small. The result is that the owl cannot move its eyes within their sockets (most birds can move their eyes 10–25°). So, in order to see sideways, the owl has to turn its whole head. Fortunately, it is able to do this infinitely better than any other animal and can turn its head through 180° or more—in other words right around so that it is looking backwards!

Owls can see extraordinarily well in the dark, but their hearing is just as good, if not better. A Great Horned Owl can hear sounds that Man cannot. When it hears something moving about in the dark, it turns its head in the direction from which the sound comes. Since its external ears (which are hidden by (feathering) are asymmetrical—one ear is larger and higher up on the head than the other—the Great Horned Owl hears a sound with one ear about 0.00003 seconds before it hears it with the other. This enables it to locate the source of a sound accurately by judging its precise distance and position.

PROFILE

Length: *51–60 cm (20–23.5 in).*
Weight: *1.0–3.0 kg (2.2–6.6 lb).*
Distribution: *North America except extreme north, south through whole of Central and South America.*
Habitat: *Mainly coniferous forests, but widespread and varied; often occurs in cities and suburbs.*
Breeding: *Rebuilds old nest of bird of prey, or nests in cave or on ground. 2–5 eggs, incubation period 28 days.*
Diet: *Small to medium-sized mammals, large birds, reptiles, insects.*
Longevity: *Insufficient information, but all owls are reputed to live long; closely related Eagle Owl (Bubo bubo) has lived to 68 years in captivity.*
Notes: *The so-called 'ear tufts' of some owls, including Great Horned, are in fact only tufts of feathers which the bird uses to convey different moods.*

SNOWY OWL

The phantom of the North

Floating silently across the snowy arctic wastes in full daylight, this ghostly white owl is stunningly beautiful yet strikes fear into the lemming population.

Of all the magnificent sights to be witnessed in the arctic summer, the spectacle of an adult male Snowy Owl (*Nyctea scandiaca*) silently hunting its prey is one of the most unforgettable. This huge owl, with a 160-cm (5.25-ft) wingspan, habitually floats over the northern tundra in search of its favourite food—lemmings and voles—looking for all the world like a ghostly snow-white apparition. Its beauty belies its true nature, for this is one of the most powerful of all owls: it is capable of killing and carrying off ten or more lemmings, each up to 15 cm (6 in) long and weighing up to 130 g (4.6 oz), in one day.

One of the most fascinating aspects of this owl's life concerns its breeding habits. It feeds primarily on voles and lemmings but the populations of these prey fluctuate, reaching a peak every four years or so and then plummeting. The Snowy Owl's food supply therefore changes from year to year. In 'good' vole years the owls may lay as many as 14 eggs, while in the 'bad' years they lay only two eggs or may even not bother to nest at all.

In some years, when the populations of voles and lemmings are at their lowest, Snowy Owls move south in large numbers; they have even turned up as far south as Bermuda and northern India. These movements are known as 'eruptions'. Even so, some Snowy Owls remain in northern Greenland throughout the arctic winter, when darkness reigns throughout the 24 hours of the day for a period of 90 days.

Snowy Owls unexpectedly bred on Fetler, Shetland, in 1967 and until 1975; since then only females have been present on the island.

PROFILE

Length: *53–66 cm (21–26 in), female larger than male.*
Wingspan: *142–166 cm (5.6–6.5 ft).*
Weight: *Male 1.2–2.5 kg (2.6–5.5 lb), female 1.5–2.95 kg (3.3–6.5 lb).*
Distribution: *High Arctic, mostly above 60°N. Some move south from northernmost areas in autumn.*
Habitat: *Arctic tundra, often with dry hummocks. Outside breeding season sometimes in other open areas farther south.*
Breeding: *Nest a small scrape on ground, usually on small hummock or rock outcrop. 2–14 (usually 3–9) eggs, incubation period 30–33 days.*
Diet: *Mostly voles and lemmings; also other mammals up to size of hare, medium-sized birds and occasionally fish.*
Longevity: *Oldest ringed bird 9 years 5 months.*

OILBIRD

The bird that navigates by echo-location

The presence of these peculiar birds in a dark South American cave is revealed by their ear-splitting screams, but they find their way about in the dark by uttering clicking sounds and listening to the echoes.

The mysterious Oilbird (*Steatornis caripensis*) is the sole member of its family (Steatornithidae) and is found only in South America and Trinidad. It looks something like a cross between a nightjar (*Caprimulgus*) and a hawk (*Accipiter*), but it feeds exclusively on fruit. It was first made known to science in 1799, when hundreds of these birds were discovered by the German scientist, Alexander von Humboldt, living by day in the Caripe cave in Venezuela and flying out at night to the fruit trees of the forest.

Over 150 years later another scientist, D. R. Griffin, made a further astounding discovery. From experiments carried out in 1954, he found that Oilbirds used echo-location to navigate in the blackness of the caves: the birds make clicking sounds and use the echoes from these to find their way around and to

avoid colliding with the cave walls or with other Oilbirds. Each click lasts for only 1/1000th of a second and is separated from the next click by 3/1000ths of a second. Oilbirds also make extremely loud screams, which is why they are called 'Guacharo'—screamer—in Venezuela.

It seems that Oilbirds feed mainly on the fruits of palms, laurels, and incense trees. They regurgitate the large seeds from the fruits on to the floor and ledges of their nesting cave; these sprout for a short while but, owing to the lack of light inside the caves, the shoots soon wither and die.

For many centuries, local natives have collected young Oilbirds, which grow incredibly fat, and have boiled them down in vats to provide an important source of oil, and it is from this that the bird gets its name.

PROFILE

Length: *35 cm (14 in).*
Weight: *400 g (14 oz).*
Distribution: *Northern South America, from western Guyana and Venezuela to Ecuador and Peru; also Trinidad.*
Habitat: *Dark caves in tropical forests, mostly in mountainous areas.*
Breeding: *Colonial. Nest a mound of debris and fruit pulp on ledge of cave. 2–4 eggs, incubation period about 33 days. Young remain in nest for up to 120 days, the longest nestling period of any bird except some birds of prey and large seabirds.*
Diet: *Fruit, mostly of palm, laurel and incense trees.*
Longevity: *Insufficient information.*

COMMON POOR-WILL

The only bird known to hibernate

The amazing discovery, on 29th December 1946, of an apparently dead Common Poor-will in a vertical crevice in rocks in southern California turned out to be the first case of hibernation by any bird species.

When a Common Poor-will (*Phalaenoptilus nuttallii*) was found by scientists in a rock crevice in the Colorado Desert, its feet and closed eyelids were cold, its heartbeat could not be detected and the bird was absolutely still: to all intents and purposes it appeared dead. Then, as it was put back in the crevice, it opened one eye briefly. Ten days later the bird was still in the same place: it was picked up again, but this time it woke up fully and flew off. The bird was found in the same condition in the same crevice in three more winters. It was obviously hibernating!

Subsequent experiments were made, both in the field and in the laboratory. These showed that the Common Poor-will's body temperature during hibernation was 18–20°C (64–68°F), sometimes dropping much lower if the air temperature fell. When the bird was active its temperature was between 35°C (95°F), and 43.5°C (110°F), itself a variation much greater than that of other birds. During hibernation at low body temperature, the bird needed about one-third less energy in terms of heat than when its body temperature was normal. So, a hibernating Common Poor-will requires only about 7 g (0.25 oz) of fat to keep alive for 70–100 days, whereas it would survive for only about a week on this amount if it had to maintain its normal body temperature of around 40°C (104°F).

The Common Poor-will gets its weird name from its song, which sounds like 'poor will', sometimes with a short 'ip' note added to the end. A name used for it by the Hopi Indians means 'the sleeper': presumably they have long been familiar with the bird's hibernating habits!

PROFILE

Length: *20 cm (8 in).*
Weight: *About 40 g (1.4 oz).*
Distribution: *West and Central North America south to Central Mexico.*
Habitat: *Arid, often hot, open country, open woodland, mountainous country.*
Breeding: *Nest a shallow scrape near vegetation. 2 eggs, incubation period uncertain.*
Diet: *Night-flying insects, e.g. moths.*
Longevity: *Insufficient information.*
Notes: *Other nightjars and some swifts and hummingbirds sometimes enter a state of overnight torpidity (deep sleep and reduced body temperature), but their torpidity lasts at most only for a few days.*

EDIBLE-NEST SWIFTLET

The bird with the exquisite saliva

The white nests of these small swiftlets are made entirely of the birds' own saliva and are collected in southeast Asia and consumed as a delicacy – bird's nest soup.

Throughout most of its range the Edible-nest Swiftlet (*Aerodramus fuciphagus*) nests in sea caves and inland limestone caves, though it also inhabits old buildings. It is remarkable in that it usually breeds in immense colonies in total darkness, up to 400 m (440 yds) from the cave entrance, but it is most renowned for its extraordinary nest. This is placed high, sometimes over 45 m (150 ft) up, on the cave roof and is made from the bird's own saliva deposited in semicircular layers which 'cement' themselves together and dry into a hard basket-shaped receptacle. Nest-building takes one month or more.

The nests have a calorific value of only 4.4 calories, weigh about 10 g (0.35 oz) each, have barely any taste and so are usually served in a soup containing spices and chicken. They have little, if any, nutritional value, yet the Chinese in particular prize them highly as a delicacy and as a medicine to aid recovery from illness. At the end of the 1950s 1 kg (2.2 lb) of nests cost over £10, while

in 1978 1200 nests weighing a total of 12 kg (26.5 lb) fetched £560.

Edible-nest Swiftlets find their way about in dark caves by echo-location (see Oilbird). During the day they feed outside, catching flying insects above the forest trees. The adults feed their young on individual balls of insects glued together with saliva in their

mouth; each 'foodball' averages about 0.57 g (0.02 oz) in weight and contains about 500 insects.

Two other swiftlets build edible nests. One, the Black-nest Swiftlet (*Aerodramus maximus*), is responsible for most of the incredible 2 million swiftlet nests built annually in the Great Cave of Niah in Borneo.

PROFILE

Length: *About 10 cm (4 in).*
Weight: *8–9.5 g (0.28–0.34 oz).*
Distribution: *Malaysia and Indonesia east to Borneo and north to south China.*
Habitat: *Caves along coasts and in tropical rainforests.*
Breeding: *Colonial. Nest of saliva, weighing about 10 g (0.35 oz), built on base of saliva. 2 eggs, incubation period about 23 days.*
Diet: *Insects, all caught in flight.*
Longevity: *Insufficient information; probably short-lived.*
Notes: *A large carnivorous cricket often lives in the nesting caves; young swiftlets that fall or are knocked from the nest are instantly devoured by these crikets or by rats and cave-dwelling snakes.*

BEE HUMMINGBIRD

Colourful master of the air

This handsome bird is only the size of a large insect, but it has complete control in flight and can fly backwards as well as forwards.

At only 6 cm (2.4 in) in length and weighing no more than 2 g (0.07 oz), the Bee Hummingbird (*Mellisuga helenae*) is the smallest bird in the world; even some beetles weigh 20 times more! The male is a beautiful glossy crimson, blue and white, but the female lacks the crimson colour and is generally duller. Like all hummingbirds, this species can move its wings in any direction—and even rotate them. Usually it moves them backwards and forwards almost horizontally in a kind of figure-of-8 motion, and this enables it to fly backwards as well as forwards. The number of wingbeats per second is about 30, but can sometimes reach as many as 80. Because of its minute size and the audible hum from the wings, the Bee Hummingbird both looks and sounds like a bee in flight.

Bee Hummingbirds feed on nectar by hovering in front of flowers and sipping from them. The number of heartbeats of this tiny jewel is as high as 1000 per minute when it is resting, and immeasurable when it is active.

PROFILE

Length: *6 cm (2.4 in).*
Weight: *1.6–2 g (0.06–0.07 oz).*
Distribution: *Confined to Cuba and Isle of Pines in Caribbean.*
Habitat: *Open woodlands and gardens.*
Breeding: *Minute cup-shaped nest of plant down, moss and cobwebs, placed on twig. 2 eggs, incubation period about 14 days.*
Diet: *Nectar, perhaps also some insects.*
Longevity: *Uncertain, probably 1–2 years.*
Notes: *At night Bee Hummingbirds sometimes enter a state of torpidity, when their body temperature drops and their heart rate slows down.*

HORNED SCREAMER

South America's feathered unicorn

One of the oddest-looking birds, this one is so named because it possesses a forward-projecting cartilaginous horn up to 15 cm (6 in) long growing out of its skull between the eyes.

The 3 species of screamer are goose-like birds but with a small head and a chicken-like bill. They all live in South America. The Horned Screamer (*Anhima cornuta*) is the size of a turkey. Its unique horn is probably a decoration but, like the other two screamers, it also possesses two spurs 2–5 cm (1–2 in) long on the wing which are used in aggressive fighting between individuals. Other peculiarities of these birds include small air cells beneath the thicker-than-normal skin, which create an audible crackling noise when the birds take off.

The screamers get their name from their voice, a loud double trumpeting note that can be heard at up to 3 km (2 miles) and is repeated incessantly. Horned Screamers also call while soaring high in the sky like vultures.

PROFILE

Length: *90 cm (3 ft); horn length up to 15 cm (6 in).*
Weight: *Male about 3 kg (6.6 lb).*
Distribution: *Tropical South America from Guianas, Venezuela and Colombia south to Bolivia and southern Brazil.*
Habitat: *Savannas, marshy areas, forest lakes.*
Breeding: *4–7 eggs, incubated for 43–45 days, in nest usually above water.*
Diet: *Sedges, grasses, seeds, aquatic plants.*
Flock size: *100s, sometimes 1000s.*
Notes: *Very little is known of this bird's behaviour. It regularly perches in trees and probably roosts there overnight. The screamers may be most closely related to ducks, geese and swans (Anatidae).*

SILVERY-CHEEKED HORNBILL

Walled in for love

When the time comes to nest and produce young, the male hornbill brings mud to his mate who then proceeds to plaster herself inside for over three months.

When a pair of Silvery-cheeked Hornbills (*Bycanistes brevis*) finds a suitable nest hole in which to rear young, the female goes inside. The male then finds some mud, swallows it and takes it back to the nest hole, where he regurgitates it in the form of small mud pellets which he passes through the hole to the female. The female then pats the mud on to the sides of the hole. After each day's session of plastering work she comes out for a break. Eventually only a narrow slit is left through which the female is too big to emerge; it is then that she lays her two eggs.

Throughout the 45 days that the female incubates the eggs, she is fed by the male through the narrow slit. When the young hatch, they and their mother continue to receive food from the male for a further 60 days until they are ready to leave the nest. The female has by then been walled up inside for as long as 3½ months! Finally the female breaks the mud with her huge bill in order to get out, and she and her young all leave together.

These big birds—76 cm (2.5 ft) long—eat almost nothing but fruit. It has been estimated that during the breeding season the male makes 1600 trips to the nest, delivering an average of 15 fruits each time. He regurgitates these and passes them through to his family. During the whole nesting period he may bring in as many as 24,000 fruits.

PROFILE

Length: *76 cm (2.5 ft).*
Weight: *About 1.3 kg (2.96 lb).*
Distribution: *Eastern Africa.*
Habitat: *Forest.*
Breeding: *In tree hole, walled up with mud. 2 eggs, incubation period 45 days.*
Diet: *Mainly fruit, occasionally insects.*
Longevity: *Insufficient information, but probably fairly long-lived.*
Notes: *These birds spend all their time in the treetops, usually in small groups, though up to 150 may roost together.*

BLACK-THROATED HONEYGUIDE

The bird that leads the way

When one of these birds finds a bees' nest it attracts other animals and human beings to it by making a loud chattering noise, then waits for the nest to be opened.

Black-throated or Greater Honeyguides (*Indicator indicator*) are extremely fond of the waxy honeycomb and grubs present in the nests of wild bees. Unfortunately they cannot get at them without some help, so they have evolved a remarkable method of obtaining their favourite food. The honeyguide, usually alone, makes a chattering call and swooping flights until another animal, generally a Ratel (Honey Badger), investigates; the bird then flies a short distance towards the bees' nest, stops and chatters again. Finally, the nest is reached and the Ratel breaks it open. The honeyguide then devours any honeycomb spilled on the ground.

As well as Ratels, baboons and mongooses may also follow Black-throated Honeyguides to bees' nests, and African natives often use these birds to guide them to sources of honey.

It is probable that Black-throated Honeyguides are nest parasites. In other words, they lay their eggs in the nests of other birds—usually hole-nesting birds—one in each nest. Little is known, however, of their breeding behaviour, but the honeyguide chick is said to have a begging call that sounds like several chicks calling together.

In experiments, Black-throated Honeyguides have survived for four weeks on nothing but wax. Conversely, they have lived for several months when deprived of wax.

PROFILE

Length: *20 cm (8 in).*
Weight: *30–60 g (1.1–2.2 oz).*
Distribution: *Africa south of the Sahara.*
Habitat: *Evergreen forest and open woodland, edges of forest.*
Breeding: *Little known. Probably lays eggs in nests of other birds. Fledging period about 40 days.*
Diet: *Wax and larvae from bees' nests; also insects.*
Longevity: *Insufficient information.*
Notes: *As these birds have been attracted by the scent of burning wax, it is possible that they locate bees' nests first by smell.*

BLACK WOODPECKER

One of Nature's head-bangers

Hammering powerfully on a tree-trunk with its bill, a Black Woodpecker would almost certainly damage its skull if it did not have a protective cushion of tissue at the base of its forehead.

The Black Woodpecker (*Dryocopus martius*) is the biggest woodpecker in Europe and Asia, and also the loudest. Clinging to the side of a hollow tree, it hammers on the trunk with its chisel-like bill in bursts of 2–3 seconds, making 14–18 'hits' per second. The noise created sounds like a machine-gun and can be heard for up to 1.8 km (1.12 miles) and exceptionally, in good conditions, as far away as 3–4 km (2–2.5 miles). In spring this woodpecker also utters a very loud, ringing call that sounds like somebody laughing, though its head-banging behaviour is hardly done for fun.

The Black Woodpecker feeds mainly on ants and their larvae and on wood-boring beetles. It has a long, hard, sticky tongue with five pairs of barbs at the tip which it can extend to 55 mm (2.2 in) beyond the tip of its bill. The bird hacks away at trees and stumps, sometimes creating massive craters in them, and then enters its tongue to spear its food. In one instance in Denmark, up to 800 rotten stumps were attacked by Black Woodpeckers in an area of only 32 ha (79 acres). This woodpecker seems able to detect the presence of ants simply by sliding its tongue over a stump or log, and it can find ants' nests on the ground in winter when they are covered by 60 cm (2 ft) of snow.

PROFILE

Length: *45–50 cm (16–20 in).*

Weight: *Male 270–460 g (9.5–16.3 oz), female 255–344 g (9.0–12.1 oz).*

Distribution: *Eurasia, from Spain and Scandinavia east to Kamchatka and south to Caspian Sea and southwest China.*

Habitat: *Forests; in winter may wander to more open country.*

Breeding: *Excavates nest hole 4–25 m (13–18 ft) up in large tree or telegraph pole. 4–6 eggs, incubation period 12–14 days.*

Diet: *Mainly ants and wood-boring beetles, also bees and wasps; occasionally fruits and seeds and (rarely) nestling birds.*

Longevity: *Oldest ringed bird lived to 7 years.*

Notes: *Old nest holes of this species are used by a wide variety of other animals, including Red Squirrels and many kinds of birds (owls, ducks, falcons, pigeons etc).*

RED-HEADED WOODPECKER

The itinerant food-storer

Although it eats a wide variety of foods in summer, this woodpecker subsists in the winter months on beechmast and acorns which it stores in cavities and crevices in case of food shortage.

Because the crop of acorns and beech-mast varies from year to year, the Red-headed Woodpecker (*Melanerpes erythrocephalus*) often has to change the areas in which it spends the winter. It seems to be so dependent on these foods that it will travel many hundreds of kilometres from its breeding areas in open parkland, wooded valleys and light woodland in order to find an adequate supply of acorns in the heavily wooded areas. This woodpecker breeds in North America from the Atlantic coast across to the mid-west, but the western half of this range is deserted in winter. Over the last 100 years it has shifted its breeding range markedly, moving in large numbers first westwards and then, much later, back eastwards again. In some years a great exodus of Red-headed Woodpeckers has taken place from the region of the Great Lakes, and similar mass movements occur in other areas when the acorn crop has failed there.

Red-headed Woodpeckers collect as many acorns as they can and store these in any handy crevice or cavity they can find. They often store many more than they can possibly eat and sometimes do not need to touch the store at all during the winter. It appears that they hide food away as a kind of insurance against shortage or bad weather later.

This species bores a nesting hole in a dead tree, telegraph pole or fence post. It has become rare in some parts of its range owing to competition from Starlings, which may evict the woodpeckers from their hole and use it for themselves.

PROFILE

Length: *24 cm (9.5 in).*
Weight: *Around 100 g (3.5 oz).*
Distribution: *North America from Lake Winnipeg east to Alberta and south to southern Texas; in winter it moves south and east in large numbers.*
Habitat: *Parkland, open woodland and river valleys; in winter often in heavily wooded areas.*
Breeding: *Bores hole in dead tree, fence post or telegraph pole. 4–7 eggs, incubation period 14–16 days. 2 broods.*
Diet: *Wide variety of insects and vegetable matter; in winter almost exclusively acorns and beechmast.*

GOLDEN WHISTLER

The world's most variable bird

Many bird species vary in appearance and size from one place to another and their different forms are often classed as subspecies or races. The Golden Whistler, however, shows the greatest geographical variation of any bird: at least 73 subspecies can be recognised.

The Golden Whistler (*Pachycephala pectoralis*) occurs around the southern and eastern coasts of Australia and on innumerable islands to the northwest, northeast and east of that country, although not in New Zealand or New Guinea. Throughout this range the bird exhibits an enormous, though subtle, variety of plumages. Males are generally bright orange or yellow on their underparts, with a black breast band; they have a white patch on the throat, but this varies in extent from a large and obvious area of white to a much-reduced or even non-existent patch, and some subspecies also lack the breast band. The Golden Whistler's length and the shape and size of its bill also show an incredible variation, as does the shape of the head. Depending on the subspecies, females can be anything from dull reddish-brown to bright yellow like the males. Conversely, males on some islands are dull brownish, like the females.

All these different-looking birds are, nevertheless, members of the same species—the Golden Whistler. They have not evolved the genetic differences necessary for them to be considered as separate full species. Interestingly, there is another bird found in North Australia, New Guinea and on islands to the east, known as the Mangrove Golden Whistler (*Pachycephala melanura*). This is almost identical in appearance to some races of the Golden Whistler – yet it is a totally distinct species!

PROFILE

Length: *Around 17 cm (6–7 in).*
Weight: *Around 35 g (1.2 oz).*
Distribution: *South and East Australia, Tasmania, eastern Indonesia, Melanesia, Kermadec Islands.*
Habitat: *Highly variable; from rainforest to eucalyptus forest, mangroves and scrubland.*
Breeding: *Well-concealed nest of twigs and bark. 2–3 eggs, incubation period uncertain.*
Diet: *Small beetles, caterpillars and other insects; also berries.*
Notes: *The loud whistles uttered by this bird can easily be triggered by any loud noise, hence one of its alternative names of 'Thunder Bird'.*

EASTERN WHIPBIRD

The recluse with the strangest of calls

The remarkable whipcrack call of these birds is familiar and quite unmistakable, yet whipbirds are so shy that they are rarely seen in the dense thickets of their Australian forest homes.

In the brush country of eastern Australia, the Eastern Whipbird (*Psophodes olivaceus*) is quite a common bird. Unfortunately it prefers to live within dense vegetation such as scrub, wooded areas and thickly wooded gullies and is therefore very difficult to see. On top of this it is exceedingly shy and skulks about inside the dense cover, so that it rarely permits even a glimpse of itself. It tends to keep near the ground, and if disturbed will, rather than fly off, run quietly through the vegetation until it is out of danger.

The easiest way to tell whether these elusive birds are present is to listen for their calls. As luck would have it, Eastern Whipbirds have the most distinctive voices. The male's song is made up of several fluty notes followed by an amazing sound just like the crack of a whip. It is this unmistakable sound that gives the bird its name. Occasionally another two short, sharp notes come straight after the whipcrack, but, despite the impression that they are made by the same bird, these notes are in fact the female responding to the male. Yet, although it is easy to recognise this species' voice and to know that it is present inside an area of vegetation, a person can watch carefully for days without seeing the bird itself.

A similar species, the Western Whipbird (*Psophodes nigrogularis*), is found only in the extreme south-west of Australia and in coastal South Australia; it is also elusive, and apparently much rarer.

PROFILE

Length: *25–30 cm (10–12 in).*
Weight: *Around 80 g (2.8 oz).*
Distribution: *Coastal eastern Australia.*
Habitat: *Dense lower vegetation of rainforests, wet wooded areas, coastal scrub.*
Breeding: *Nest of twigs and roots built low in a bush. 2–3 eggs, incubation period unknown.*
Diet: *Mainly insects.*

CAPE SUGARBIRD

A life dependent on just one type of flowering shrub

Wherever protea shrubs grow in southern Africa these birds are also present, for they are almost totally dependent on the plants for their food and nesting requirements.

Protea shrubs have spectacular flowers which are justly famous for their beauty. They grow only in southern Africa, and here they are almost inevitably surrounded by parties of Cape Sugarbirds (*Promerops cafer*). These rather dull birds with distinctively long tails spend all or most of their life at the proteas. The shrubs grow mainly on slopes of mountains, and they blossom at different times according to the altitude. The Cape Sugarbirds feed mostly on nectar and insects from the flowers; they therefore move up and down the mountain, following the variations in the blossoming times of the proteas.

Sugarbirds also nest in the protea bushes, placing their cup-shaped nests of grass and small twigs 90–160 cm (3–5.3 ft) up in a dense bush. Even the nest-lining is made up of fluff and seed pappi from proteas. The birds are extremely territorial when breeding. The male Cape Sugarbird performs a highly conspicuous display in which he flies up above the protea bushes, with his long tail arched over his back, and claps his wings loudly; if another male intrudes into his territory, he flies straight at it to chase it off.

PROFILE

Length: *Up to 45 cm (18 in) including tail, which in male may reach 30 cm (12 in) in length.*

Weight: *Up to around 25 g (0.9 oz).*

Distribution: *Southern Cape Province in South Africa.*

Habitat: *Hilly country and mountain slopes with protea bushes.*

Breeding: *Nests in dense protea bush. 1–2 eggs, incubation period 17 days.*

Diet: *Nectar and insects, mainly from protea bushes.*

Notes: *The only other species in this genus is Gurney's Sugarbird (Promerops gurneyi), which is found only in eastern parts of South Africa.*

DUSKY SEASIDE SPARROW

The world's loneliest bird

Found nowhere in the world outside a small remote area in eastern Florida, USA, this species' lonely existence has brought it near to extinction.

A small saltmarsh area near Titusville on the east coast of Florida, not far from the Cape Canaveral rocket base, is home to the few Dusky Seaside Sparrows (*Ammodramus nigrescens*) left in the world. At the last count only one of these small dark birds was found living among the grasses of the tidal marshland. It was a male, about 13–15 years old, so this bird looks certain to become extinct within a very short time unless an undiscovered population exists somewhere in America.

Although it seems that the Dusky Seaside Sparrow has always had a very restricted range in Florida, reclamation work on the coast has altered the saltwater nature of its habitat and contributed to its decline.

A very similar species, the Cape Sable Sparrow (*Ammodramus mirabilis*) also has a small range, being found only in southwest Florida. Both this and the Dusky Seaside Sparrow are nowadays usually considered to be subspecies of the Seaside Sparrow (*Ammodramus maritimus*), which is more widespread and occurs along the whole of the south and east coasts of the USA apart from central and southern Florida.

PROFILE

Length: *15 cm (6 in).*
Weight: *19–28 g (0.7–1.0 oz).*
Distribution: *Confined to small area near Titusville, Florida, USA.*
Habitat: *Tidal saltmarsh.*
Breeding: *Cup-shaped nest in salt-marsh grasses. 3–4 eggs, incubation period 11–12 days.*
Diet: *Seeds and arthropods.*
Longevity: *Mortality probably high, about 30–35% of adults dying each year. Some, however, live to at least 15 years of age.*
Notes: *There are over 30 native 'sparrows' in North America, all of which are in fact buntings (family Emberizidae).*

BANANAQUIT

The fussy sleeper

Unlike most birds, these tropical songsters roost inside nests all year, but these nests are built specially for sleeping in—and the Bananaquit always sleeps alone.

One of the most intriguing features of the Bananaquit (*Coereba flaveola*) is its roosting habits. The birds spend the night inside specially built nests, the male and the female each in a separate one. These 'dormitory nests' are similar to the ones this species uses for breeding: a spherical construction of grasses, with a downward-facing entrance like a small doorway at the side. Usually each Bananaquit builds its own dormitory nest, but the female may sometimes use the one in which the young have previously been reared. Many dormitory nests are used for very long periods of time; when they eventually become too tatty, the bird builds another one. Bananaquits' nests are often sited at the outer end of branches and are therefore quite easy to find, but because most are used only for roosting in and are then abandoned the majority found are empty!

These small birds, 11 cm (4.3 in) in length, are quite common in tropical America, where their high-pitched song may be heard throughout much of the day. One of their natural foods is flower nectar and fruit juice, but they often come into gardens of houses and take sugar solution from special feeders put up to attract such birds as hummingbirds. An alternative name for the Bananaquit is 'Sugarbird'.

PROFILE

Length: *11 cm (4.3 in).*
Weight: *8.0–10.5 g (0.3–0.4 oz).*
Distribution: *Most of southern Central America and West Indies (but not Cuba) and throughout tropical South America.*
Habitat: *Open country with scattered low trees and shrubs, forest edges and gardens (including in cities).*
Breeding: *Spherical nest with side entrance. 2–3 eggs, incubation period 12–13 days.*
Diet: *Nectar, juice of fruits, insects.*
Notes: *There are over 40 races of Bananaquit, and in the Caribbean almost every island has its own race of this bird.*

RED-EYED VIREO

Top songster of the avian world

Whereas other birds cease all activity during the hottest hours of the day, the song of this small woodland bird continues without a break throughout the length of the summer's days.

Although no more than 15 cm (6 in) long, the Red-eyed Vireo (*Vireo olivaceus*) makes its presence known by singing non-stop throughout the summer. Its song is by no means the most beautiful of bird songs; if anything, it is rather dull, being a series of short variable phrases. It is, however, notable for being sung with such persistency and tirelessness that nobody could possibly ignore it. Indeed, it is quite remarkable that the Red-eyed Vireo can keep up a constant outpouring of self-advertisement — with all the energy that it consequently uses up — right through

from dawn to dusk, day after day. Perhaps it wants to make certain of gaining the distinction, as it recently has, of being the commonest woodland bird of eastern North America!

Red-eyed Vireos migrate south in autumn, some flying over 4800 km (3000 miles) well into southern South America. When they return in early spring, guess what: they immediately sing!

Another vireo, Bell's Vireo (*Vireo bellii*), is almost as persistent a singer, but its song is more unpleasant, being a fast, harsh chatter.

PROFILE

Length: *15 cm (6 in).*

Weight: *15–21 g (0.5–0.7 oz).*

Distribution: *Breeds from Canada south to mid South America; North American breeders all migrate south.*

Habitat: *Deciduous forest and woodland.*

Breeding: *Nest suspended from small branch. 2–5 eggs, incubation period 11–13 days.*

Diet: *Insects, berries and fruits. In Amazonian winter quarters, apparently fruits and berries only.*

Longevity: *Insufficient information, but probably maximum 4–5 years.*

BROWN-HEADED COWBIRD

The laziest bird in the world

Not only does this parasite lay its eggs in the nests of other birds and let them raise its young, it also gets cattle to help find its food for it.

Flocks of Brown-headed Cowbirds (*Molothrus ater*) can often be seen following cattle and catching the insects disturbed by their feet. This habit has given them their name, though they are just as likely nowadays to be seen foraging in city parks and suburbs or in open woodland. In winter, however, up to 90% of their food may consist of seeds.

These birds are, however, best known for their breeding habits—or perhaps bad habits. Brown-headed Cowbirds watch other birds building nests, and as soon as the rightful owner has laid two eggs the female cowbird lays one of her own in the same nest. In this way, the

cowbird will lay up to 25 eggs, one per day, in other birds' nests. Normally she lays only one or two eggs in each nest, though 12 have been found in the nest of one unfortunate Wood Thrush (*Hylocichla mustelina*). As many as 206 different bird species are known to be parasitised by Brown-headed Cowbirds; these are mostly warblers and sparrows (buntings), but the Red-eyed Vireo is one of the commonest victims.

The nestling cowbird, unlike the young Cuckoo (*Cuculus canorus*), does not eject the chicks of its host from the nest. As a result, the host is able to raise its own young as well as the young cowbird.

PROFILE

Length: *18–19 cm (7.0–7.5 in).*
Weight: *40–70 g (1.4–2.5 oz).*
Distribution: *Breeds from Central Canada to southern Mexico; winters from mid USA south to South Mexico.*
Habitat: *Grassland, farmland, open woodland, city parks and suburbs.*
Breeding: *Lays up to 25 eggs, in nests of other birds (1–2 in each); incubation period 10–12 days.*
Diet: *Seeds, grasshoppers and other insects.*
Longevity: *Insufficient information, but probably averages 1–2 years.*
Notes: *This species has increased in numbers enormously in the last 50 years.*

RED-BILLED QUELEA

The 'feathered locust'

Just one flock of these small sparrow-like birds can totally destroy a whole field of cereal crops, doing as much damage as a plague of locusts.

The most notable feature of the Red-billed Quelea (*Quelea quelea*) is the size of its population. Feeding flocks are gigantic and number tens of thousands—often millions—of individuals. Together the birds can destroy in a matter of days 30–50% of a crop—and not infrequently the whole lot. It is not surprising that another name for this bird is 'Locust Bird'. Queleas nest in massive colonies which may contain up to 10 million nests and cover areas extending over 10 square km (4 square miles). It has been estimated that the total world popula-

tion of this species may be of the order of 100,000 million individuals, putting it well in line for the title of the world's most numerous bird.

Queleas do in fact prefer to eat the seeds of wild grasses, but, because there are so many of these birds, from time to time they exhaust their natural food supply. It is then that they turn to cultivated fields, where they eat the ripening seeds of millet, corn, wheat and rice. In fact, the Red-billed Quelea affects the economies of 20 or more African countries, most of which are

greatly dependent on a good harvest.

Various methods have been employed to try to reduce the population of this species, including dynamiting the roosts (which are several million birds strong), destroying their nest colonies with flame-throwers and spraying both roosts and colonies with poison. In one year 183 million Red-billed Queleas were killed by poison-spraying in South Africa alone; amazingly, this had no noticeable effect on the species' population nor on the amount of damage done to crops in the following years.

PROFILE

Length: *12–13 cm (5 in).*
Weight: *About 15 g (0.53 oz).*
Distribution: *Africa south of the Sahara.*
Habitat: *Savanna and other grassland areas.*
Breeding: *Immense colonies of oval-shaped nests built of grasses in thorn and acacia trees. 2–4 eggs, incubation period 12 days.*
Diet: *Seeds of wild grasses and of cultivated cereals and rice; also insects.*
Longevity: *Averages about 1.5 years.*
Notes: *Undertakes migration according to the rainfall, flying up to 1600 km (1000 miles) in search of crops ripened by rainfall or irrigation.*

STARLING

The world's most successful bird

At the end of the 19th century just over 100 Starlings were released in Central Park, New York, but 60 years later this species had spread across the whole of the United States.

Although originally confined to Europe and West Asia, the Starling (*Sturnus vulgaris*) is such an adaptable bird that it rapidly colonises new areas and increases its population. From just over 100 Starlings introduced into New York in 1890, by 1950 this species had reached all parts of North America; and now, in the 1980s, the total Starling population of North America—from Alaska to Mexico—numbers something like 150 million, nearly a third of the world population of 500 million. Yet the bird was unknown throughout North America less than 100 years ago!

Starlings have also been introduced into South Africa, southwest Australia, New Zealand, Fiji and the Caribbean, with similar success. One of this bird's secrets is that it takes advantage of Man's activities: the large areas of forest felled and replaced by grassland for stock grazing make ideal habitat for Starlings to find their food (largely worms and other soil invertebrates), while roofs of houses provide many suitable nesting sites.

One of Nature's most spectacular sights is that of Starlings at their winter roost sites. The birds fly in from various feeding areas up to 32 km (20 miles) away. Before settling down for the night they often perform fantastic aerial manoeuvres, when they appear as great swirling clouds of smoke. Starlings roost in city centres, in trees and in reedbeds and sometimes the gatherings are immense, numbering several million birds. Their droppings often damage trees and can form a carpet 50 cm (20 in) deep on the ground below. The weight of so many Starlings can cause tree branches to break off, while up to 500 birds totalling about 35 kg (77 lb) within each cubic metre of a reedbed will soon be more than the reeds can support.

PROFILE

Length: *21–22 cm (8.5 in).*

Weight: *70–100 g (2.5–3.5 oz).*

Distribution: *Europe, Azores, Canary Islands, and Asia east to Lake Baikal; northern populations move south or west in autumn. Introduced into North America, Caribbean, South Africa, Australia, New Zealand and Fiji.*

Habitat: *Varied: open grassland and farmland, parkland, urban areas, rubbish tips – virtually anywhere near human habitation.*

Breeding: *Untidy nest of straw, grass and leaves in hole or other cavity. 4–6 eggs, incubation period 12 days.*

Diet: *Varied: mainly soil invertebrates, but in autumn and winter also fruit and berries, seeds, refuse, garden scraps.*

Longevity: *Oldest ringed bird 21.3 years; most live only up to 18 months.*

Notes: *The Starling is an excellent mimic capable of imitating not only many other birds but also mechanical sounds such as creaking doors or ringing telephones.*

SATIN BOWERBIRD

The Don Juan of the avian world

Having spent much time and care building and decorating its bower, the male bowerbird then displays to a visiting female, but his fidelity is not all that it should be.

Bowerbirds (family Ptilonorhynchidae) are well known for their intriguing habit of building bowers to attract a female. What is not so well known is that they are highly promiscuous birds. Males display to and mate with as many females of their species as they can lure to their bower. What is more, the males do not even bother to help in the subsequent nest-building, incubation and care of the young. Insufficient is known of the mating systems of most of the 18 species of bowerbird, which are found only in Australia and New Guinea, but it is apparent that most are polygamous.

There are several different types of bower built by these birds. Some species construct an elaborate roofed tower of sticks. The Satin Bowerbird (*Ptilo-norhynchus violaceus*), one of the better known of its family, builds an avenue of two stick walls and decorates the pathway between with up to 100 different objects; these include feathers (especially of parrots), bottle tops, cigarette packets, old bags, biro tops and the like. It also 'paints' the inside walls with a mixture of saliva and crushed vegetation. The Satin Bowerbird has a distinct preference for blue objects, the same colour as the adult male's plumage. Rival males often steal objects from others and even wreck other bowers.

The immature males, which take seven years to acquire adult plumage, practise at being Don Juans by displaying to one another and to females. They sometimes 'borrow' the bowers of their elders for added effect.

PROFILE

Length: *27–33 cm (10.5–13 in).*
Weight: *About 100–250 g (3.5–8.8 oz).*
Distribution: *Southeast and northeast Australia.*
Habitat: *Rainforest and forest edge.*
Breeding: *Nest a shallow twig saucer, built by female in forest tree. 1–3 eggs, incubation period 19–24 days.*
Diet: *Mostly fruits and berries; adult feeds young on insects.*
Longevity: *Up to 15 years.*
Notes: *Apparently the walls of this bird's bower always face in a north-to-south direction, perhaps so that the male can get the best view of the female—and also be most visible to her—in the early morning.*

FISHES

There are more kinds of fishes than there are mammals, birds, reptiles and amphibians together. Estimated to number around 22,000 different species, the precise number cannot be exact for years yet because scientists are still sorting them out, identifying previously undescribed species and reviewing those described in the past. Every year, a few species which are genuinely unrecognised are added to the total.

Fishes are superbly designed to take advantage of living in water, which covers more than three-quarters of the earth's surface. The essential features common to all are the possession of gills by which they absorb oxygen from the water, the presence of a backbone made up of separate units or vertebrae, and swimming by means of fins. Variations include having a primitive lung so that some can breathe air, or having such minute fins that others swim by means of serpentine wriggling.

Fishes present many contrasts. Their size varies from the gigantic, like the 18 m (59 ft) Whale Shark, to the miniscule—the Luzon Goby is only 10 mm (0.39 in) when mature. Their feeding habits vary from the monstrous flesh-eaters such as the Great White and hammerhead sharks, through the parasitism of the lampreys, the Slime Eel and the Candiru, to the gentle jellyfish-eating Ocean Sunfish and the insect-eating Archer Fish. Sometimes their behaviour seems extraordinary. The Climbing Perch and the Asian Walking Catfish come out of the water and can progress overland, but this is a neat way of finding a new place to live when the old one becomes untenable. In the case of drought, which can sometimes last for more than a year, some African lungfish stick it out by burrowing deep into the mud and survive by breathing air. In the sea lifestyles vary enormously.

There are few variations on body form or lifestyle which fishes have not successfully exploited.

SEA LAMPREY

Vampire of the fish world

The Sea Lamprey has been described as looking like a yard of hosepipe which has been left out in the garden all winter, and this is apt for it has an elongated body with minute, blotchy yellow and black eyes and a round sucker disc instead of a mouth.

The sucker disc of the Sea Lamprey (*Petromyzon marinus*) is one of several features which show that this unattractive animal is not a true fish at all, for fishes have jaws. It is a member of the primitive pre-fish group, called agnathans or jawless fishes. Other features are a lack of paired pectoral and pelvic fins; no bony rays in the other fins; and a series of seven holes on the side of the body which connect to separate gill pouches instead of a single gill cover on each side.

What makes the Sea Lamprey seem a particularly repulsive character is its feeding habits, for it is a blood-sucking parasite on other fishes. The sucker disc is armed with quite strong, conical, blunt teeth with, in the centre, a set of extremely sharp fangs. While the lamprey fastens onto a larger fish by its sucker and the blunt teeth give it purchase, these fangs are driven into the fish's flesh. Glands in the lamprey's throat produce a form of saliva which contains an anticoagulant, so the victim's blood will not clot. The lamprey then proceeds to suck its victim dry, stopping when there is insufficient blood to flow. The victim often dies, because in its weakened state it falls prey to bacterial or fungal infections.

Sea Lampreys breed in fresh water. The young are blind, slender, eel-like creatures which bury themselves in mud and feed by filtering micro-organisms out of the mud. After three to five years, they change to the adult form and migrate to the sea. In the sea, and in estuaries, they become parasites on other fishes. In some areas, as in the Great Lakes of North America, they migrate from the rivers into the lakes and substitute the lake for the sea.

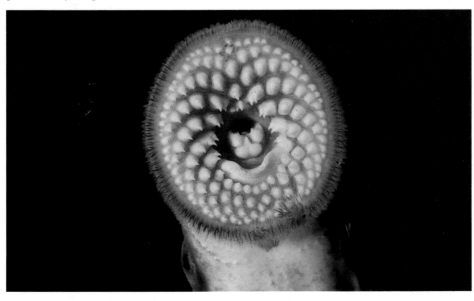

PROFILE

Length: *Grows to 90 cm (35 in).*
Distribution: *Both sides of the North Atlantic, and in the western Mediterranean; also in major rivers within this range.*
Habitat: *Coastal waters. Young hide in mud and muddy weedbed; adults behave as parasites on fishes in the sea and in estuaries.*
Breeding: *Hollows out a nest in a stony riverbed in which the eggs are laid.*
Diet: *Larvae take diatoms, bacteria, protozoa; adults suck blood of fishes.*
Notes: *Through much of its range this species has become rare.*

WHALE SHARK

The fish with skin like armour plating

The Whale Shark has several claims to fame on account of its massive size but unaggressive nature, and its wide tropical distribution yet apparent rarity, but despite these noteworthy features it is still poorly known to science.

The Whale Shark (*Rhincodon typus*) is huge. The largest measured accurately was 12.65 m (41.5 ft) long, but there are many reported estimates and approximate measurements of these sharks reaching up to 18 m (59 ft). It is probable that only a few exceed 12 m (39.4 ft) in length.

Despite its size this shark is inoffensive to Man, its main impact being that if entangled it may destroy a fishing net in its struggle to escape. On the other hand, the presence of Whale Sharks is often taken to be an indicator of plentiful plankton and good fishing, so some fishermen actually set their nets near them.

This is a highly characteristic shark, with a flattened head and immensely broad mouth. The gill slits are wide. It feeds by pumping sea water into its scoop-like mouth, through a net-like filter formed by the gill rakers in the throat, with the water being forced out of the gill slits. In this way the Whale Shark concentrates the minute animal life of the plankton. Whale Sharks have, however, been watched snapping up small bonitos and other sizeable fishes which are also attracted to the plankton and the smaller fish which feed on it.

The Whale Shark has prominent ridges running along its back, the lowest one of which forms a keel along the side of the tail. The function of these ridges is uncertain, but they help to make the skin thicker and, with its fine tooth-like denticles also, the skin is so hard as to be almost armour-plated.

Although the Whale Shark has been reported in all tropical seas and is widely distributed, it is evidently not a common shark.

PROFILE

Length: *Adult 12–18 m (39.4–59 ft).*
Weight: *More than 8165 kg (18,000 lb), but never accurately weighed.*
Distribution: *All tropical seas.*
Habitat: *Mainly surface-living in the oceans, but approaches the coast.*
Breeding: *Probably gives birth to young about 55 cm (22 in) long.*
Diet: *Animal plankton and fish.*
Longevity: *Not known, but if comparison with other large sharks is valid probably at least 50 years.*

GOBLIN SHARK

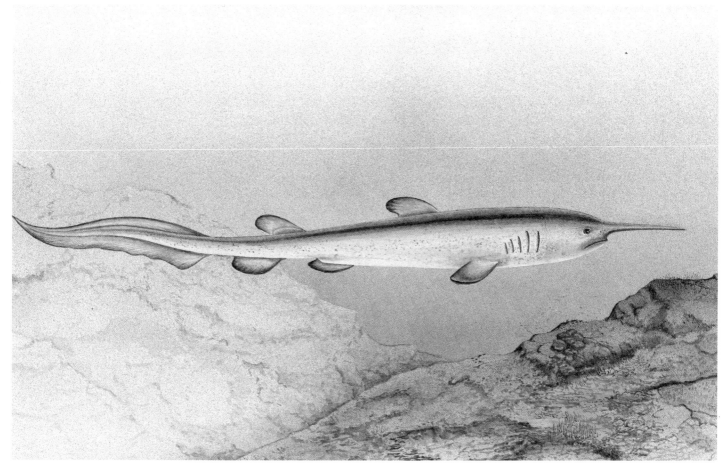

Japan's weird bottom-dweller

One of the world's mystery fishes, this shark's natural history is virtually unknown; moreover, it seems to be closely similar to a fossil shark whose remains, found in Syria, date back to 90–140 million years.

One of the several extraordinary features about the Goblin Shark (*Mitsukurina owstoni*) is its very long, flattened, blade-like snout which projects like a hood above the protruding jaws. Unfortunately there seem to be no observations on the feeding behaviour of this shark, but the whole structure of its head end suggests an unusual, if not unique, diet and means of finding food. As its eyes are very small, its vision is unlikely to be particularly acute. The snout and area around the jaws have plentiful sensory organs and must be the principal means of locating food.

Its teeth are long and slender, with very sharp points in the front and sides of both upper and lower jaws, but towards the angle of the jaws they are smaller and modified for crushing.

These teeth suggest that this shark feeds on soft-bodied prey such as fish, squids, and shrimps. The jaws seem to be capable of rapid and extensive projection forward from the head, and no doubt are used to snap up prey.

The Goblin Shark is best known from Japanese waters, where it has been reported on a number of occasions and even photographed alive (the photographs show that it is pinkish-white, although museum study specimens always seem to be dull brown). It has also been captured off southern Australia, off southern Africa, in the eastern Atlantic and in the western Atlantic: clearly, it is widely distributed but never common. It lives on the upper continental slope down to depths of 550 m (1805 ft).

PROFILE

Length: *Up to 3.35 m (11 ft).*
Distribution: *Eastern North Atlantic (Biscay to Madeira), western Atlantic (off northern South America), off southern Africa, southern Australia, and Japan.*
Habitat: *Continental shelves near deep water.*
Breeding: *Probably bears living young.*
Diet: *Deduced from the shape of its teeth to be fish and squid.*
Notes: *The natural history of this bizarre shark is virtually unknown; it will probably be reported elsewhere in suitable depths of continental shelves.*

MEGAMOUTH

The giant shark with a built-in scoop

The first-known specimen of Megamouth was caught by accident when an extraordinary-looking shark, 4.46 m (14.8 ft) in length and with a huge scoop-like mouth, got itself tangled up in a parachute of the sea anchor of a US Navy oceanographic research vessel off the Hawaiian Islands in November 1976.

The Megamouth (*Megachasma pelagios*) has a rounded thickset body, large long head, blunt, rounded snout and a huge scoop-like mouth. Its teeth are small, very numerous and slightly hooked, and it has densely packed gill rakers on the gill arches inside the throat. These and the massive scoop-like mouth show that it is a plankton feeder: it cruises in middle depths of the sea with its jaws swung open, filtering plankton on the gill rakers as the water flows out of its five gill slits on each side.

The stomach of the Megamouth caught in Hawaii contained a mass which looked like thickened tomato soup, but was, in fact, concentrated small reddish euphausiid shrimps. These shrimps are most common at 350–750 m (1150–2460 ft) during the day, but come near the surface at night; they give a clue as to the depth at which the Megamouth prefers to live.

The shark itself was dark grey to blue-black on the back and lighter below and on the sides. Its mouth was bright silvery inside with small circular pores, which, it has been suggested, could be light organs. Perhaps they are used to lure the shrimps into its throat.

The Megamouth's flesh is very soft and flabby: the Hawaiian specimen's tail came off as it was hoisted out of the water! This specimen had also been attacked by the Cookiecutter Shark, which had taken several bites out of it.

A second Megamouth was captured off the coast of California in 1984, but, with only these two specimens to go on, very little is known about this species' biology.

PROFILE

Length: *Grows to 4.46 m (14.8 ft).*
Distribution: *Known only from off Hawaii and southern California.*
Habitat: *Probably lives in mid-water.*
Diet: *Small planktonic crustaceans and other small animals.*
Notes: *This is the least well-known but most exciting shark to be discovered in the present century.*

GREAT WHITE SHARK

PROFILE

Length: *Often to 5 m (16.4 ft), possibly to 8 m (26.25 ft).*

Weight: *Measured to 1208 kg (1.2 tons); probably reaches 2030 kg (2 tons).*

Distribution: *All warm-temperate and tropical seas.*

Habitat: *Surface-living in ocean, but often in shallow water.*

Breeding: *Virtually unknown; believed to be a live bearer.*

Diet: *Large marine invertebrates, fish, turtles, marine animals.*

Longevity: *Not known, but probably lives up to 40 years.*

Notes: *Known to attack Man, but the danger of attack is usually greatly exaggerated.*

The swimmer's nightmare

This aggressive giant has been responsible for many attacks on swimmers, divers and surfers, and so great is its size and strength that these are frequently fatal; it often attacks small boats.

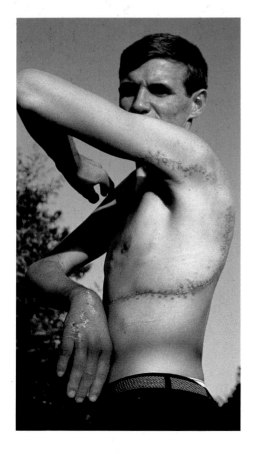

The stout spindle-shaped body, with its broad half-moon-shaped tail and wide gill slits, are typical of a shark which has mastered efficient, long-distance swimming. The Great White Shark (*Carcharodon carcharias*) is also capable of high-speed attacks over a short distance and occasionally will leap out of the water. It has a strong keel along the sides of its body, and its teeth are also highly distinctive, being (at least in the main part of the jaws) triangular and erect with serrated edges.

The Great White Shark is a massive fish. As always with large animals, there is substantial doubt about its maximum size. Specimens of 6.4 m (21 ft) have been measured, and it possibly grows to over 8 m (26.25 ft). Weights of sharks this size can only be guessed at, but a 5.134-m (16.8-ft) Great White Shark caught off South Australia weighed 1208.38 kg (1.2 tons), so weights above 2030 kg (2 tons) are probable.

The preferred food of the Great White Shark is in fact fish including many species of shark, seals, sea lions, sea otters, porpoises and dolphins, and even small whales. It also attacks turtles, seabirds, and marine invertebrates such as squids. In effect, this powerful and voracious predator will attack almost any living creature in the sea. For all its ferocious reputation it does not attack Man very often; indeed, more Great White Sharks are killed by Man each year than ever humans are eaten by sharks.

This is not a particularly common shark. Usually it occurs singly, sometimes in pairs, and very rarely up to ten at a time, but these do not form schools. The Great White Shark may perform trans-oceanic migrations, for it can swim at a steady 3.2 km/h (2 mph) for days on end.

GREAT HAMMERHEAD SHARK

The bulldozer of the sea

Hammerheads are truly one of the most bizarre of the sea's creatures: their head is flattened from top to bottom, with the eyes and nostrils opening at the far sides of the expanded hammer head.

Why these sharks have such an extraordinary head is uncertain. Some scientists have argued that it acts as a bow rudder, giving the shark stability when swimming; others see it as a means of separating the paired eyes and nostrils, providing a broader-based triangulation for finding food. It is certainly extremely sensitive to scents, as these are usually the first sharks to investigate the bait on long-lines. Whatever its function, the head resembles the shovel of a bulldozer.

The Great Hammerhead Shark (*Sphyrna mokarran*) is a specialist feeder on stingrays, rays, small sharks, and a wide range of fishes including sea catfishes, and many have been caught with the spines of catfishes embedded in their mouths and throats; it must also be immune to the venom in the spines.

Most Great Hammerheads reach a length of about 3.5 m (11.5 ft), but some grow to more than 6 m (19.6 ft). At this size they are, of course, extremely powerful and prove hard to handle if accidentally caught in a fisherman's net. One is also reputed to have attacked a swimmer, but it is not certain that it was this species of the 9 known species of hammerhead.

This shark occurs in all tropical and subtropical seas, both inshore and in the open sea, and around oceanic islands. It is usually caught in shallow water between 1 m and 80 m (3 ft and 262 ft) deep. It is migratory, moving towards the north or south seasonally (depending on the time of year); huge schools, sometimes numbering thousands and all heading in the same direction, have been reported from passing ships in several parts of the world.

PROFILE

Length: *Usually 3.5 m (11.5 ft), rarely to 6 m (19.7 ft).*
Weight: *Up to 770 kg (1700 lb).*
Distribution: *All tropical and some subtropical seas.*
Habitat: *Coastal waters of the continents and offshore islands, occasionally offshore.*
Breeding: *Viviparous: number of young 13–42.*
Diet: *Mostly fish, especially stingrays, small skates and other sharks.*

COOKIECUTTER SHARK

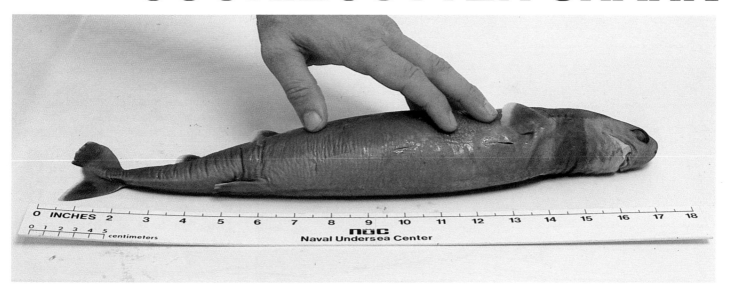

The finny horror that attacks whales

Despite its small size, this fearsome sharp-toothed dwarf takes chunks out of much larger sea creatures as its staple food.

The Cookiecutter Shark (*Isistius brasiliensis*) grows to only about 50 cm (19.7 in), and has the most amazing feeding method of all sharks. It has fleshy lips like suction-discs, with incredibly sharp, triangular, blade-like teeth in the lower jaw and small, narrow, erect cusps in the upper jaw. It feeds by taking a firm hold on any large fish, dolphin or whale it encounters, using its lips to fix it in place, then drives its lower teeth into the flesh of its victim, twisting its body while doing so, so that a neat circle of flesh or blubber is removed.

The Cookiecutter was known to science for 150 years before anyone realised that it fed in this bizarre manner. Once the discovery had been made, however, it became obvious that this shark was the cause of the crater-like wounds on many deep-water fishes and cetaceans. It is also reported to have attacked the rubber covering on the sonar apparatus on a US Navy nuclear submarine!

The whole of the Cookiecutter's underside is covered with luminous organs which at night cause it to shine with a green phosphorescent glow. The suggestion that this glow might attract its larger prey to attack it, whereupon the little shark turns on its attacker and sinks its teeth in, is quite plausible. This shark's fins are too small to drive it along at speed, but its massive oil-filled liver gives it near neutral buoyancy in the sea, which means that it does not need to use much energy during the enormous daily vertical migrations it makes: at night it has been caught 100 m (328 ft) from the surface, but in daytime it lives at 3000–4000 m (9843–13,124 ft).

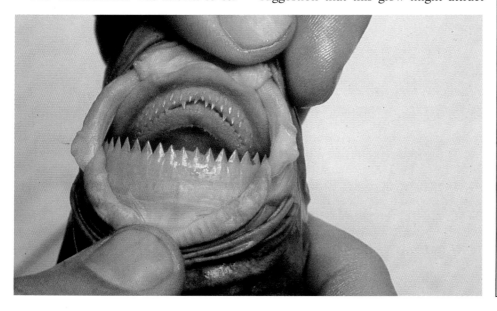

PROFILE

Length: *Maximum 51 cm (20 in); male sexually mature at about 35 cm (13.8 in), female at 40 cm (15.8 in).*

Distribution: *Reported in deep water mainly in the tropical Atlantic and Pacific Oceans, and near oceanic islands.*

Habitat: *Free-ranging in the deep sea from 4000 m (13,124 ft) to near the surface.*

Breeding: *Probably gives birth to live young.*

Diet: *Chunks bitten out of whales, dolphins, marlin, tuna and dolphin fishes.*

Notes: *The remarkable feeding habits of this shark make it one of the few known vertebrate parasites.*

WEST AFRICAN LUNGFISH

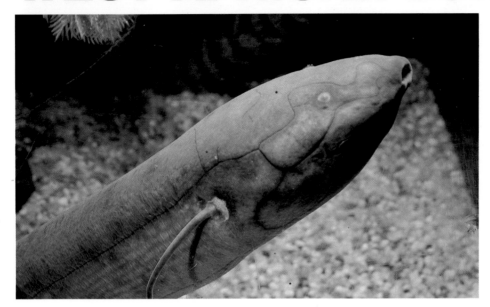

The fish that must breathe air

Even though it has gills like other fish which extract oxygen from the water, this peculiar swampland creature has to come to the surface from time to time to breathe air in order to survive.

Lungfish live in the fresh waters of South America, Australia and Africa, but each continent has its own unique family. The African family is represented by 4 species, one of which, *Protopterus annectens*, lives in West African swamps, creeks and backwaters associated with rivers.

It is a long slender fish with a cylindrical body and a low dorsal fin which runs around the pointed tail to join the equally low anal fin. The pectoral and pelvic fins are long and whip-like. The body is covered with moderately large scales which are overlain with thick slime.

Lungfish live in swamps at the edge of the water, areas which dry out early in the dry season. When this happens the fish burrows deep into the swamp, curls its tail over its head, and secretes copious mucus which dries out to form a cocoon, leaving only a small opening near its mouth. Not only can it survive during the months of drought, when the water level has fallen below its burrow, but it can live for up to four years in this condition.

The lungfish spawns during the wet season, laying whitish eggs about 4 mm (0.16 in) in diameter in a nest hollowed out in the bed of the swamp or backwater.

STINGRAY

The stabbing assassin

If one of these fishes, lying buried in sand, is stepped on by an unsuspecting bather or fisherman, it stabs the intruder at incredible speed with its venomous tail, often with fatal results.

Stingrays belong to the group of cartilaginous fishes which also includes the skates and sharks. They are flattened from top to bottom, so that the body has the form of a diamond with, at its rear end, the tail. Stingrays are special in that the tail is long and whip-like, with one or more long, dagger-bladed, serrated-edged spines about half way down the back.

Stingrays occur in all tropical and temperate oceans of the world. Europe has the species *Dasyatis pastinaca*, which may be 2.6 m (8.5 ft) long; the Atlantic coast of North America has *Dasyatis centroura*, which may grow to 3.66 m (12 ft) in length and 2.14 m (7 ft) broad. These, however, are mini-fish compared with the related stingarees of tropical Australia, which can weigh as much as 340 kg (750 lb).

Normally, stingrays are harmless and inoffensive creatures. They live close to the sea bed, usually on sand, muddy-sand or gravel, and do not travel far as a rule. They eat crustaceans and molluscs.

Despite their generally gentle lifestyle, stingrays can be very dangerous indeed. When caught in a trawl, they have been known to lash out madly with their tails and have inflicted severe wounds on fishermen who were sorting their catch.

PIKE

The world's most maligned fish

Frank Buckland, Britain's first Inspector of Salmon Fisheries, wrote 'more lies . . . have been told about the pike than any other fish in the world'. Even after he wrote this in 1880 more lies continued to be told.

The Pike (*Esox lucius*) is one of the larger freshwater fishes of the northern hemisphere. Its range extends right across Europe, northern Asia and into North America (where it is known as the Northern Pike, to distinguish it from the three other North American species).

Exaggerations focus around its size, its longevity and its ferocity. In large lakes and big rivers where there is abundant food, Pike can weigh as much as 34 kg (75 lb), though most of the population never attain half that. But there are reports of Pike as heavy as 65 kg (143 lb). If such stories are true, these are veritable monsters, but they are probably examples of misremembered weights or inaccurate scales (two 'accidents' that anglers are still prone to).

Size is also expressed in length, and there was the famous case of the Mannheim Pike with a skeleton 5.2 m (17 ft) long. This, unfortunately, had three times as many vertebrae as any other Pike reported!

Europe was also the home of the Pike which lived for 267 years after a German Emperor had marked it by putting a brass ring around its body. No one now can prove that it did not live that long; if it did, it was about ten times older than any Pike aged by modern methods.

COELACANTH

A fossil resurrected from the dead

When, in 1938, a live specimen of this fish was landed in a net off South Africa, scientists were astounded to find that it belonged to a family believed to have become extinct 90 million years ago.

The Coelacanth (*Latimeria chalumnae*) is perhaps the best known of fishes which no one has seen alive and healthy in its native habitat. The name means 'hollow spine' and was given to a group of common and well-known fossil fishes which lived from 300 to 90 million years ago, after which they seemed to become extinct.

The scientific world was therefore both astonished and sceptical when the capture of a live Coelacanth was announced in 1938 off South Africa. It had been captured in a trawler's nets off the mouth of the River Chalumna near East London at 67 m (220 ft) depth.

This led to the belief that further Coelacanths might live in this region, but it was not until December 1952 that the puzzle of their hiding place was

solved. The Coelacanth's home ground is at moderate depths off the coast of the Comoro Islands, northwest of Madagascar. Here, unknown to scientists, native fishermen have been catching the 'Gombessa' (as they know it) for centuries.

The Coelacanth lives in the much-creviced nearly vertical rock and coral drop-off into the deep water of the Indian Ocean. It is a heavy-bodied fish with a spiny first dorsal fin, while the second dorsal, pectoral, pelvic and anal fins all appear to be placed on short 'wrists' (this feature can be seen in many fossil coelacanths). It is a very slimy fish which also contains huge quantities of oil, both in its bones and in its muscles. This oil helps it remain neutrally buoyant in the water, where it positions

itself by making gentle sculling movements of its fins. It can also swim very powerfully.

PROFILE

Length: *Grows to 1.9 m (6 ft).*
Weight: *Up to about 90 kg (200 lb).*
Distribution: *Western Indian Ocean, near the Comoro Islands.*
Habitat: *Lives on the upper continental shelf among rock and coral.*
Breeding: *A live bearer; gives birth to litters of at least 5 young, at birth about 30 cm (12 in) in length.*
Diet: *Believed to feed on fish.*
Notes: *The only surviving species of a group of fishes which were abundant in the Devonian period.*

EUROPEAN EEL

The fish that cannot swim

Although it migrates vast distances, this eel cannot really swim at all and instead has to wriggle through the water.

This eel, which is so abundant in the rivers and lakes of Europe and also very common on northern sea coasts, is in many ways still an animal of mystery. After years of study and research, the greatest mystery of all, how and where it breeds, is still not known in detail. What is known is that the mature adults swim virtually the width of the Atlantic Ocean to get to their breeding grounds, which are to the south and east of Bermuda, in the area that is known as the Sargasso Sea.

Despite this immense migration the European Eel (*Anguilla anguilla*) can scarcely be said to swim. Its long slender body has a long, low fin on the back which joins with the rather shorter low fin under the tail, and it moves by wriggling its body through the water, each loop of the body and erect fins forcing it along. It uses exactly the same wriggling motion, but with its fins depressed, when it wants to make progress overland.

The young eels pass through a remarkable larval and post-larval period during which they are carried to Europe in the Atlantic currents. When they arrive on the coast, at 2½–3 years of age, they change into baby eels (elvers), and then begin another migration far upstream into the rivers. Females may live in fresh water for up to 19 years, and males up to 9 years. Once they move down towards the sea their colour changes to silver, and in the sea their eyes increase in size. This suggests that they migrate at considerable depths, but so few have been caught on their return migration that this phase of their life is a virtual blank.

PROFILE

Length: *Grows to 1.5 m (5 ft), usually nearer 1 m (30 in).*
Weight: *Up to about 9 kg (20 lb).*
Distribution: *The rivers and lakes of Europe from the Arctic Circle to the Black Sea, and North Africa; also common on the sea shore in the north of this range.*
Habitat: *Usually lies hidden in bottom mud or in crevices in rocks.*
Breeding: *Eggs are shed in the sea in the Central Atlantic.*
Diet: *Invertebrates and small freshwater fishes; also scavenges on carrion.*
Longevity: *In the wild perhaps to 25 years; in captivity up to 60 years.*

BELUGA

PROFILE

Length: *Up to 5 m (16 ft).*
Weight: *Infrequently to 1228 kg (2707 lb), rarely more in the present century.*
Distribution: *Caspian Sea, Black Sea, Sea of Azov and northern Adriatic.*
Habitat: *In rivers for spawning winter and spring, migrating downstream to estuaries and the sea during summer.*
Breeding: *A large fish produces up to 8 million eggs.*
Diet: *When young, riverine invertebrates; as adult, mostly fish.*

The world's most valuable fish

Rubbed gently on a screen to remove mucus, washed in wine or vinegar, dried out and salted, the Beluga's eggs become caviar, the most expensive fish dish in the world.

The Beluga (*Huso huso*) is a sturgeon which in late spring spawns in fresh water on rocky bottoms.

Its migration upriver is the opportunity for trapping the adult females for the sake of their roe. At one time the fish were killed and the eggs removed, but to save the stocks the eggs are now collected without killing the fish. Only the eggs are used, but they make the Beluga the world's most valuable fish.

This is also one of the largest freshwater fishes in the world, growing to a length of 5 m (16 ft) and a weight of 1524 kg (1.5 tons), although heavier weights have been reported. A Beluga of just over 1016 kg (1 ton) contained 145 kg (320 lbs) of eggs, and one of 1228 kg (1.2 tons) contained 246 kg (542 lb).

Unlike other sturgeons, the Beluga has a wide mouth. It feeds extensively on fish, particularly the herring-like fishes which are abundant in the Caspian Sea basin. Large Beluga have occasionally eaten young seals. A slow-growing fish, it takes 14–18 years to reach sexual maturity. Its lifespan is therefore possibly as long as 25–30 years. Taking so long to reach maturity is likely to cause conservation problems in an area where commercial fishing takes place; the Beluga has become scarce and is now reared in fish farms.

RED PIRANHA

South America's river shark

This fearsome-looking fish has an evil reputation, though this is based on legend rather than on knowledge of the natural history and biology of the species.

The Red Piranha (*Serrasalmus nattereri*) is found in South America from the River Plate to the Orinoco. It is an ugly-looking fish, with a deep, blunt head and short powerful jaws armed with razor-sharp, interlocked teeth. It is highly carnivorous, but there are some species that feed only on fruits and seeds.

In larger lakes and lagoons, swimmers and bathers go unmolested by these fishes; similarly, riverine populations represent no great threat. Dangerous situations occur in the dry season, during low water, when the lakes and lagoons shrink, allowing the Red Piranhas to congregate in large numbers. Any animal or human entering these waters would be readily attacked. Swimmers and bathers avoid such waters, which are easily detected by the commotion caused by the Red Piranhas attacking fishes stranded on the shoreline. Ultimately, the piranhas become stranded themselves and the shore is littered with the rotting corpses.

It has always been thought that blood was the major stimulant to Red Piranhas and that a wounded animal entering the water would be devoured by them. It seems, however, that Red Piranhas are more readily attracted to noise and splashing, by which they recognise a disadvantaged prey.

COMMON HATCHETFISH

PROFILE

Length: *6.5 cm (2.5 in)*.
Taxiing distance: *Up to 12 m (40 ft)*.
Flight distance: *1.5 m (5 ft)*.
Flight altitude: *90 cm (3 ft)*.
Diet: *Insects*.
Distribution: *Amazon region and Guianas*.
Habitat: *Fresh water*.

The fish that flies

This unusual fish, probably the best known of the freshwater hatchetfishes, has a deep body, narrow tail, and extremely long pectoral fins which gives it the capacity for powered flight.

The Common Hatchetfish (*Gasteropelecus sternicla*) is very popular with aquarists, not only for its brilliant silver coloration but also for its ability to fly. Its chest is very deep because it houses lots of muscles that power the fins, so that they act like wings during the flight. Before taking off, the Common Hatchetfish will 'taxi', with the pectoral fins beating up and down in preparation for flight while the chest and tail trail in the water. On take-off, the flapping of the pectoral fins is increased and provides the lift to get the little fish airborne. The movement of the fins during the flight sequence is so rapid that they produce a distinct buzzing sound. The flight is rarely very prolonged and the fish takes to the air only when endangered.

It is interesting that a species of herring is often found in association with the Common Hatchetfish. This herring also has a very deep chest and is similar in profile to the Common Hatchetfish, the only difference being in the length of the pectoral fins; these are short in the herring, and it is clearly unable to fly. It seems that the herring is a mimic of the Common Hatchetfish, with which it swims on the premise that any predator would fail to recognise it and would not attack the shoal, believing that they would all take to the air.

PROFILE

Length: *40 cm (16 in)*.
Weight: *2 kg (4.4 lb)*.
Distribution: *Guianas and Amazon basin*.
Habitat: *Lakes and rivers*.
Volume of bite: *16.4 cubic cm (1 cubic in)*.
Notes: *Almost nothing is known of the spawning behaviour of Red Piranhas in the wild. It appears that they spawn during the annual floods, but their preferred habitat for spawning is still unknown. It has been reported that these fish guard their young in aquaria, and this is presumed also to be the case in the wild.*

ASIAN WALKING CATFISH

The fish that should never have been introduced into Florida

Between 1964 and 1966, a number of these fish were imported to a fish farm near Deerfield Beach, Fort Lauderdale, Florida, but some escaped to found a thriving population which feeds on native fishes.

The Asian Walking Catfish (*Clarias batrachus*) can breathe oxygen in the water using its gills like all other fishes, but it also has a special air-breathing organ in each of the paired gill chambers. This feature makes the species very popular with aquarists, so a supply of the catfish was imported to a Florida fish farm and placed in outside holding tanks. The climate in Florida proved ideal for the Asian Walking Catfish, and the tanks were very similar to the type of ponds they inhabited in their native Thailand. In the wild, these fish migrate and spawn during the monsoon period. The rainy season of subtropical Florida simulated the climatic conditions of their homeland, and the captives walked out of their holding tanks to spawn in the canals of Florida.

Asian Walking Catfish have no natural enemies and a very high reproductive rate in Florida. They feed on the eggs and young of native fishes such as bass, bluegills and sunfishes. In the dry months they eat all forms of life in the ponds and waterways. If the droughts are long enough, they become sluggish and may even aestivate.

During January 1970, the temperature in Florida dropped to −2°C (29°F) and in a number of places the Asian Walking Catfish died. The cold snap lasted only a few days, however, and many survived in deeper, therefore warmer, pools. These survivors began to reproduce and replenish the numbers. Florida is subject to cold spells every few years, but the Asian Walking Catfish is gradually becoming hardened

to them and less susceptible to fungal infections. It is now successfully established in Florida. A lesson: to beware of introducing fishes into non-native countries!

PROFILE

Length: *40 cm (16 in).*
Distribution: *India, Pakistan, Nepal, Sri Lanka, Bangladesh, Burma, Thailand, Malaya, Molucca, Philippines, Java, Sumatra and Singapore.*
Diet: *Fish eggs, small fish and insects.*
Notes: *The adipose fin is absent, the dorsal and anal fins are elongate; albinism is common.*

WELS CATFISH

The catfish that eats children

Some of these big, ugly fish in the River Danube have been found to contain not only small dogs but even the remains of children in their stomach.

The name catfish is given to a very large group of mainly freshwater fishes which have barbels in varying number around the mouth. The association with the long whiskers of the domestic cat must be the only reason for the name, for catfishes in general are scaleless, slimy, rather ugly fishes totally dissimilar to the sleek, furry cat.

The Wels Catfish (*Silurus glanis*) is widespread through Europe but most abundant in the Danube and the Rhine, although it has been introduced to many rivers and lakes elsewhere, including England. It is also one of the largest catfishes known: a specimen in the Dnieper River, USSR, was reported to be 5 m (16 ft) long and 306 kg (674 lb) in weight.

Naturally a fish of this size can tackle large food items. When young it eats bottom-living invertebrates, then graduates to frogs, fishes of all sorts, birds and small mammals. There are also sinister reports from the Danube of very large specimens which, when caught by fishermen, were found to contain the bodies of small dogs, and even the remains of children. Whether such an event was due to a Wels gobbling up a swimmer or merely followed an earlier tragedy is not recorded, but a fish of 5 m (16 ft) would surely be large enough to swallow a child.

The Wels usually lives in hiding under overhangs of the bank, among roots of bankside trees, or beneath fallen trees in the river. It is most active at night. Surprisingly for such an unpleasant-looking fish, the male is a devoted parent. He guards the pale yellow eggs, laid in a backwater out of the current, for up to three weeks.

PROFILE

Length: *Up to 5 m (16 ft); usually around 1.5 m (5 ft).*

Distribution: *Rivers and still waters of the USSR and eastern Europe; introduced to western Europe, including England.*

Habitat: *Lives in large rivers and still waters, usually close to the bottom or under cover.*

Diet: *Invertebrates when young; fish, frogs and aquatic mammals and birds as an adult.*

Notes: *This is an important food fish in the Danube basin; it has white, flaky flesh.*

CANDIRU

The only vertebrate that parasitises Man

The head and gill covers of this rather unpleasant fish have numerous erectile, hooked spines on them, with which the fish damages the skin of other vertebrates so that it can feed on the blood.

The Candiru (*Vandellia cirrhosa*) is a tiny South American catfish that lives hidden away from the sunlight, burrowing into the sand or mud beneath stones or sunken logs. It uses its spines to pierce the skin of other fishes and mammals, including humans, which may enter the water. The spines may be used only to graze the skin, the Candiru then eating the blood from the surface wound. The Candiru may also enter the body of its victim: it passes under the gill cover and between the gills of other fishes, using its sharp teeth and opercular spines to tear the delicate skin and start a flow of blood, which it then sucks up. The erectile spines on the head hold the Candiru in position by hooking on to the surrounding tissues.

The Candiru is attracted to the gill opening of a fish by the respiratory current of its unfortunate victim, so that, as the water passes over the gills and out through the operculum, the Candiru nips inside.

In some parts of South America, the Candiru is dreaded by the local people because of its unpleasant habit of entering the human urinary tract. It has been suggested that it is attracted either by urine or by the flow of urine, which it mistakes for a respiratory current from another fish. Once inside it cannot be pulled out, because of the erectile spines on the head and gill covers; the only way it can be removed from humans is by surgery. In some areas the Candiru is such a serious pest that both men and

women wear special sheaths to protect themselves from the fish when they enter the water.

PROFILE

Length: *2.5 cm (1 in).*
Distribution: *Amazon.*
Habitat: *Unknown.*
Breeding: *Unknown.*
Notes: *Candiru are notorious for stealing fish from the Amazonian fishermen; if the line is not hauled in immediately a fish is hooked, they will rapidly strip it of flesh.*

ELECTRIC EEL

The fish that uses shock tactics

The most distinguishing feature of this remarkable fish is its ability to produce and use electricity: it can emit an electrical discharge of 500 volts.

The first account of the Electric Eel (*Electrophorus electricus*) was by a Frenchman, J Richer, in 1729, but it was not until the 1920s that C W Coates of the New York Aquarium began to investigate the electrical potential of this truly remarkable fish. It has three electric organs occupying about four-fifths of its body. The organs are made of wafer-like electroplates arranged in rows. These electroplates are usually connected in a series so that, although the individual electrical output is small, their effect is cumulative and they add up to a considerable voltage. The effect of a full electrical discharge is strong enough to fell a mule and probably to put a human being in hospital. The Electric Eel uses this electrical discharge to shock and stun or kill the smaller fish that constitute its diet.

The Electric Eel has very small eyes and cannot see very well. In order to compensate for its poor vision, part of the electric organ is used as an electro-sensor. This emits small pulses which are bounced back towards the Electric Eel from objects and other fishes in the water. The skin of the Electric Eel has special electro-receptors in it to detect the returning signal.

The electric organ has another vital function in its use for communicating with other Electric Eels. The pulses emitted are recognised by other members of the species. Dominant males make the loudest and most frequent emissions; the females respond by shor-ter bursts of pulses. The slightly different pulse emission by the female is to inform the male that she is near and not to mistake her for a rival male.

PROFILE

Length: *2.4 m (8 ft).*
Distribution: *Guianas, the Orinoco, the middle and lower Amazon basin.*
Habitat: *Turbid waters.*
Diet: *Adults eat other fishes, juveniles eat aquatic insects.*
Electric organ discharge: *500 volts.*
Notes: *This fish lacks dorsal, tail and pelvic fins and swims by undulation of the anal fin.*

ANGLERFISH

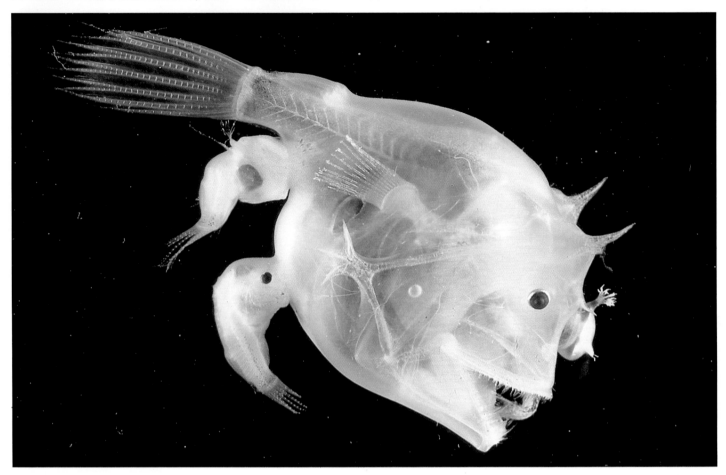

Mated for life

Once a male anglerfish has made contact with a female, he fastens onto her body with his jaws; in time his blood supply becomes connected to that of his mate and he becomes wholly dependent on her for nourishment and oxygen.

The Deep-sea Anglerfish (*Ceratias holboelli*) is one example of a group of perhaps 20 species in which the male is parasitic on the female. It is a lifestyle which is unique among vertebrate animals. Odd as it may seem, it is a very practical solution for fishes which cannot be strong swimmers and which live in the pitch-black, three-dimensional space of the deep sea.

From its appearance *Ceratias* is not an athletic fish, and probably floats through life using its small fins to make fine adjustments to position and level in the ocean. Like other anglerfishes, it has the fascinating habit of luring its prey to within snatching distance. Because it lives in the deep sea below the level that light penetrates (although it may come nearer the surface at night), it has a light

organ at the tip of its 'fishing rod'. The female's eyes, however, are small, so it is probable that she has to use other senses to detect the close approach of prey.

Female Deep-sea Anglerfishes can grow to 120 cm (47 in); the males are rarely longer than 6 cm (2.5 in). The discrepancy in length means that the female is about 1000 times heavier than her mate.

It seems certain that the females give off a special scent (pheromone) which the males recognise and are attracted to. There is no fixed place where attachment occurs; the male may be fastened to her side, or belly, or even her back. Occasionally two or more males are attached to a single female. It is presumed that anglerfish mate for life, but

many details of their biology are not known.

ATLANTIC NEEDLEFISH

Living javelin of the sea

These long-beaked hunters have caused many nasty accidents by leaping out of the water and stabbing people in boats.

The needlefishes belong to the family Belonidae and are therefore relatives of the European Garfish (*Belone belone*), which grows to a length of 94 cm (37 in). A common needlefish that lives off North America is the Atlantic Needlefish (*Strongylura marina*), a rather larger species which ranges from Maine to the Gulf of Mexico, although it is rare for it to be found at the northern end of this range.

Like all garfishes, this is an active surface-living hunter which, in the frenzy of hunting smaller fishes, occasionally hurls itself out of the water. When hooked by a fisherman it often leaps clear of the water, 'tail-walking' along the surface while trying to dislodge the hook.

It is this habit of leaping clear of the water that has caused accidents in various parts of the world. Needlefishes are all long, slender fishes with very long, sharply pointed beak-like jaws. If one strikes a fisherman, the force with which they leap causes the jaws to penetrate deeply, leaving a severe stab wound which frequently becomes complicated by the beak snapping off in the wound. Cases of serious injury, and on rare occasions death, have occurred in the tropical Atlantic and in the East Indies. The needlefishes can indeed be thought of as living javelins.

Like their relatives, the flying fishes, the needlefishes lay small, round eggs the surface of which is covered with long hair-like filaments. These filaments tangle in seaweed or flotsam until the young hatch. The young fishes have only the lower jaw elongate. Not until they are about 5 cm (2 in) long does the upper jaw equal the lower jaw in length.

PROFILE

Length: *1.2 m (4 ft).*
Distribution: *Inshore waters of the western Atlantic, from Maine to Texas and the Gulf of Mexico.*
Habitat: *Surface-living, often in shallow water and penetrating into river estuaries.*
Breeding: *Lays eggs which are attached to plants and flotsam by long threads.*
Diet: *Feeds mainly on small surface-living fishes, some squids and crustaceans.*
Notes: *These notes apply to the Atlantic Needlefish but, apart from the distribution, are also valid for many of the 20 or so species of needlefish.*

DEVIL'S HOLE PUPFISH

PROFILE

Length: *2 cm (0.79 in)*.
Devil's Hole pool length: *20 m (65 ft)*.
Devil's Hole pool width: *2.5–3.1 m (8–10 ft)*.
Devil's Hole pool temperature: *32.8–33.9°C (91–93°F)*.

The world's most restricted fish

This fish has been the subject of a great deal of concern to scientists, as well as being the focal point of the media, all because it is known from only a single pool in California's Death Valley.

The Devil's Hole Pupfish (*Cyprinodon diabolis*) is a very small fish that was discovered as recently as 1930 and has earnt its common name from the pool, known as Devil's Hole, where it lives. This pool is in the Nevada Desert and was once part of a water-formed cave, but the collapse of the roof, probably hundreds of years ago, has exposed it to the desert sun. The only plantlife at the pool is a green alga growing on a single ledge, and the fish are usually seen swimming in the shallow part of the pool near the algal growth.

The algal growth shows great seasonal variability. In the winter months Devil's Hole does not receive any direct sunlight, but in the spring the sun's rays touch the surface of the pool; as the day length increases, the alga begins to grow at a tremendous rate. The Devil's Hole Pupfish feasts on the growing alga and it seems that the abundance of food and increased day length trigger these fish to reproduce. The highest numbers of Devil's Hole Pupfish are found in late summer and autumn.

The Devil's Hole Pupfish is entirely dependent on this single pool for its survival. Should anything, either man-made or natural, damage this unique habitat, this remarkable little fish would be doomed to extinction.

GRUNION

The fish that beaches itself to spawn

These fish allow themselves to be swept ashore so that they can lay their eggs on land, and then have to wait for the next wave to return them to the sea.

The Grunion (*Leuresthes tenuis*) is a very unremarkable-looking fish with the most remarkable spawning habits. Spawning takes place only for three or four nights following a full or new moon, and then for only a few hours after high tide. The spawning season extends from late February to early September. Schools of Grunion come into shallow water and, swimming in the surf, are swept onto the beach and strand themselves. The females bury themselves partially in the sand and shed their eggs, which are fertilised by the males as they are shed. The adults are carried out to sea by the next wave, while the eggs are buried by the shifting sand of the ebbing water.

The eggs lie hidden in the sand until the next set of high tides two weeks later, when, if disturbed by the surf, they hatch out and disperse. If not so disturbed, they stay hidden until the next spring tides — a month after they were laid — and hatch then, remaining in a state of suspended animation until they are uncovered.

During spawning season Grunion are vulnerable to predators, chief of whom is Man. Along California's beaches, catching them by hand is a popular night-time sport, but it may be done only under licence.

OARFISH

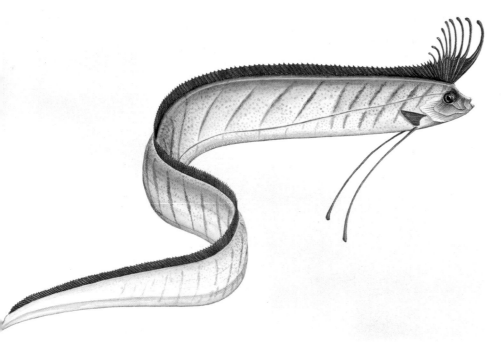

The sea serpent of legend

There are few more striking-looking fishes than the Oarfish, which is literally a flattened silvery band, with a dull red fin along its back, large eyes and an intensely gloomy expression.

The Oarfish (*Regalecus glesne*) is presumed to be an inhabitant of the open ocean, living in mid-water at depths of 300–600 m (980–1960 ft). Almost all those that have been described and examined by scientists have, however, been stranded on the shore or found swimming feebly near the surface, and were probably sickly or dying fish. Young specimens have been captured in special nets, and more have been taken from the stomachs of deep-dwelling tuna and lancetfishes.

When seen drifting at the surface, particularly if struggling to swim away, an Oarfish looks like a sea serpent. This impression is heightened by the crest on the head, where the first rays of the dorsal fin are elongate with fleshy tips, and bright red in colour: nothing could look more like a mane. Several of the 'giant sea serpents' sighted were certainly Oarfish, which, at 7.6 m (25 ft), are the longest bony fish known to science.

Although the pelvic fins are elongate streamers with paddle-like fleshy flaps at their tips and along their length, they are unlikely to be used for swimming, even though they give the name Oarfish to the animal. Swimming is probably achieved by a serpentine wave-motion along the body; this would give powerful thrust through the water.

DWARF SEA-HORSE

The slowcoach of the fish world

With a rigid body and limited in its movements, this diminutive animal is the slowest swimmer in the seas.

Sea-horses are possibly the most remarkable fishes of the oceans. Their amazing body form gives them the appearance of a horse's head on a comma-shaped tail. Their mobility is very limited and their swimming ability is governed by a rigid body structure, so that the only freely moving parts are the pectoral fins on either side of the back of the head and the fin along the back.

Swimming is effected by wave-motion of the dorsal fin rays: this makes a ripple which drives the fish forward in an erect posture, but very, very slowly.

In still water sea-horses move in a deliberate, steady fashion with all the grace of a minuet, but in a current they are lost, and quite incapable of swimming against the stream. Despite this feeble performance they are quite common, especially in tropical and warm temperate seas. They hang on to coral and marine plants by their prehensile tail, their coloration matching their surroundings.

The Dwarf Sea-horse (*Hippocampus zosterae*) by reason of its size — maximum length 42 mm (1.6 in) — must be the slowest swimmer on record. It inhabits the turtle-grass flats of Florida and the Gulf of Mexico, clinging to the plants and rarely moving more than a few feet before stopping and hanging on to another frond. Occasionally it clings to floating vegetation, but this must be a hazardous habit because currents can sweep it out to sea.

In common with other sea-horses, the male has a pouch beneath his abdomen in which he carries his mate's eggs until the young are well developed, at about ten days old.

PROFILE

Length: *Maximum length 42 mm (1.6 in).*
Distribution: *Tropical Atlantic coast of the USA and the Gulf of Mexico, possibly also off Cuba.*
Habitat: *Lives in shallow water in bays among turtle grass and floating weeds.*
Breeding: *March to October; males carry up to 55 eggs or developing young in special pouch on upper tail.*
Diet: *Small crustaceans.*
Longevity: *Average lifespan possibly 3–4 months; few individuals survive to 1 year.*

STONEFISH

Largest venom glands of any fish

Hidden on the bottom in shallow water, this dangerous fish inflicts excruciatingly painful wounds on anybody unfortunate enough to step on it.

The Stonefish (*Synanceia horrida*), which lives in the Indian and West Pacific Oceans and grows to 61 cm (2 ft), has huge venom glands at the base of each of its dorsal fin spines. It belongs to the scorpionfish family (Scorpaenidae), all of which have venom glands, but the Stonefish is the most venomous of the lot.

It is an inshore species found on coral reefs, mudflats and outer estuaries. It is particularly dangerous to Man because it lives in such shallow water, between and just below tidemarks, and because, when alarmed, it freezes in hiding and erects its spines. Not surprisingly, therefore, most injuries caused by this fish are inflicted on the feet of people such as fishermen who are wading in shallow water.

The short, incredibly sharp spines are grooved and connect directly to the venom glands, so pressure on the spine, such as when it is trodden upon, automatically injects venom into the wound. The pain from such a wound is immediate and agonising. It continues for hours as the venom spreads through the limb, and the victim usually becomes delirious. Cases of death owing to cardiac arrest have been reported; other deaths have been due to the victim losing consciousness and drowning in the sea. Even if the victim survives, unless medical help is immediately available, the wounded region often becomes gangrenous and permanently deformed.

With its rough, craggy head, small lappets of skin and wart-like surface, together with drab brownish colouring with grey mottling, the Stonefish blends perfectly into its background. It is almost impossible to see this fish as one wades through the water — which makes it all the more dangerous.

PROFILE

Length: *Grows to 61 cm (2 ft).*
Distribution: *Coasts of India, the East Indies, northern Australia, and northwards to the Philippines.*
Habitat: *Shallow water, down to 10 m (30 ft) on coral reefs, shallow mudflats and in estuaries.*
Diet: *Small fish, which the well-hidden Stonefish seizes.*
Notes: *Two other species of stonefish live in the Indo-western Pacific, so that these fishes occur from East Africa to Australia and north to the Philippines.*

BLUEFISH

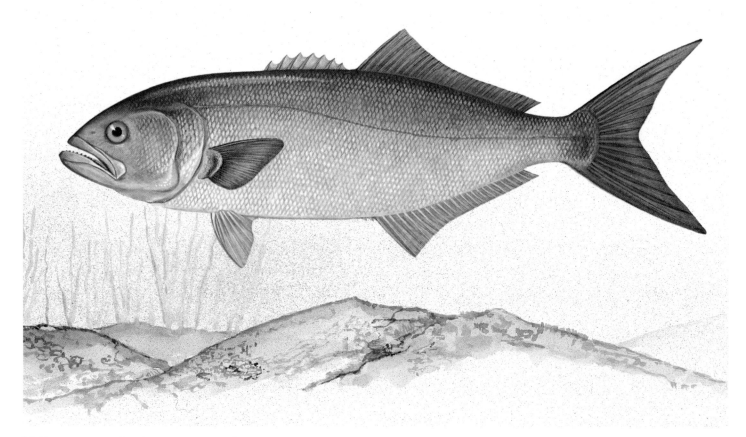

The world's most ferocious marine fish

Off the east coast of the USA, frenzied schools of these vicious fish have been reported attacking schools of other fish and slashing millions of them to death with their long, sharp teeth.

What marks out the Bluefish (*Pomatomus saltatrix*) from many other sea fishes is its strong, conical, canine teeth — up to 0.64 cm (0.25 in) long in a 4.5-kg (10-lb) fish — lining both its upper and its lower jaws. These and its athletic build have given the Bluefish its reputation as a vicious slayer of smaller fishes. A schooling fish itself, it sometimes forms packs numbering thousands, and in 1901 one school was estimated to be 6.5–8 km (4–5 miles) in extent.

Although very widely distributed in the warmer seas of the world, the Bluefish is best known on the east coast of the United States. The schools are seasonal in occurrence there, being off Florida in late winter and working their way northwards to appear off New Jersey by April to May. At first they stay in deep water, moving inshore only during summer. It was in these waters

that Bluefish schools were reported to form maddened feeding frenzies, attacking schools of mackerel, menhaden, herring and other fish, snapping at their prey to bite and slash indiscriminately, and leaving a trail of dead and dying fish. So wastefully extravagant was their feeding behaviour that Bluefish were estimated to kill 1200 million fish each year!

Bluefish feed on practically any kind of smaller fishes which are common in the area in which they live; they also eat swimming crustaceans and marine worms. Young Bluefish enter shallow water in summer: even when only finger length they are extremely speedy swimmers with well-developed teeth.

This species is captured in huge quantities by commercial fishermen, but its sharp teeth play havoc with the nets. It is also a favourite sporting fish.

PROFILE

Length: *Maximum about 1.2 m (4 ft).*

Weight: *Reported up to 20.385 kg (45 lb).*

Distribution: *Tropical and warm-temperate seas of the world except for the eastern Pacific.*

Habitat: *Adults along continental shelf; young inshore in estuaries and shallow water.*

Breeding: *Mainly over the outer continental shelf in spring; 112,000–195,000 eggs per female.*

Diet: *Mostly fishes, especially schooling species, but also crustaceans and squid.*

Longevity: *Largest individuals are probably 10 years and more old.*

Notes: *Strongly migratory with seasonal warming of the sea; moves into temperate waters during summer.*

REMORA

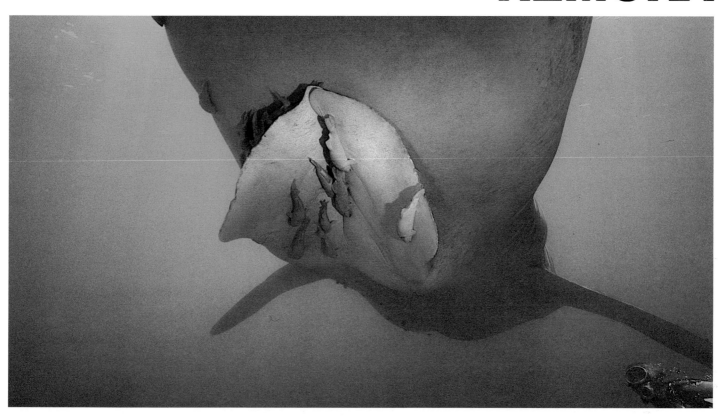

The hitchhiker of the oceans

This streamlined fish has a powerful suction-disc on the top of its head which it attaches to other large fishes, sharks, whales, turtles or even boats, and so hitches a ride.

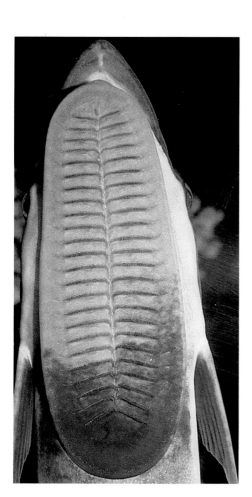

The suction-disc of the Remora (*Remora remora*) is a greatly modified spiny dorsal fin, and is formed by a series of transverse plates resembling the slats of a venetian blind. When these plates are raised, a vacuum is created between the Remora's disc and the host. Often large fish, sharks and rays may have two or more Remoras attached to them.

There are three possible reasons why the Remora attaches itself to larger fishes: the host protects it from its enemies; the Remora feeds on scraps left over or missed by its host; or the Remora is transported to new feeding grounds. They are not always attached to the outside of the host's body, but may be found inside the mouth or under the gill covers of swordfish, tuna and sunfish. Remoras sometimes remove parasites from the bodies of sharks and, interestingly, sharks never seem to eat them.

The food of Remoras consists largely of other fishes such as herring and sardines. When travelling with a shark, they will feast on the bits dropped by their feeding host. When hunting, the Remora is still transported by its host fish, but, on spotting a suitable meal, it lets go of the host and swims after its prey.

It seems that Remoras hate to swim alone. Groups swim together stacked one on top of the other, rather like a large pile of plates. The Greeks and Romans were much anguished by Remoras, believing that if one attached itself to a boat it could slow it down or even stop it altogether.

PROFILE

Length: *46 cm (18 in)*.
Distribution: *Tropical and warm-temperate seas.*
Disc laminae: *14–20*.
Notes: *Little is known of this species' biology apart from its hitchhiking habits.*

ARCHER FISH

The underwater crackshot

This pretty little fish is renowned for its habit of shooting down insects from overhanging leaves and branches into the water and eating them.

The Archer Fish (*Toxotes jaculator*) is very popular with aquarists because of its unusual technique for catching its prey. Strictly speaking the word 'archer' is incorrect, as the fish literally spits drops of water at the insect. The water drops are ejected rather like pellets from an airgun and with a great deal of force. It is not unknown for this fish to shoot down an insect in flight.

The mouth of the Archer Fish is specially adapted for shooting drops of water with force and accuracy. The roof of the mouth is grooved. The tongue is thick and muscular at the back with a fleshy protuberance on it, while the front is thin and whip-like. The back

part of the tongue fits the groove, converting this part of the mouth into a tube. This tube-like section creates the necessary pressure and the flexible, whip-like part of the tongue acts like a valve. By manipulating the latter the Archer Fish causes the drops of water to be ejected in rapid succession and with considerable force.

The Archer Fish has exceptionally good eyesight. Swimming at the water's surface if it is muddy or just slightly below if it is clear, and pointing its head towards its prey, it approaches an insect on a plant. This ability to see in air is more important than seeing underwater, since, although the Archer Fish

will also eat aquatic creatures such as worms and shrimps, it has a definite preference for insects that hover over the water or inhabit overhanging plants.

PROFILE

Length: *23 cm (9 in).*
Distribution: *Salt and fresh waters of India, Malaysia and northern Australia.*
Habitat: *Murky waters.*
Range of shooting: *1.5 m (5 ft).*
Notes: *This fish was first discovered in 1763 by Governor Hommel of Batavia.*

JACK DEMPSEY

The only fish named after a heavyweight boxer

This small fish, very popular with aquarists, is so aggressive that it has been given the name of a famous boxer.

The Jack Dempsey (*Dichlasoma octofasciatum*) is named after the famous American boxer who in 1919 beat Jess Willard to win the world heavyweight title, which he then retained until 1926, when he lost it to Gene Tunney. These fish have earned their common name because they are so aggressive. Except when small, they are certainly not recommended for community tanks.

Many of the fishes of the Cichlidae family, such as the Jack Dempsey, that originate from South America, are popular with aquarists. This is because they grow to quite a large size, are very colourful, especially when breeding, and are easy to breed in captivity. The

Cichlidae family has as many as 680 individual species and is the second largest family among the Perch-like fishes. The Jack Dempsey is a mottled brown colour with bright blue spots at the head, these becoming paler towards the tail.

Like all cichlids, the Jack Dempsey has a perch-like body that is slightly compressed; the dorsal and anal fins have a series of spines at the front, while the rest of the rays are soft. The older males develop a large bulge on their heads, but it is not known what its function is; probably the females find it very becoming! The most characteristic features of the cichlids are two discontinuous rows

of lateral-line scales, and a single nostril on each side of the head, and this clearly distinguishes them from the perches.

PROFILE

Length: *18 cm (7 in).*
Distribution: *Middle Amazon.*
Breeding: *Both parents nurse eggs and young.*
Diet: *Fish eggs, fish fry, insects and worms.*

CLOWNFISH

The fish that lives dangerously

These conspicuous little fishes are unusual in that they live in close association with a sea anemone, a creature that normally feeds on small fishes.

Clownfish (*Amphiprion percula*) have a bright orange-brown body with three irregularly shaped white stripes edged with black running vertically across it, and all the fins have white edges with a black stripe. They form a lifelong association with a large type of sea anemone, and so are also called Anemonefish. Sea anemones have thousands of special stinging cells along the tentacles and a fish, if it touches one of the tentacles, is usually stung to death and then fed into the anemone's mouth. It is therefore somewhat remarkable that the Clownfish lives among the tentacles, apparently immune to their sting. Initially it was thought that Clownfish were agile enough to avoid the tentacles, but

it was later realised that they actually rub against them and that if danger threatens they dart among the tentacles for protection. If the Clownfish are experimentally taken away from the anemone, they are very soon eaten by other fish. It seems that the Clownfish gains its immunity to the anemone's sting from its mucus coat. All fish feel slimy to the touch, which is a result of the mucus coat. The Clownfish's mucus apparently lacks the amino-acid glutathione, and it is this substance that triggers the anemone's sting cells.

While the Clownfish gains protection from its enemies, it is not really known what benefits the anemone from this association. Possibly the fish eats par-

ticles of food debris which would otherwise allow harmful bacteria to accumulate on the surface of the anemone.

Newly hatched Clownfish live at the water's surface, feeding on plankton, and are only later found associating with anemones.

PROFILE

Length: *6 cm (2.5 in).*
Distribution: *West and Central Pacific.*
Habitat: *Coral reefs.*
Breeding: *Spawns on clean coral or rock beside anemone. Both parents guard eggs.*

SAILFISH

The fastest fish in the sea

This large oceanic fish has a torpedo-shaped body and is streamlined for fast swimming, being able to reach speeds of as much as 100 km/h (62 mph).

The Sailfish (*Istiophorus platypterus*) is an extremely fast swimmer. Its dorsal fin rays are elongate and form a sail-like structure on the fish's back; when speeding through the water, this fin is laid flat against the back. The upper jaw is extended into a spear-like bill or 'sword' that is longer than the head. The bill is round in cross-section, unlike that of its relatives in the swordfish family, whose bill is flattened in this plane. The jaws of young Sailfish are short and equal in length, and armed with small, conical teeth; the edge of the head above each eye has a series of short bristles and the dorsal fin is like a short fringe. As the fish grows, the upper jaw becomes longer, the teeth disappear, the dorsal fin splits into two fins, and the bristles above each eye disappear.

Sailfish are migratory, undertaking largely seasonal movements from cooler to tropical regions. They are surface-living fish, often found near the shore feeding on locally abundant fish and squid. On calm days, the Sailfish is reported to bask at the water's surface with its dorsal fin fully erected and apparently being used as a sail, this giving rise to their common name.

The Sailfish is very popular as a sporting fish, although it does not grow to a great weight. It is a strong fighter, and the spectacular leaps it makes when hooked sadly makes it a target for angling.

PROFILE

Length: *3.6 m (12 ft). Bill length (fully grown) 5 cm (2 in).*
Weight: *Averages 32 kg (70 lb); maximum 125 kg (275 lb).*
Distribution: *Tropical Atlantic, Indian and Pacific Oceans.*
Habitat: *Surface-living, often close to shore.*
Swimming speed: *Up to 100 km/h (62 mph).*
Notes: *As with many fishes, little is known of the biology and habits of this species.*

CLIMBING PERCH

The fish that climbs trees

This fish was first discovered in 1791 in India by a Dutch naturalist called Daldorff, who found it about 1.5 m (5 ft) up a palm tree, enjoying a trickle of water that ran down the trunk.

In addition to the fleshy gills that all bony fishes have for breathing in water, the gill chambers of the Climbing Perch (*Anabas testudineus*) have a special 'labyrinth organ' which enables it to breathe atmospheric air. The word 'climbing' is actually incorrect because these fish do not climb trees, although they are occasionally found in trees. These unfortunate ones have usually fallen prey to a bird that has taken them to a convenient perch to eat; possibly the fish manages to escape and becomes stranded in the tree, or the bird changes its mind about eating the Climbing Perch as the front of its dorsal and anal fins and the gill covers have sharp spines on them.

The ordinary gills of the Climbing Perch are not so efficient as those of other bony fishes, so it has to rise to the surface of the water every half hour or so to gulp in atmospheric air. This ability to breathe air enables it to live in water that contains very little oxygen. If the water becomes stagnant, however, the Climbing Perch comes out on to the land and sets off to look for cleaner water. It moves across the land using wriggling movements of its tail, while the front end of the body is propped up by the pectoral fins and spiny gill covers. The Climbing Perch can endure long periods out of the water, so long as the labyrinth organ remains moist.

In Thailand, Climbing Perches are considered good to eat and are offered for sale alive on the market stalls, or transported in special jars and sprinkled with water every so often to keep them alive—until supper time!

PROFILE

Length: *25 cm (10 in).*
Distribution: *South China, Philippines, Indo-China, Malaysia, East Indies, India and Sri Lanka.*
Habitat: *All kinds of fresh water, but especially canals, ditches, lakes and ponds.*
Diet: *Crustaceans, insects and plant matter.*
Notes: *This fish can survive out of water for 12 hours, so long as the gill chamber is kept moist.*

SIAMESE FIGHTING FISH

A spectator sport in Thailand

This beautiful fish has been bred for its fighting qualities for more than a century, and has earned its name because of the exciting, dramatic and prolonged fights that occur between rival males.

In the wild, the Siamese Fighting Fish (*Betta splendens*) is an inconspicuous, shy and rather retiring little animal. It hides among and beneath aquatic plants to shelter from the sun's glare and to avoid predators such as kingfishers and herons. Like its relative the Climbing Perch, it has a 'labyrinth organ' and must periodically go to the water's surface to gulp in atmospheric air. If another male swims along, this shy fish becomes a transformed personality. It spreads its fins wide, expands it gill membranes so that they look like a ruff, and the body becomes a lustrous reddish-blue — then it attacks its rival. The handsome coloration of the enraged male has been selectively bred in aquarium specimens, producing a beautiful red or bluish fish. When two rival males in an aquarium confront each other, their colour becomes even more brilliant.

The fighting tendencies of this fish develop at two months, when the males are less than half grown. In Thailand, Siamese Fighting Fish are cultivated for their fighting abilities. In the wild they lose interest in each other in a matter of minutes, but domesticated ones can fight on for up to two hours. During the contest the fish bite each other. Fins are usually the main casualties and may be reduced to stubs, reducing the fish's ability to swim, steer and balance; scales and flesh may also be nipped off. The winner is decided when one of the males becomes too fatigued to continue. The fish are then placed in separate jars and their fins grow again within a few weeks. Needless to say, large amounts of money are wagered on these arranged fights.

PROFILE

Length: *6 cm (2.5 in).*
Distribution: *Thailand.*
Habitat: *Ponds, drainage channels and sluggish rivers.*
Diet: *Adults take tens of thousands of mosquito larvae; young feed on crustaceans.*
Notes: *The Siamese Fighting Fish is greatly valued because of its capacity for eating large numbers of mosquito larvae and thereby is very important in the control of the disease malaria, which is transmitted by mosquitoes.*

TRIGGERFISH

Champion snoozer of the fish world

So leisurely is the life of some triggerfishes that one species even jams itself between rocks and appears to fall asleep.

Triggerfishes are found mostly in tropical shallow inshore waters, but some species occur in temperate seas, while others inhabit the open ocean and have been caught far offshore. Such variation suggests that they are very successful fishes and that their body form and lifestyle are designed for survival.

However, they are not powerful swimmers. Their normal means of locomotion is a leisurely progress by flapping their long-based, many-rayed second dorsal fin and anal fin synchronously from side to side, but they can also sprint over a short distance by lashing their tail stiffly from side to side. Several species, including the Gray Triggerfish (*Balistes capriscus*), are even more laid back. This triggerfish jams

itself between rocks or in crevices in the coral and lies there apparently snoozing quietly.

Triggerfishes have a flat-sided deep body, covered with heavy interlocking scales, and a characteristic spiny dorsal fin. The first spine is long and strong, the second shorter and thinner, while the third spine is minute. Once the spines are erected, however, this third spine acts as a lock, keeping the stronger spines upright. Only by depressing the third, small trigger spine can the fin be lowered (although the fish can do this at will).

The fish backs tail first into a crevice or cranny until it is snugly jammed in, then, by erecting its spiny fin, it is locked in place. No predator can get at

it, especially as triggerfishes have formidable rat-like front teeth which they do not hesitate to use.

PROFILE

Length: *Up to 41 cm (16 in).*
Distribution: *Both sides of the Atlantic Ocean, from northern Argentina to Nova Scotia and from West Africa to Britain.*
Habitat: *Usually in open water, but also around rocks and reefs.*
Diet: *Hard-shelled animals, but as it is often caught in crab pots it may also be a scavenger.*
Notes: *Little is known of the breeding biology of these fishes.*

PORCUPINE FISH

The swimming fortress

This fish has a beak-like mouth and well-developed spines on its body; when frightened it inflates itself so that all the spines stick up, thus providing a very effective deterrent against any would-be predator.

The Porcupine Fish (*Diodon hystrix*) is one of the largest members of its family. The well-developed spines to which it owes its common name are actually modified scales with a double root and normally lie flat against the body. Porcupine Fish are closely related to pufferfishes and, like them, are capable of inflating their bodies. When inflated, the spines of the Porcupine Fish are erected automatically and project out from the body. The result is that any predator is deterred by the apparent size and prickly appearance of the fish.

The teeth of each jaw of the Porcupine Fish are fused together to form a beak (the word *Diodon* means two teeth). This beak is used for crushing and crunching up the sea urchins, snail-like molluscs, crabs and hermit-crabs which are this fish's favourite food.

When caught by fishermen, the Porcupine Fish is dried out while inflated and sold as a curio, or it may suffer the final indignity of being turned into a lampshade!

PROFILE

Length: *91 cm (3 ft).*
Distribution: *Tropical Pacific, Indian and Atlantic Oceans.*
Habitat: *Shallow water with turtle grass or sandy flats.*
Diet: *Sea urchins, molluscs and crabs.*

OCEAN SUNFISH

The most fertile of all fishes

One female Ocean Sunfish was estimated to contain 300 million eggs, and some individuals may well contain many times this number.

The Ocean Sunfish (*Mola mola*) has several claims to fame. Its extraordinary shape is perhaps the most remarkable: it seems to be three-quarters head and the remaining one-quarter tail fin. Practically circular in side view, it has two matching oar-shaped vertical fins, one on the back, the other behind the vent. The tail fin consists of a wide fringe of thick skin.

The Ocean Sunfish swims very slowly. It feeds mostly on jellyfish and has been observed to nip chunks out of these creatures as they pulsate along at the surface; biting around the bell's edge until most of the jellyfish is consumed, the sunfish does not need to swim fast to keep up with its prey. This diet is not very nourishing as jellyfish are about 98% water, so it must spend most of its life feeding. It is therefore all

the more surprising that sunfishes grow so large; one struck by a ship in southern Australian waters was 4 m (13.1 ft) long and weighed more than 1500 kg (1.8 tons).

Apart from its size and its curious diet the Ocean Sunfish has another claim to fame: it is one of the most fecund fishes known. According to one scientist, a sunfish 1.37 m (4.5 ft) long contained 300 million eggs; one the size of the Australian specimen might have had 100 times this number.

The spawning grounds of the Ocean Sunfish are unknown, and even their larvae have not been caught. Post-larvae about the size of a pea have been caught in the open ocean; they are strange little animals, covered with broad plates which have jutting triangular spikes all over them.

PROFILE

Length: *Up to 4 m (13.1 ft); usually around 91 cm (3 ft).*
Distribution: *Found throughout the open oceans except for polar seas.*
Habitat: *In mid-water and near the surface in the open sea; occasionally drifts inshore with tides and currents.*
Breeding: *Lays enormous numbers of eggs in the open ocean; other details unknown.*
Diet: *Jellyfish, combjellies and, rarely, young fish.*
Notes: *Sunfishes have a very thick, tough leathery skin, but their skeletons are paper-thin and extremely lightweight.*

DEATH PUFFER

The gourmet's equivalent of Russian roulette

The flesh of this fish is edible, but its blood and some of its organs are highly poisonous; if not prepared properly for the table, it can kill anybody who eats it.

Few fishes are more fascinating than the puffers. They have a singular ability to inflate themselves into a balloon shape by swallowing water. Some have very bold rounded markings on their sides or back which look like the eyes of some threatening creature when they are inflated. Their bodies are also covered with prickles, which stand out more formidably on inflation. To crown it all, the body organs and fluids are extremely toxic to Man.

Known as puffers, toadfishes, toados, tobies and, in Japan, fugu, these fishes are common in all tropical and warm-temperate seas, but a few species also live in fresh water in Asia and Africa. Many live in shallow water around reefs, in estuaries, and in sea-grass beds, but a few are inhabitants of the open ocean. They are slow-swimming fishes which tend not to be very active, and the pelagic species are frequently carried long distances by ocean currents.

Arothron hispidus, sometimes called the Death Puffer, is wide-ranging in the Indian and Pacific Oceans. It grows to about 50 cm (20 in), and is one of the highly toxic pufferfishes. It eggs (especially when nearly ripe), liver, gut and blood contain a virulent poison, which can kill a man who eats even a moderate quantity. The body flesh is edible, but if, during its preparation, it is contaminated by any of the toxic organs or fluids it can be dangerous to eat. Despite this, pufferfishes are esteemed to be a great delicacy in Japan, and specially trained and careful fugu cooks prepare otherwise toxic fishes for human consump-

tion — a form of gastronomic brinksmanship that many people would cheerfully forgo.

PROFILE

Length: *Up to 50 cm (20 in).*
Distribution: *Indian Ocean from the East African coast and Red Sea to Australia; Pacific Ocean islands to Hawaii and Japan.*
Habitat: *Around reefs; young fish in estuaries.*
Diet: *Feeds on invertebrates associated with coral.*
Notes: *Inflates itself very quickly when alarmed; once blown-up, it is very prickly to handle.*

AMPHIBIANS AND REPTILES

Amphibians and reptiles are both vertebrates but they are two quite separate groups of animals. The amphibians include the frogs, toads, salamanders, newts, as well as a limbless group known as caecilians. All have soft moist skins and all are ectothermic, that is, they obtain their body heat from the environment. The life cycle of most amphibians includes three stages: an egg, a free-swimming larval or tadpole stage, and the air-breathing adult. The eggs of amphibians have to be incubated in water or in moist surroundings because they do not have membranes or a shell to prevent desiccation.

The evolution of amphibians over about 300 million years has given rise to a group of more that 3000 highly successful species. Many are brightly coloured, a few produce poisons from skin glands, some such as the toads and frogs have complex vocalisations, and some have quite remarkable forms of reproduction.

Included among the reptiles are the snakes, lizards, crocodiles, turtles and the lizard-like Tuatara. Reptiles have a dry scaly skin, but differ fundamentally from amphibians in the structure of the egg. This has three protective membranes and a calcareous or parchment-like shell which allows incubation to take place without water. Although most reptiles lay eggs, some retain them until the young are born as miniature adults.

Although only a few groups of reptiles have survived the great age of the dinosaurs, many of the 6100 species are highly specialised in their defence, feeding and reproduction. Reptiles have also been remarkably successful in colonising a wide range of habitats, ranging from dry deserts to the oceans and from high mountains to the Arctic.

We still know very little about most amphibians and reptiles. New species are still being discovered, but many species are endangered and many will become extinct within a few years as the world's forests and other natural areas are destroyed.

GREEN TURTLE

The turtle with remarkable navigation

The best-known turtle is the large Green Turtle, which, although cumbersome on land, is graceful in water and has amazing navigating abilities which take it many hundreds of miles out in the Atlantic.

The Green Turtle (*Chelonia mydas*) is the turtle of turtle-soup fame. It feeds on seaweed around the warm, coastal shallow waters of the Americas, Africa, northern Australia and in the Indian Ocean, and so has been the easy target of overexploitation. So serious has been this species' decline that many efforts have been made to protect both it and its nesting beaches.

Green Turtles feeding in different parts of the world travel great distances to various beaches where they lay their eggs. For example, those which feed off the coast of Brazil travel some 2080 km (1300 miles) to the island of Ascension in the middle of the Indian Ocean. Tags placed on some of these turtles have shown that the adults migrate to the same beaches every season to breed. How they are able to find this tiny island, which is only 13 km by 9 km (about 8 × 5.5 miles), has not been fully discovered. It is possible, however, that they navigate by the stars and the sun, while chemical odours in the sea water may also provide navigation clues. These long journeys are arduous, be-

cause their speed through the water is relatively slow — only about 1–3 km/h (0.6–1.8 mph).

The female Green Turtle may nest several times, at intervals of 12–14 days. Each clutch of up to 100 round white eggs is laid in scoops about 0.6 m (2 ft) deep. The maximum number of clutches estimated is 11, resulting in a very large number of eggs.

The eggs and the young suffer a very high mortality. Their predators include lizards, snakes, cats, crocodiles, sharks and even crabs.

PROFILE

Length: *1 m (3.3 ft).*
Weight: *140–180 kg (about 300–400 lb).*
Distribution: *Coasts of Central America, Africa, Australia and Asia.*
Habitat: *Coastal warm waters where there is an abundance of seaweed.*
Breeding: *Females prepare scoops and lay several clutches on nesting beaches.*
Diet: *Entirely herbivorous, feeding on 'turtle grass' or seaweed.*
Notes: *The turtle hatchlings also have excellent navigating abilities: even on dark nights they seem to know in which direction to travel to reach the sea.*

MATAMATA

The most bizarre of all chelonians

Although a very remarkable-looking turtle when seen in captivity, the Matamata's incredible nose, corrugated shell, and colour make it well camouflaged in its natural murky habitat, where it surprises its prey.

The Matamata (*Chelys fimbriatus*) is the strangest-looking of all the 30 species of snake-necked turtles. This group of turtles has long flexible necks, and they withdraw the head and neck in a sideways fashion, leaving the neck still exposed. The Australian Snake-necked Turtle has a neck about three-quarters the length of its body.

The sluggish, aquatic Matamata of Guyana and Brazil, which has three rows of humps and knobs on its shell and shaggy lobes of skin on its neck, has the appearance of a pile of debris. The most bizarre feature of the Matamata is its grotesque and flat head, ending in a flexible, extended nose or proboscis which seems to be used as a snorkel. With a very long neck and an extended nose, it can remain submerged in shallow water. Matamatas are well camouflaged when they remain motionless, and they wait in murky ponds, marshes and streams for their prey. They store oxygen in the body tissues and can hold their breath for as long as 40 minutes.

Snake-necked turtles are carnivorous and most catch their prey by suddenly extending their long neck. In contrast, the Matamata has the ability to suck up water together with its prey. As a fish swims past, the Matamata suddenly opens its gaping mouth and a powerful suction sweeps the fish into the turtle's mouth and throat. The jaws snap shut and the fish is then swallowed whole.

During the day, the Matamata remains hidden in the murky water. It is not until twilight that it seeks out suitable underwater hiding places where it can surprise its prey.

PROFILE

Length: *Up to 40 cm (18 in).*
Weight: *22 kg (48 lb).*
Distribution: *Brazil and Guyana.*
Habitat: *Ponds, swamps and murky streams.*
Breeding: *16–20 spherical, brittle eggs, each 34 × 37 mm (1.4 × 1.5 in); incubation takes 208 days.*
Diet: *Mostly fish.*
Notes: *The Matamata's eyes are lined with a reflective substance, evidence that the species is more active at night than during the day.*

SNAPPING TURTLES

PROFILE

Length: *Alligator — mostly up to 75 cm (2.5 ft), but occasionally reaching 90 cm (3 ft); Common — mostly up to 36 cm (14 in).*

Weight: *Alligator — mostly up to 100 kg (220 lb); Common — 20 kg (44 lb).*

Distribution: *Southeastern United States and Central America. The Alligator species has the smaller range of the two.*

Habitat: *Muddy ponds, lakes and rivers.*

Breeding: *15–20 eggs, laid in small holes or burrows discarded by rodents.*

Diet: *Fish, birds, snakes and carrion.*

Notes: *These are the only chelonians which use algae and mud for camouflage in murky waters.*

Right: Alligator Snapping Turtle.

Below: Common Snapping Turtle.

Chelonians that sniff out human corpses

Up to 100 kg (220 lb) in weight and 90 cm (3 ft) in length, the ugly and aggressive snapping turtles have powerful hooked jaws which can easily maul a human while swimming.

There are 2 species of snapping turtles, both of which have large heads which cannot be withdrawn into the shell. They live in stagnant ponds, swamps and slow-running rivers in the eastern regions of North America. Thriving as they do in muddy, dirty habitats, a captive snapping turtle which escaped was able to survive very successfully in the sewers of a large city.

The Alligator Snapping Turtle (*Macroclemys temminckii*), some of which grow to 100 kg (220 lb) and 90 cm (3 ft) in length, is the largest of the freshwater turtles. Its shell has keeled ridges and is covered in slime and algae, and its jaw has a powerful hooked beak like a bird of prey. This species does not actively hunt prey, but lies in wait with its mouth wide open. It has a brightly coloured 'worm-like' tongue which is used as a lure to attract unsuspecting fish and even ducklings.

The Common Snapping Turtle (*Chelydra serpentina*), although smaller — it weighs up to 20 kg (44 lb) and its shell reaches about 36 cm (14 in) in length — has the most distasteful feeding behaviour. It eats dead bodies, plants, small birds, fish, carrion, and even attacks swimmers. This species can detect dead and rotting flesh and on occasions it has been attached to a leash and used to help sniff out human corpses in swamps and lakes. Feeding on fish has brought these turtles into conflict with fishermen and today their numbers have greatly diminished.

ESTUARINE CROCODILE

The greatest man-eater of them all

The Saltwater or Estuarine Crocodile is the world's largest living reptile and the most dangerous crocodile, often acquiring a taste for human prey.

Thirteen species of crocodiles and their close relatives, the alligators and caimans, are all that remain of a once great group of reptiles which flourished during the age of the dinosaurs. The fierce nature of crocodiles is best known in the Estuarine Crocodile (*Crocodylus porosus*), which is the most dangerous of them all. The fact that crocodiles can kill humans has resulted in many exaggerated stories about crocodiles as maneaters. Crocodiles do, however, attack Man and many hundreds of people are

thought to be killed by the Estuarine Crocodile each year. It is not known why this species is so aggressive, but its size and its abundance over a large area have made it the most feared of all crocodiles.

Young crocodiles feed on a variety of small animals, particularly fish, and as they grow older they prey more and more on birds and small mammals which inhabit swamps, estuaries and rivers. Lying in wait and submerged in the water with only its eyes and nostrils

visible above the surface, an Estuarine Crocodile can suddenly launch itself at an unsuspecting prey. Large animals, including Man, are dragged into the water and drowned or killed by the Crocodile twisting and rolling over.

The Estuarine Crocodile is known to reach lengths of 5 m (16 ft), but it is now rare to find such large animals because they have been hunted and exploited so much in the past. As its name suggests, this crocodile lives mainly in and around coastal areas, estuaries and swamps, from India to northern Australia. It is not unknown for some Estuarine Crocodiles to swim out to sea, and some have been known to travel hundreds of kilometres from one coast to another.

PROFILE

Length: *Often exaggerated: most commonly grows to a length of 5 m (16 ft), but some 7 m (25 ft) individuals have been recorded. Maximum authenticated length 8 m (27 ft).*

Weight: *Adult bulls weigh up to 600 kg (1300 lb).*

Distribution: *Estuarine and brackish waters from southern India to the Philippines, New Guinea and northern and northeastern Australia.*

Habitat: *Brackish water of coastal rivers, swamps, estuaries.*

Breeding: *Average of 50 (25–90) eggs, laid high up on river banks; incubation lasts for 90 days.*

Diet: *Opportunistic, but mostly fish; also mammals (including Man) and birds.*

Longevity: *Not well known, but some live for at least 50 years and possibly as long as 100 years.*

Notes: *Estuarine Crocodiles take in a lot of salt in their food, and the well-known tears of a crocodile have a high salt content and are produced by salt-excreting glands.*

GHARIAL

The crocodile with the 'frying pan' head

The crocodilians are the most ancient of reptiles (fossil Gharials were the largest known crocodiles) and the most singular living species is the one and only Gharial, which has the most slender and unusually shaped snout of all crocodiles.

The class Crocodilia is made up of 3 families, the crocodiles, the alligators and the Gharial. The last is the only species in the family Gavialidae, and is now an endangered species. The Gharial or Indian Gavial (*Gavialis gangeticus*) has ancient origins and has remained basically the same for over 200 million years. Its most amazing feature is the long and very slender snout which sticks out from a round flat head. The head and snout, viewed from a distance, look not unlike a long-handled frying pan. Even more striking is the male Gharial, with its nostrils centred in a large, hollow, pot-like hump at the tip of the snout. The female Gharial has a simple, long slender snout.

Although there is now only one species in the family Gavialidae, there are fossil crocodilians which date from

very early times and which have the characteristic 'frying pan' heads. These were the sea-dwelling Mesosuchia, which became extinct about 130 million years ago. The Gharials as we know them evolved about 70 million years ago, and some of the many species which lived back in those ancient times grew to lengths of 12–15 m (about 39–49 ft), making them the largest crocodilians that have ever lived.

The Gharial has 54 teeth in the upper jaw and 48 in the lower jaw. It uses these very sharp teeth and the pincer-like slender jaw to seize small fish as it sweeps its jaws through the water. The fish are typically first seized across their middle, then the Gharial raises its snout out of the water and, with a few snaps of the jaw the fish is turned and swallowed.

PROFILE

Length: *Male up to 6.5 m (21.3 ft), female up to 4.5 m (14.7 ft).*
Weight: *Average-sized Gharials weigh about 200 kg (440 lb).*
Distribution: *Rivers of India, such as the Ganges, Indus and Brahmaputra.*
Habitat: *Relatively clear water of deep, fast-flowing, sinuous rivers.*
Breeding: *Female lays about 40 eggs in specially prepared 'nest'. The young are 38 cm (15 in) long when they hatch, and their tail is slightly longer than the body.*
Diet: *Mostly fish.*
Notes: *Now an endangered species (extinct in many areas), owing to modification to its habitat and exploitation for skins.*

TUATARA

The world's most amazing reptile

The lizard-like Tuatara has a third eye, remains in a burrow for most of the day, and the few remaining animals represent a species which has survived unchanged from the age of the dinosaurs and which has existed for over 200 million years.

The rare Tuatara (*Sphenodon punctatus*) lives on a few isolated islands off New Zealand and is the sole survivor of what was once a widespread and abundant group of reptiles which lived during the age of the dinosaurs. It is not a lizard, and compared with other reptiles it has a very strong skull, a primitive backbone and strangely shaped ribs.

The most fascinating feature about the Tuatara is its third 'eye' or pineal eye. Externally this appears as a tiny spot on top of the animal's head, but there is an internal 'eye' with a retina which is situated on top of the animal's brain and just below a small hole in its skull. No one really knows why the Tuatara has a third 'eye', but perhaps it is a kind of light meter (which was a common feature and an important sense organ in many ancient reptiles).

Tuataras do not breed until they reach the age of about 20 years. An adult male of about 60 cm (2 ft) could be more than 60 years old (the species may live for as long as 100 years or more). Tuataras spend most of the day in a burrow, which they sometimes share with a petrel, and emerge to feed between dusk and midnight. They feed on almost anything they can find, including beetles, spiders, earthworms and even birds' eggs and chicks.

The Tuatara has the longest incubation period for any reptile. The female lays about ten eggs in a shallow scoop and, apart from covering the eggs with dirt, she takes no further care of them. The eggs may take 15 months to hatch. At hatching, the young Tuataras weigh only about 4 g (0.14 oz) and may take as long as nine hours to break free of the shell and climb through the soil to the surface.

PROFILE

Length: *45–60 cm (18 in–2 ft), male larger than female.*
Weight: *500–1000 g (1.0–2.2 lb).*
Distribution: *A few small offshore islands around New Zealand.*
Habitat: *Lives in burrows on rocky islands.*
Breeding: *About 10 eggs.*
Diet: *Almost anything it can find, but mostly insects and spiders.*
Longevity: *Fully grown males are about 60 years old, but some may live for at least 100 years.*
Notes: *The features of this reptile make it so unlike any other reptile that it is put in a special group of its own. Slow-moving, its body temperature (20–25°C, 68–77°F) is the lowest of any reptile.*

WORM LIZARDS

Reptiles which can move forwards and backwards with ease

The origins and affinities of worm lizards, a group of burrowing reptiles, have puzzled scientists for many years: although they look like plump worms, they are highly specialised burrowing reptiles.

The one species of worm lizard to be found in Europe, *Blanus cinereus*, is fairly abundant on the Iberian Peninsula, but little is known about its biology. These highly specialised, strange burrowing animals are often found sheltering under rocks or logs. They could easily be mistaken for worms because not only are they similar in size, they are also similar in colour.

Worm lizards or Ring lizards belong to the group of reptiles called Amphisbaenids. They are not really closely related to either snakes or lizards, although they were previously thought to be lizards. Most recent studies, however, classify the class Reptilia into 6 groups: the chelonians, the crocodilians, the Tuatara, the snakes, the lizards—and the worm lizards, of which there are about 130 species.

The name Amphisbaenid comes from the Greek, and roughly means 'going

both ways'. It refers to the ability of these animals to move forwards and backwards, with ease, in their burrows.

Apart from one genus (*Bipes*), the Amphisbaenids have no limbs; *Bipes* has very short forelegs. The soft skin of *Blanus* and other Amphisbaenids is worm-like because of the ring-shaped folds in it. Amphisbaenids have powerful jaws and large teeth, but the eyes of the adults are partly covered by an opaque skin. The skull is specially strengthened for burrowing in the ground, where these reptiles spend most of their time.

Many species of Amphisbaenids are about 30 cm (12 in) long, but one species in Central Africa (*Monopeltis*) grows to a length of 65 cm (26 in). They are found in both South America and Africa as well as Spain; a distribution in both the Old World and the New World is good evidence that these strange reptiles come from ancient times.

MARINE IGUANA

The only lizard to feed at the bottom of the sea

The most biologically unique islands in the world have some of the strangest animals, one of which is the only true marine lizard: in the Marine Iguana, breathing rate, heart rate, body shape and a strong tail are all specially adapted for feeding on seaweed in cool waters around the Galapagos Islands.

The remarkable Marine Iguana (*Amblyrhynchus cristatus*) lives in a strange habitat, on the Galapagos Islands off the coast of Ecuador. Made famous by the naturalist and explorer Charles Darwin, these islands are a home for many ancient and strange plants and animals. Isolated on the islands for millions of years, the Marine Iguana has learnt how to swim and dive —and to feed almost entirely on seaweed. Growing to about 1.75 m (about 5.6 ft) in length, these iguanas have robust bodies, short legs and well-developed flattened tails. They are dependent on the sea for their survival because they feed only on algae and seaweed on the rocks above and below the water. Feeding takes place at low tide every three to five days and, while

foraging, the iguanas swim gracefully and with ease, using their powerful tail for propulsion. During a dive, which may last for 20 minutes, the heart rate and blood flow slow down so that the oxygen in the lungs is then used as slowly as possible. Diving to depths of 4.7 m (15 ft) is not unusual, and some Marine Iguanas have been recorded at depths of 9.3 m (30 ft).

Many visitors to the islands have found that the Marine Iguana, when chased towards the sea, is reluctant to enter the water. It would seem that this lizard, although dependent on the sea for its food, has not adjusted fully to spending time in the sea.

Hordes of Marine Iguanas bask for many hours on the black rocks and in the hot tropical sun. Occasionally large

males engage in head-on clashes, though neither lizard seems to get hurt and eventually one will rapidly depart from the conflict.

PROFILE

Length: *Up to 1.75 m (5.6 ft).*
Weight: *3.4 kg (7.5 lb).*
Distribution: *Some islands in the Galapagos archipelago .*
Habitat: *Rocky shores and shallow seas.*
Breeding: *Average of only 2–3 eggs laid each year.*
Diet: *Marine algae and seaweed.*
Notes: *Marine Iguanas regulate their body temperature very precisely, and within 35–37°C (95–99°F), by basking.*

HORNED TOADS

An optician's nightmare

The most bizarre lizards of North America are the so-called horned toads, which look as if they have been flattened and which, when alarmed, will squirt blood from their eyes.

The horned toads are not toads at all but are lizards, yet they have the shape and appearance of a toad: they are flat, almost circular, large-bodied, short-tailed and grotesque in appearance. They form a group of seven North American Iguanid lizards, most of which have horns or large spines projecting from the back of the head. There are no other lizards like them in the world, apart from the Thorny Devil of Australia, which is described on page 177.

The well-known species *Phrynosoma douglasii* has a rather bloated appearance. It is grey or brown, but is expert at camouflage and can change colour to match the desert sand or to look like a piece of stone.

At night this species of horned toad wriggles below the sand and hides, but during the warmer parts of the day it moves slowly about, feeding mainly on ants and other insects.

When disturbed, horned toads flatten themselves on the ground and remain motionless — making them difficult to see. They have many frightening means of defence when danger threatens, including the ability to inflate themselves and jump forwards and hiss. Snakes and other predators do well not to eat them because their horns can pierce the attacker's gut when it tries to digest them.

Most curious of all is the ability of the horned toad to eject blood from its eyes. No one knows how this is achieved, though some accounts tell how blood not only appears around the eyes but seems also to be squirted with a characteristic sound from the eyes. There is even a report that describes blood being squirted in fine droplets as far as 1 m (3.3 ft).

PROFILE

Length: *4–13 cm (1.6–5.2 in).*
Weight: *10–32 g (up to about 1 oz).*
Distribution: *Dry areas of western North America and as far north as Canada.*
Habitat: *Sandy areas, deserts and short-grass plains; some now found in urban areas.*
Breeding: *Some species lay eggs and some give birth to live young. Phrynosoma douglasii gives birth in August to 5–31 young, each weighing less than 1 g (0.035 oz) at birth.*
Diet: *Insects, particularly ants.*
Notes: *The most prolific lizard known, with an average of 15 young.*

BASILISK

The lizard that runs across water

Travelling at speeds of up to 12 km/h (7.5 mph), the Basilisk or 'River Crosser' can swiftly cross a 400-m (440 yd) wide lake on its strong hindlegs without sinking.

The Basilisk (*Basiliscus basiliscus*) is an olive-brown Iguanid lizard found in the tropical regions of America. These are handsome lizards — fearfully handsome because legend says that the glance of a Basilisk could be fatal to Man and all other animals. They grow to lengths of 80 cm (32 in) and have a long, crested, tapering tail as well as a dorsal casque on the head and a crest on the back. The long, powerful hindlegs end in long, fringed toes and in some ways are similar to the powerful hindlegs of a toad.

Basilisks live among the dense vegetation lining rivers and streams. There they move about with great agility while feeding on small animals and fruit. When confronted by danger, they drop to the ground and immediately run on their hindlegs. Many other species of lizards can run on their hindlegs, but they need first to accelerate on all four legs. Rivers and lakes are no barrier because the Basilisk just keeps running —and it moves so fast that it does not sink. The lizard's speed and the rapid movement of its legs and fringed toes enable it to skim across the surface of the water at speeds of 12 km/h (7.5 mph). One Basilisk was seen to cross a 400-m (440-yd) wide lake without sinking.

Crossing water is one method of escaping from landbound predators, but the Basilisk can swim equally well and will sometimes stay submerged for long periods of time to avoid danger.

PROFILE

Length: *Up to 80 cm (32 in).*
Weight: *288 g (10 oz).*
Distribution: *Central America.*
Habitat: *Dense vegetation on the banks of tropical rivers and lakes.*
Breeding: *Female prepares hole and lays 18 eggs, which are then covered. Incubation takes about 3 months and the young, each 7–8 cm (3 in) long, can take up to 3 hours to hatch and leave the nest.*
Diet: *Small animals, particularly invertebrates and fruit.*
Longevity: *4–5 years.*
Notes: *Has the most developed form of bipedal locomotion among the lizards.*

THORNY DEVIL

A lizard that drinks from its body

The Thorny Devil is the most bizarre Australian desert lizard (appropriately given the scientific name horridus*) and takes a delight in eating ants one at a time.*

The Thorny Devil or Moloch (*Moloch horridus*) is found in many desert regions of Australia. It is easily identified by the many large spines which entirely cover its fat body and tail. Because of its very strange appearance, it was given the name Moloch, which was also the name of a devil and a god to whom children were sacrificed. Its weird appearance, however, is nothing but bluff, because it is completely harmless; it is slow-moving, and when frightened it tucks its head between its front legs. It is a very small lizard, only about 15 cm (6 in) in length, but its prickly appearance makes it appear much larger.

In the harsh desert environment, the Thorny Devil has a most unusual way of collecting water. On the surface of the animal's skin there are thousands of tiny grooves which allow water to spread and move very quickly over the lizard's body as if it were made of blotting paper. It was once thought that the water was absorbed through the skin into the lizard's body, but such an idea has been discarded because, if the skin could absorb water, then it would equally well lose water, particularly during the hot part of the day. Deserts become very cold at night and dew forms on the lizard's skin; the tiny droplets then spread rapidly over the entire body and reach the lizard's lips, where they can be sipped.

Ants are a favoured food of the Thorny Devil and it may sit for hours by a nest, flicking up one ant at a time with its sticky tongue. Thousands of ants may go into one meal, and the Thorny Devil has been known to take about 45 ants a minute.

PROFILE

Length: *15 cm (6 in).*
Weight: *About 37 g (1.5 oz).*
Distribution: *Arid and desert regions of Australia.*
Habitat: *Sandy deserts of dry scrub regions.*
Breeding: *In December/January the female lays about 8 eggs in a specially prepared tunnel. Compared with the small size of the adult, newly hatched Thorny Devils are large — about 6 cm (2.2 in) in length.*
Diet: *Favours ants, and eats one ant at a time.*
Notes: *Many predators will avoid spiny-looking prey and in this respect the Thorny Devil has unique protection from its enemies.*

CHAMELEONS

PROFILE

Common Chameleon

Length: *The species grows to between 25 and 28 cm (10 and 11 in).*
Tail: *Prehensile and used like a limb, length 12 cm (4.7 in).*
Weight: *40–60 g (1.5–2.0 oz).*
Distribution: *North Africa, southwest Asia, Mediterranean.*
Habitat: *One subspecies of the Common Chameleon has become a ground-dweller, but the main species lives in trees.*
Breeding: *Lays parchment-shelled eggs on the ground.*
Diet: *Insects, spiders and small birds, lizards and mammals.*
Longevity: *Rarely more than 4–5 years.*

Nature's most amazing tongue

Chameleons are highly specialised reptiles with modified feet, a prehensile tail, the ability to change colour, remarkable eyes and the longest and stickiest tongue of all lizards.

The members of the family Chamaeleontidae are descendants of an ancient group of reptiles. Today there are about 50 different species, occurring mainly in various parts of Africa, Madagascar (where more than half the total species can be found), the Mediterranean and the Middle East.

Chameleons such as the Common Chameleon (*Chamaeleo chamaeleon*) are flattened from side to side, and have a very granular skin which changes colour according to mood (rage brings on dark colours) and camouflage requirements. The actual mechanism which brings about the colour change is not fully understood, but it is due in part to pigments moving about in different layers of the skin. The eyes, housed in cone-like turrets, can be moved independently, giving the best all-round vision of any reptile. Most of these animals' life is spent crawling slowly and erratically along branches, for which the feet are modified by fusion of five toes into two groups (one group of two and one group of three) so that they look like pincers.

Most remarkable of all is the tongue,

which can be suddenly catapulted forward and extended to a length as long as the animal's body. A special bone with its own muscle is used to propel the tongue forward and different muscles retract it. Only very high-speed photography can catch the long sticky tongue

in action, for it can be extended and retracted in less than half a second. The actual mechanism by which the prey is secured is not clear, but sticky saliva, minute hairs and hooks and the grasping tip of the tongue all contribute to holding the prey.

ALPINE WATER SKINK

The lizard with antifreeze in its blood

For most lizards, a temperature of 10°C (50°F) or lower results in cold torpor, but the Water Skink of Australia has antifreeze in its blood and is sometimes active in snow-covered areas late in the autumn before eventually going into hibernation.

The Alpine Water Skink (*Spheno-morphus*) is a small lizard that is active on sunny days throughout the summer, but during winter, when the ground is snow-covered, it seeks shelter up to 1 m (3.3 ft) below the ground.

Cold snaps can occur without warning during the spring and summer, and it is then that this species has special protection from the cold. Normally active with a body temperature of 26–34°C (79–93°F), it can still move about even when its temperature drops below freezing. With body temperatures as low as −1.2°C (29.8°F), the Alpine Water Skink does not freeze because it has small amounts of an antifreeze agent (glycerol) in its blood.

PROFILE

Length: *12–16 cm (4.7–6.3 in).*
Weight: *8–12 g (0.28–0.42 oz).*
Distribution: *Subalpine and montane regions of southeast Australia.*
Habitat: *Low-lying vegetation in moist or wet areas.*
Breeding: *Viviparous; 4–5 young born late summer to early autumn.*
Diet: *Insectivorous.*
Longevity: *4–5 years.*
Notes: *Regulates its body temperature very precisely by alternately spending short intervals of time in the sun and then in the shade.*

WHIPTAIL LIZARDS

A world without males

Fertilisation of the egg is fundamental for animal reproduction, but some lizards have evolved a method of reproduction which requires no males or fertilisation of the eggs.

Whiptail lizards are common lizards of North America. They have powerful legs, pointed heads and streamlined bodies—well suited for scurrying about their habitat at speeds of up to 30 km/h (18 mph). They are extremely agile, and when disturbed they suddenly vanish into the undergrowth. There are more than 40 species with greatly varied lifestyles, and some have even yet to be described. Many live in colonies, where there are often territorial displays and conflicts.

Some species reproduce parthenogenetically. Parthenogenesis is the development of a new individual from an unfertilised egg and without the need for males and fertilisation.

PROFILE

Length: *Most whiptail lizards are between 20 cm and 45 cm (8–18 in) long.*
Weight: *13–28 g (0.5–1.0 oz).*
Distribution: *Northern and Central America.*
Habitat: *The many species live in varied habitats; typical is dry open terrain in forest clearings and along banks of rivers.*
Diet: *As varied as the habitats, but mainly insects.*
Breeding: *Sexual and parthenogenetic reproduction; 1–7 eggs, depending on age of female.*

PALLAS'S GLASS SNAKE

The legless lizard that breaks up into pieces when struck

With no legs, a tail longer than its body and the appearance of a snake, Pallas's Glass Snake, at 1.5 m (4.9 ft) long and 5 cm (2 in) thick, is the largest legless lizard and indeed a remarkable animal.

Glass snakes are not in fact snakes but are lizards. Of the many lizards which have evolved to do away with legs, Pallas's Glass Snake (*Ophisaurus apodus*) is the largest. This European lizard was first discovered by a naturalist called Pallas. Its size—1.5 m (4.9 ft) long and as thick as a man's wrist—and its ability to clamber among the undergrowth are enough to make anyone believe that it is a snake. Although it has no legs, the remnants of hindlegs still

exist—a pair of small stumps 2 mm (0.08 in) long where the tail joins the body.

The thick skin of Pallas's Glass Snake is matched by the animal's blunt, broad teeth, which are well adapted for crushing hard prey such as snails and insects with tough cuticles.

Whereas snakes have short tails relative to the length of the body (the junction of the body and tail being marked by the cloaca or vent), legless

lizards have very long tails. Pallas's Glass Snake is spectacular in this respect because the tail amounts to two-thirds the length of the body. Each tail vertebra has a pre-fracture joint which allows any part of the tail to be shed. If hit with a stick, the unfortunate lizard will cast its tail in bits and all the pieces will continue to wriggle and writhe while the 'body' of the lizard escapes. The tail is so long that the effect is one of the lizard breaking into pieces.

KOMODO MONITOR

The dragon of Indonesia

The giant Komodo Monitor with its huge head and solid-looking body is the largest of all the lizards and is one of the largest lizards that have ever lived.

There are about 30 species of different-sized monitor lizards and because they are similar in appearance they are all included in one group, the Varanids. The smallest kinds of monitors are only 20 cm (9 in) in length, but the largest of all is the Komodo Monitor or Komodo Dragon (*Varanus komodoensis*). The biggest Komodo Monitor ever recorded had a length of 3.2 m (10.5 ft) and weighed 140 kg (about 300 lb). This is

the largest living species of lizard.

The Komodo Monitors are found only on a few very small islands east of Java in Indonesia, and early this century their presence gave rise to rumours about large, fierce, land crocodiles. It was not until 1912 that the first scientific description was made of this giant lizard. Their discovery and description created a sensation, and even today it is hard to believe that such giant-sized

lizards still exist. Komodo Monitors search for food early in the day. Their characteristically forked tongue, which is rapidly flicked in and out, is used to help detect the odours or scent left by their prey.

Living on only a few islands, it is perhaps not surprising that there are probably fewer than 1000 Komodo Monitors alive today. They are strictly protected in their natural habitat.

GILA MONSTER

PROFILE

Length: *60 cm (23 in).*
Weight: *1.4 kg (3.2 lb).*
Distribution: *Arizona and Mexico.*
Habits/habitat: *Active mainly at night in desert regions.*
Breeding: *About 10 long, cylindrical eggs, laid in a hole dug by the female; eggs hatch after about 30 days.*
Diet: *Invertebrates, birds' eggs, other small reptiles and small rodents.*
Longevity: *20 years.*
Notes: *The gaudy colours of this lizard function as a warning that it is venomous.*

The lizard that keeps a larder in its tail

The distinctive coloration of pink and black spots and the large bony scales add to the strange appearance of the fat, short-legged and venomous Gila Monster.

The Gila (pronounced 'heela') Monster (*Heloderma suspectum*) is one of the two lizard species aptly called the beaded lizards. The backs of these lizards are covered in bead-like bony scales. The Gila Monster is found in the southwestern United States, where it lives in the desert regions, being active mainly at night.

Food in the desert is not always abundant and the Gila Monster, because it is a slow-moving lizard, must eat as much

as possible when food is available. It feeds mainly on invertebrates, other small reptiles, birds' eggs and small rodents, and is able to store fat in its large tail. Well-fed Gila Monsters have very fat tails and, during times of food shortage, they are able to survive off the fat stored in the tail. After a long period without food, the girth of the tail can become reduced by as much as 80%; within six months, and with ample food, the Gila Monster is capable of doubling

the size of its tail.

The Gila Monster and its close relative, the Mexican Beaded Lizard, are the only two venomous lizard species. Powerful jaws and venom are very necessary for these slow-moving lizards if they are to overcome their prey. Small animals such as rodents are detected by these lizards with their great sense of smell and the Gila Monster, when seizing its prey, chews, rather than injects, venom into its victim.

PROFILE

Length: *Up to 3.2 m (10.5 ft), but average 2.5 m (8 ft).*
Weight: *Maximum 165 kg (365 lb), average 82 kg (180 lb).*
Distribution: *Has the smallest distribution of all monitor lizards: occurs on the island of Komodo and a few other nearby islands.*
Habits/habitat: *Spends the night in caves or in dense jungle and forages by day in forests and grasslands.*
Breeding: *Lays about 15 eggs, each about 10 cm (4 in) long with a parchment-like shell; the eggs take as long as 8 months to hatch.*
Diet: *Carrion, small deer and wild boar, as well as other small animals.*

ANACONDA

The 'bull-killer' of the Amazon

The Anaconda or Water Boa kills large mammals by drowning and constriction, and is the longest reptile in the world as well as being the largest of the boa family.

The boa family is a group of about 90 species of so-called primitive snakes. The family includes pythons and boas, some of which are massive semi-aquatic species and others of which are small desert species. They are called primitive snakes partly because they have not developed the complete snake skeleton and body muscles, and partly because they retain vestiges of the hindlimbs in the form of spurs on either side of the cloaca. This is good evidence to indicate that snakes have evolved from reptiles with limbs.

The great size of the Anaconda (*Eunectes murinus*) has caused it to be surrounded in myth and fantasy. There are many exaggerated stories about this snake's length, some telling of lengths of 42 m (138 ft). The usual maximum length stated is 9 m (under 30 ft), with some records of 9.6 m (31.5 ft). A

closely related species, the Yellow Anaconda (*Eunectes notaeus*), is a much smaller species, reaching only 3.3 m (10.8 ft).

Spanish explorers called the Anaconda the 'Matatoro' (bull-killer), obviously as a result of exaggerated stories about the Anaconda's length and general body size. Although an aquatic snake and an expert swimmer, the Anaconda preys on terrestrial mammals and birds which have come to the river to drink. Sluggish in its movements, it is very strong and can easily overcome very large prey. There is one record of an Anaconda killing a 2-m (6.5-ft) long caiman. Some mammals, such as small species of deer, are known to be easily overcome by Anacondas, as are large rodents such as Agoutis. As the Anaconda is an aquatic animal, fish form a large part of its diet.

PROFILE

Length: *9 m (29.5 ft) is the maximum usually recognised, although 9.6 m (31.5 ft) is sometimes stated.*
Weight: *126 kg (278 lb).*
Distribution: *Mainly in the Amazon and Orinoco basins of South America.*
Habits/habitat: *Aquatic, living in tropical rivers.*
Breeding: *Gives birth to 4–39 live young, each about 80 cm (32 in) long.*
Diet: *Fish, large rodents, mammals, and reptiles such as crocodilians.*
Longevity: *29 years has been recorded.*
Notes: *Skins taken from killed specimens are dried and stretched, resulting in lengths greater than in the living snake.*

CUBAN TREE BOA

The only snake that feeds extensively on bats

The rare Caribbean boas feed mainly on small rodents, birds, lizards and frogs, but one, the Cuban Tree Boa, has developed a liking for bats which it catches at the entrances to caves.

The family Boidae includes 39 species found in western North America, South America, the West Indies, North Africa, New Guinea and some Pacific islands. There are 5 forms of Caribbean boas, some of which, like other island reptiles, are unique to certain islands; most are also now very rare. Three species of the genus *Epicrates* have more recently become so endangered that intensive captive breeding prog-rammes have been established to try and save them.

The Cuban Tree Boa (*Epicrates angulifer*) is one of the species which has been the subject of captive breeding, since much of its natural habitat on Cuba has been lost to agriculture and cane cultivation. Because this boa is greatly disliked and has, in the past, frequently been killed by local people, it is now completely protected.

Cuban Tree Boas are the longest of the Caribbean *Epicrates* species, reaching lengths of 5 m (16.4 ft). Their colour and markings are extremely variable, making them inconspicuous among the branches of trees where they spend most of their time.

All snakes are carnivores, but many have specialised diets and some have specialised feeding techniques. Most remarkable is the feeding behaviour of some Cuban Tree Boas which have rejected an arboreal life and have become predators on a species of bat (*Phyllonycteris poeyi*) in the caves on Cuba. These boas lunge and strike at the bats as they fly through small openings in the caves, and are mostly very successful at catching them. What is not known is how the boas are able to detect the bats in the dark confines of the caves.

PROFILE

Length: *Up to 5 m (16.4 ft).*
Weight: *2 kg (4.4 lb).*
Distribution: *Cuba (other* Epicrates *species occur on other West Indies islands).*
Habits/habitat: *Inhabits holes and rock piles in cultivated areas, but mainly an arboreal species.*
Breeding: *Gives birth to on average up to 5 live young (not more, as is often quoted), each weighing about 200 g (7 oz).*
Diet: *Mostly rodents and birds, but some feed almost entirely on bats.*
Longevity: *Unknown; many large snake species live for up to 25 years in captivity.*
Notes: *Each snake is extremely large at birth, and weighs 14 times more than the newborn young of other Caribbean boas. The adult's vestigial hindlimbs (spurs) are used during courtship; the male rubs the spurs along the flanks of the female prior to mating.*

COMMON KING SNAKE

The harmless reptile that dines on venomous snakes

The smooth scales, attractive markings and small head, so typical of the Common King Snake and its close relatives, contrast with its remarkable predatory behaviour as a killer of rattlesnakes.

The king snakes are found in North America. Although most are medium-sized, the large, handsome Common King Snake (*Lampropeltis getulus*) reaches 2 m (6 ft) in length. Sometimes called the Chain Snake or Thunder Snake, it has shiny, smooth black or brown scales with yellow or white bands. Other king snakes are banded in bright colours of red, yellow and black or contrasting black and white. The vivid colours of some species mimic the colours of some very venomous snakes such as the coral snakes.

Active between March and October and mostly ground-dwelling, the Common King Snake is harmless to Man (as are other Colubrid snakes) and is a favoured pet. It is, however, an excellent predator of small mammals, lizards and frogs. Most remarkable is its ability

to overcome and swallow whole, venomous snakes: Common King Snakes are the deadly enemies of rattlesnakes and other deadly species, and are also immune to rattlesnake venom.

These snakes coil themselves aggressively around other snakes and kill the prey by choking it. As the Common King Snake is immune to snake venom, the deadly rattlesnake has but one other method of defence: by raising part of its body off the ground, it tries in vain to beat off its attacker with blows from its body while at the same time attempting to keep its head well protected, because the Common King Snake will try to swallow its victim head first.

The Common King Snake of North America is a close relative of the rarely seen, harmless Smooth Snake (*Coronella austriaca*) of Britain and Europe.

PROFILE

Length: *Up to 1.8 m (6 ft).*
Weight: *Typical for adult, 500–540 g (1.1–1.2 lb).*
Distribution: *Southeastern North America.*
Habits/habitat: *Ground-dweller in wilderness areas, such as moist pine woods and lowland meadows.*
Breeding: *5–24 parchment-shelled eggs laid among woodland litter; incubation takes 70 days. Young 9–11 cm (3.6–4.3 in) long.*
Diet: *Mainly snakes, also small rodents, turtle eggs, birds, lizards.*
Longevity: *6 years.*
Notes: *Scent-gland secretions produced by this snake act as a repellent in defence, as well as a sex-attractant in courting.*

EGG-EATING SNAKE

The reptile with a saw in its gullet

Many snakes eat eggs, but this species is a specialist because its jaws and throat can expand to an extraordinary size and a sharp-edged 'saw' at the back of its throat slits open the shell of the egg.

The Common African Egg-eating Snake (*Dasypeltis scabra*) is one of a subfamily (Dasypeltinae) of 6 Colubrid snakes which have become egg-eating specialists; one is an Indian species and the rest are found in Africa. It is rarely seen during the day, and at night it goes in search of birds' nests. Most individuals reach a length of 75 cm (2.5 ft).

African Egg-eating Snakes have small heads and slender bodies, but the head and mouth are so flexible that they can swallow whole eggs as big as large-size chicken eggs and which are larger than their own head. Following a few yawns to limber up the throat muscles, the snake slowly 'walks' its mouth over the whole egg by allowing the lower jaw muscles to be pushed apart. Egg-eating snakes have small weak teeth and so the egg remains whole as it is slowly engulfed within about 15 minutes. Projecting down from the back of the snake's throat are sharp spines, which are extensions of the vertebrae; about 30 sharp saw 'teeth' slice through the egg's shell as it passes on down the snake's gullet, and the shell is then regurgitated as a neat white pellet.

Egg-eating snakes are so highly spe-cialised that they are of little danger to any other animal. Some are so harmless and vulnerable to attack by predators that they mimic venomous vipers by way of colour and behaviour. Although harmless to Man, they will put on a fierce display (hissing, inflating the body and striking like a cobra) if anything should happen to disturb or threaten them.

KING COBRA

The snake that can kill an elephant

Commonly around 4 m (13 ft) in length but reaching 5.5 m (18 ft), the King Cobra is the largest and most feared venomous snake, with a startling ability to move forward while standing on its tail.

Many legends and fascinating stories have come out of encounters with the most feared snakes in the world, the cobras. The true cobras are in the genus *Naja* and these are the species which characteristically rise up and sway in front of snake-charmers. The King Cobra (*Ophiophagus hannah*) is found in India, southern China, Malaysia and the Philippines, where it inhabits dense forested areas. A secretive and normally quiet species, it is easily excited and angered: it then raises the forepart of its body off the ground, erects the skin around its neck on 'neck ribs', and gives a prolonged hissing; and, most frighten- ingly of all, the King Cobra can move forward while in this posture. Given the chance to escape, it will quickly flee and if necessary will even take to water.

King Cobras have very large poison glands containing highly potent neuro- toxic venom, and without treatment a man can die within 15–20 minutes of being bitten. As they live in forested areas King Cobras are not easily de- tected, and many 'work' elephants in Thailand and India have died after being bitten on the trunk. Bites from King Cobras occur most frequently dur- ing these snakes' breeding season, be- cause at that time both sexes aggressive- ly guard their eggs. Although the female does not incubate the eggs, she does stay with the hatchlings—each about 0.5 m (20 in) long—until they leave the nest.

The generic name of this species gives us a hint about its diet. *Ophiophagus* means 'snake-eater': King Cobras prey on other snakes, as well as on large lizards, rodents and birds.

PROFILE

Length: *4 m (13 ft) not unusual, and record is 5.5 m (18 ft).*
Weight: *Large individuals 2.8 kg (6.2 lb).*
Distribution: *India (not Sri Lanka), southern China, Malaysia, Philip- pines and other small island groups.*
Habitat: *Forests and areas containing rural agriculture.*
Breeding: *Mates January/February. Usually 20 eggs, but may produce up to 41–51.*
Diet: *Mostly other snakes, but also rodents, lizards and birds.*
Venom: *Neurotoxin.*
Longevity: *Probably about 7–8 years.*
Notes: *This is the only snake which is known to construct a nest. The nest is very simple in construction and is made of leaves and twigs.*

BLACK MAMBA

The world's fastest-moving snake

4 m (13 ft) of Black Mamba travelling at speeds of up to 23 km/h (14 mph), with a potent venom and fangs 6.5 mm (0.25 in) long, make this snake the most feared in Africa and the fastest in the world.

The largest venomous snake in Africa is the Black Mamba (*Dendroaspis polylepis*), which can reach lengths of up to 4 m (13 ft), although most large specimens are a little under 3 m (9.8 ft). It is a very keen-sighted, agile species which can move at lightning speed over branches and through undergrowth. A large slender snake racing quickly over branches and on rough ground always appears to be moving much faster than it really is, an illusion which has led to exaggerated recorded speeds of the Black Mamba. Although they *seem* to move at up to about 40 km/h (25 mph), the maximum speeds known are short bursts of 23 km/h (14 mph), while the usual speed is about 11 km/h (7 mph) — still making this species the fastest snake in the world.

As well as being the fastest snakes, Black Mambas are extremely vigorous and can bite and hold their head 50 cm (20 in) above the ground while moving forward. They are very accurate when striking, and have the remarkable ability to throw their head and the forepart of their body 1 m (3 ft) upwards off the ground.

The Black Mamba is in fact dark brown in colour and is the larger of 2 mamba species found in Africa. Another common species is the Eastern Green Mamba (*Dendroaspis angusticeps*). which is equally venomous but slightly smaller than its close relative.

The high speeds and very active behaviour of the Black Mamba mean that it requires plenty of food as often as possible. Black Mambas are voracious snakes and catch birds with ease, as well as preying on birds' eggs, small mammals and lizards. They have a very high rate of digestion and have been known to digest a large rat completely within nine hours.

PROFILE

Length: *Maximum 4 m (13 ft), but usually reaches 3 m (9.8 ft).*

Weight: *Large specimens weigh 1.6 kg (3.5 lb).*

Distribution: *Southern Ethiopia, south to southwest Africa and Natal.*

Habits/habitat: *Ground-dwelling species, but sometimes climbs into trees.*

Breeding: *10–15 white oval eggs, laid in a burrow or hollow tree stump. Newly hatched young are about 51 cm (20 in) and can kill rats and mice immediately.*

Diet: *Small rodents (including squirrels), birds, bats and lizards.*

Venom: *Neurotoxin resulting in death by asphyxia.*

Longevity: *One specimen in captivity lived for 12 years, probably lives for much longer in wild.*

SPITTING COBRA

Death comes in not one but two jets

The most feared of all the venomous African cobras is the Black-necked Spitting Cobra, which, as a means of defence, rears up off the ground and with deadly accuracy squirts two jets of potent venom at its enemy's eyes.

The cobras are a family (Elapidae) of front-fanged snakes and are the most feared of all. The well-known display of raised body and outspread hood is not only characteristic but is performed by the young snakes as soon as they leave the egg. The most unique form of defence is found in the spitting cobras, particularly the Black-necked Spitting Cobra (*Naja nigricollis*), which is found throughout many parts of the African continent.

Powerful jaw muscles squeeze the venom from large glands on either side of the cobra's head, and the venom is ejected as two jets (these turn into a fine spray within a short distance) from a tiny hole near the tip of each fang. The

fangs enclose venom canals and the venom is under such pressure that, when suddenly released from the tiny holes, it can be sprayed to a distance of up to 2.5 m (8 ft) and in an arc spanning 70 cm (about 2 ft). Cobra venom is extremely potent and 1 g (0.035 oz) of dried venom alone could kill 165 humans or over 160,000 mice. The Black-necked Spitting Cobra, when milked of its venom, can yield as much as 350 mg (0.012 oz), far more than many other venomous snakes.

The average size of this species is 1.5 m (5 ft), but there is a record of one massive Black-necked Spitting Cobra which was 2.8 m (9 ft) long and had a girth of 20 cm (8 in).

PROFILE

Length: *Usually about 1.5 m (5 ft); many are 2 m (over 6 ft), and there is a record of one at 2.8 m (9 ft).*
Weight: *3.9 kg (8.6 lb).*
Distribution: *Widespread throughout Africa except around the Sahara.*
Habits/habitat: *Ground-dwelling species in savanna and rural areas, but will climb trees to raid birds' nests.*
Breeding: *Large females lay about 30 eggs.*
Diet: *Small mammals, birds' eggs, lizards and other snakes.*
Longevity: *11 years or more.*
Notes: *The spitting is a form of defence and the species may spit many times in quick succession to try to blind the enemy.*

SAW-SCALED VIPER

The most dangerous snake in the world

Widely distributed, common, highly venomous, aggressive, alert and quick, this viper has all the features required to make it the most feared and dangerous of all vipers.

Vipers have a wide distribution throughout Europe, Asia and Africa, and number about 150 species. They vary from ground-dwelling forest forms to arboreal (tree-dwelling) and burrowing forms. All are venomous and all are predators, feeding on a wide variety of vertebrates. One of the most widely distributed species is the Saw-scaled Viper (*Echis carinatus*), which occurs in Africa north of the Equator, in the Middle East and across to India and Sri Lanka. As well as having an extensive range, it is found in very dense populations, particularly in agricultural and rural areas.

Comparisons with the King Cobra (*Ophiophagus hannah*) demonstrate the dangerous nature of Saw-scaled Vipers.

These two species are equally dangerous, but, over a period of four years of monitoring snake bites, only 5% of King Cobra bites were fatal compared with 36% fatalities from Saw-scaled Vipers. One adult Saw-scaled Viper has sufficient venom to kill as many as eight human beings. The combination of its aggressive behaviour, agility, abundance and extensive range makes this species the most dangerous in the world.

Despite its dangerous nature, this viper is small. They are extremely variable in colour, but most are brown, grey or olive with light and dark patches on the dorsal side. Their small size, colour and pattern, together with the rough texture of the scales, make them very difficult to detect.

PROFILE

Length: *40–60 cm (16–24 in), with some up to 80 cm (32 in); female larger than male.*
Weight: *90 g (3.2 oz).*
Distribution: *West Africa north of the Equator, Middle East, India, Sri Lanka.*
Habitat: *Under stones or logs in semi-desert and dry arid regions.*
Breeding: *Gives birth to live young.*
Longevity: *12 years.*
Venom: *Highly toxic.*
Diet: *Small mammals and lizards.*
Notes: *When molested, this species rubs its body scales together while moving in a sidewinding fashion, producing a rasping noise.*

GABOON VIPER

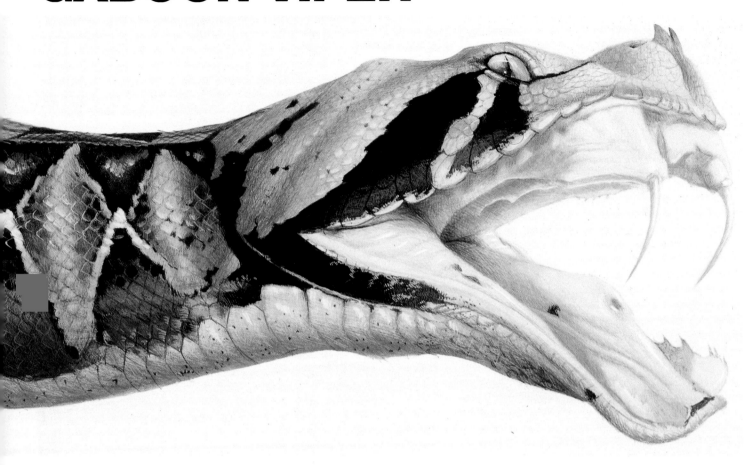

The world's longest-fanged snake

Large, robust, beautifully coloured and venomous, this is a very docile snake when in its natural habitat, but the magnificent recurved fangs of a 1.8-m (5.5-ft) Gaboon Viper are a massive 500 mm (1.9 in) in length and they have sufficient venom to kill 20 people.

The Gaboon Viper (*Bitis gabonica*) is a kind of puff adder, which are the most impressive and dangerous African snakes. They belong to the Viperidae family, of which there are 160 species, and their name comes from their habit of hissing and puffing through their nostrils. Not only is the Gaboon Viper the most dangerous of all puff adders, it is also the largest, fattest, most beautifully coloured and most commonly encountered. Reaching lengths of 1.8 m (5.5 ft), the thick body is equally as impressive as the coloration: resembling a piece of oriental carpet, it is sometimes as thick as a man's calf.

Like all vipers, the puff adders have a highly sophisticated venom apparatus and possess exaggerated front fangs on the upper jaw. When at rest the fangs lie folded against the roof of the mouth,

but when about to strike are raised and extended. Many vipers have fangs over 10 mm (0.4 in) long, but one Gaboon Viper's fangs were found to be a massive 500 mm (1.9 in) in length. It is possible, therefore, for the Gaboon Viper to deliver its deadly venom deep into the body of its victim. There have been many deaths resulting from Gaboon Viper bites, but cattle are more at risk than are humans. Rodents and other small animals are the main prey, and the Gaboon Vipers lie in wait for their victims while partially hidden among leaves on the forest floor.

Gaboon Vipers do not lay eggs; instead the young are born enveloped in a membrane, only to break loose soon after birth (giving birth to 30 young is not unusual among puff adders). The newborn young are as deadly as adults.

PROFILE

Length: *1.2–1.8 m (3.6–5.5 ft), female larger than male.*
Weight: *6.5–12.0 kg (14.3–26.4 lb).*
Distribution: *Forests of eastern, central and western Africa.*
Habits/habitat: *Active at night or in shady areas of rainforest and jungle floors.*
Breeding: *20–40 live young, each 30 cm (12 in) long, born about March.*
Longevity: *11 years in captivity and probably longer in wild.*
Diet: *Rodents and other small mammals, including bats; frogs and lizards.*
Venom: *Haematoxic and neurotoxic.*
Notes: *Large amounts of fat stored in body are sometimes taken from specimens and sold for medication.*

SIDEWINDER

The snake that moves in a series of little jumps

Instead of moving as do other snakes, the Sidewinder has adopted the sidewinding movement, which is a particularly efficient and rapid method of movement on dry loose sand, easily allowing speeds of up to 4 km/h (2.5 mph) to be reached.

Rattlesnakes are highly advanced, specialised snakes which have reached the peak of their evolution. One relatively small species is the Sidewinder (*Crotalus cerastes*), growing only to about 70 cm (2 ft) in length. Its body is stout and it has sharply protruding eyebrow shields. Its tail tapers to the characteristic rattle, which is a feature of all rattlesnakes. Although venomous, its venom is not particularly powerful and its prey is limited to other reptiles, particularly small lizards, and small rodents.

Snakes move by one of three methods. There is the well-known serpentine movement in which the body of the snake slips over the surface while scales grip on any rough features on the ground. The concertina movement involves the hind part of the body gripping the ground while the head and front are thrust forward. Sidewinding is a special adaptation to desert environments and involves just two points of the body momentarily touching the ground, resulting in graceful, continuous, stepwise movements or a continuous series of little jumps. The track left by the Sidewinder is like that left by a coiled wire rolled along the sand—leaving parallel separate tracks, 7.5–15 cm (3–6 in) apart, angled in the direction of the snake's movement. The sidewinding method of locomotion is particularly suitable where there is dry shifting sand, and Sidewinders avoid competition with other kinds of rattlesnakes by adapting to these parts of the desert.

The Sidewinder catches prey by lying partly concealed beneath the sand. Coiled like a spring, it has no difficulty snatching and overcoming its prey.

PROFILE

Length: *60–70 cm (24–28 in).*
Weight: *170 g (6 oz).*
Distribution: *Southwest United States.*
Habitat: *Dry sandy, brush deserts — even on loose sandy soil.*
Breeding: *Average of 7–13 live young born, September to October.*
Longevity: *10 years in captivity, but longer in the wild.*
Diet: *Small lizards and rodents such as deer mice* (Peromyscus), *and occasionally other snakes.*
Notes: *Has a reputation for being aggressive, but is moderately tranquil in captivity. Is able to change colour with temperature and so match the colour of the desert sand.*

OKINAWA HABU

The snake that likes to bite people

Many species of snake occasionally enter houses, but the most feared snake to do so is the 1.6-m (5.2-ft) long, irritable, venomous and notorious house invader, the Okinawa Habu or Yellow-spotted Lance-head Snake.

In some tropical localities where human activity has not been too extensive, many snakes are known occasionally to enter and even stay in houses and other dwellings. The names of such snakes sometimes indicate their habits: for example, the African House Snakes (*Lamprophis fuscus* and *Boaedon* species). Warmth, shelter and of course food (such as rats and mice) are the obvious attractions to snakes which share Man's dwellings.

One of the Asian lance-head snakes, the Okinawa Habu (*Trimeresurus flavoviridis*), is a slender, ground-dwelling snake which often enters houses in forested regions but also in urban areas, where it is no welcome guest. This notorious species is one of the Asiatic pit vipers which has heat-seeking organs as well as a potent venom. Many vipers and related species have pit organs beside each nostril and

these can detect warm-blooded prey at night. Many people have died from the bite of this aggressive and greatly feared snake, but the most serious problem concerning the Habu is that a large percentage of the 400 attacks which occur each year take place indoors or in the garden. Found on only a few islands such as Okinawa and Ryukyu, the Okinawa Habu is related to more than 30 other species which share the same habit of entering houses and biting people. Little can be done to keep them out because they can crawl through even the smallest hole or crevice in a wall or door.

For many years, scientists have investigated the invasive behaviour of the Habu but, although much is now known about the biology of this species, little can be done to prevent the large number of bites which continue to occur each year.

PROFILE

Length: *Usually up to 1.6 m (5.2 ft), but some specimens as long as 2 m (6.6 ft).*

Weight: *Up to about 470 g (about 1 lb).*

Distribution: *Limited to southwestern islands of Japan, including Okinawa and Ryukyu Islands.*

Habits/habitat: *Ground-dweller in forested regions. Has notorious invasive behaviour in residential areas.*

Breeding: *3–17 eggs laid between June and July; incubation takes 40–41 days.*

Diet: *Small rodents and frogs.*

Venom: *Haematoxin.*

Longevity: *Male 10 years, female 7 years.*

Notes: *Much research has been undertaken to prevent invasion by the Habu: some houses surrounded by concrete walls have fewer invasions than do houses with other types of walls or fences.*

CAECILIANS

The amphibians that look and behave like a worm

An amphibian without legs does not seem possible, but caecilians are limbless amphibians despite the fact that they look remarkably like worms — complete with a smooth, slimy skin and annulations along the length of a long, cylindrical body.

Amphibians are the group of animals which includes frogs, toads, newts and salamanders. They differ from reptiles in not having a dry scaly skin and in the fact that their eggs lack protective membranes. There is one other member of the amphibian class and that is the caecilians (*Caecilia*), the little-studied group of amphibians which have become specialised for a life without limbs.

There are more than 160 species of caecilians and other closely related species (Apoda), found mainly in tropical forested regions throughout the world. The various species, often brightly coloured, range in size from the smallest, 7 cm (2.8 in) and found in West Africa, to the longest, which occurs in Colombia and reaches 1.5 m (nearly 5 ft).

All caecilians have a worm-like body, with tiny eyes set below the surface of the skin. From their internal anatomy it is known that they are related to frogs and salamanders, but that many millions of years ago they underwent a dramatic change: they have since become burrowing amphibians and have lost all traces of limbs and limb girdles. They are the only survivors of an ancient group of early land animals. The young have external gills.

It seems that these burrowing animals feed mainly on earthworms and other invertebrates such as ants and termites. The bones in a caecilian's skull are very strong and enable it to push its head into the soil, rather like a garden trowel, when searching for food. Caecilians have a powerful jaw lined with rows of sharp teeth, suitable for grasping and cutting prey.

Some of the larger caecilians feed on small snakes, but large snakes will in turn feed on caecilians.

PROFILE

Length: *Most species are 24–30 cm (9.6–12 in).*

Weight: *Most species weigh 16–23 g (approximately 0.5–1.0 oz).*

Distribution: *Warm-temperate areas from Mexico to Argentina, in southern and southeast Asia, parts of Africa and in the Seychelles.*

Habitat: *Mainly forest; some in savanna areas, but only near rivers.*

Breeding: *Internal fertilisation; some produce eggs in a sticky string, but most species are viviparous (developing young are retained in the oviducts until metamorphosis is complete).*

Diet: *Earthworms, termites and other insects, small snakes and possibly young of small mammals.*

Longevity: *Not well researched.*

Notes: *Caecilians have an unusual sense organ, a tentacle on each side lying in a groove running from the eyes to the tip of the snout; this is thought to be for either olfaction or tactile senses.*

SHARP-RIBBED SALAMANDER

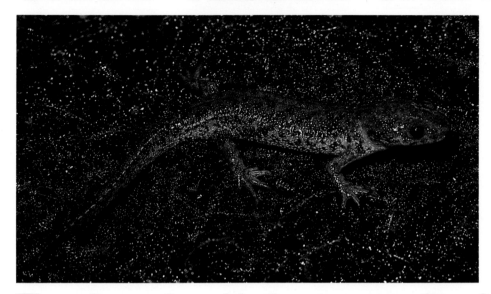

PROFILE

Length: *Up to 30 cm (12 in).*
Weight: *A specimen of 20 cm (8 in)
would weigh 16 g (0.6 oz).*
Distribution: *Morocco, and Iberia
except north and northeast regions.*
Habits/habitat: *Nocturnal species
inhabiting slow-moving rivers,
ponds, ditches.*
Breeding: *Eggs laid in clusters on
stones or aquatic plants.*
Diet: *Voracious, eating almost any
small invertebrate animal.*
Longevity: *Up to 20 years in captivity, but probably far less in the
wild.*

The salamander with the strangest ribs of all

Inoffensive-looking Sharp-ribbed Salamanders have an unusual means of defence in the form of ribs which are not only strong and well developed but actually stick through the animal's own skin.

The Salamandrids are a widespread family found throughout Europe, eastern Asia and both Atlantic and Pacific coasts of North America. Known from ancient times, the European species were thought by some to be able to live in fire. This myth arose because during winter salamanders escape the cold by sheltering underground or in cracks and holes of rotting logs; used for firewood, the logs would sometimes give forth salamanders as the flames warmed the once dormant animals.

Sharp-ribbed Salamanders (*Pleuro-deles waltl*) are robust, olive-coloured, rough-skinned animals, with strong tails which are at least as long as the body. They have a row of wart-like protuberances on the flanks which mark the position of the rib ends. When handled, the ends of the ribs can easily be detected where they push against the skin, and in some individuals the ribs actually pierce the skin and look like rows of teeth. The ends of these protruding ribs are sharp and can easily draw blood.

Why Sharp-ribbed Salamanders should have such unusual ribs is a mystery. Although strong swimmers, they have many potential predators, including a large variety of snakes; perhaps the sharp, sometimes protruding ribs of this strange salamander may just prevent it from being swallowed and so act as an excellent defence.

OLM

The doubtful amphibian

Living in the caves and underground streams and pools of Europe, the Olm is the strangest amphibian known to science and indeed scientists have not always been sure if it is an amphibian or a fish.

Not only is the Olm (*Proteus anguinus*) the strangest-looking amphibian, it also has the strangest habits of any amphibian. Olms are blind, white-coloured amphibians related to salamanders. They have a slender, cylindrical-shaped body, with short, feeble, thin legs. The front legs have three toes and the hindlegs two. Olms live in underground water systems where there is no light, and so the eyes have degenerated to tiny spots, just below the skin. The body of the Olm lacks pigment and is slightly translucent, but the external, feathery gills are red with blood.

Olms are strictly aquatic amphibians living in the underground streams of Yugoslavia and northern Italy, where they spend much of the time partially buried in mud or sand. Because they are strictly aquatic, they retain the feathery gills all their life.

Early records of the Olm refer to them as being the young of dragons swept out from underground rivers. Later, a more scientific examination pronounced that Olms had both fish-like and amphibian characteristics but, because they did not fit neatly into the classification of animals, Olms were sometimes omitted from books on animals or were referred to as either 'fish-lizards' or 'fish-newts'.

BLACK ALPINE SALAMANDER

PROFILE

Length: *15 cm (6 in)*.
Weight: *14 g (0.5 oz)*.
Distribution: *European Alps and mountainous regions of Yugoslavia and Albania.*
Habits/habitat: *Montane, wooded habitats; although mainly nocturnal, may be active in shady areas during the day.*
Breeding: *Becomes sexually mature after 2 years and gives birth to 1–4 young.*
Diet: *Primarily beetles, spiders and millipedes, and not earthworms as is often claimed.*

The only salamander whose young are cannibals before birth

The Alpine Salamander can breed without returning to water because it gives birth to live young miniature salamanders which have survived intra-uterine cannibalism and have been nourished on developing eggs and young within the parent's body.

Salamanders and newts are the so-called tailed amphibians, because the adult retains a long powerful tail. They are found in a variety of habitats and, although some are fully aquatic, the majority of salamanders are terrestrial. The skin of salamanders has no scales and is moist and soft, making it impossible for them to live in warm and dry habitats. The life cycle of salamanders typically includes three stages: egg, larval or tadpole, and adult.

Alpine Salamanders (*Salamandra atra*) are found in the mountains of Europe between 800 m (2600 ft) and 3000 m (9800 ft). They are not dependent on water but prefer to inhabit cool moist areas.

The Alpine Salamander is viviparous and gives birth to between one and four young, despite the fact that as many as 60 eggs would have been fertilised. The remarkable fact is that only the first few eggs develop fully, because the embryos feed on developing eggs and devour their own siblings while still in the mother's body; even some blood cells produced by the reproductive system provide some nourishment for the developing young. The surviving embryos metamorphose before birth, and so, therefore, this species of salamander does not need to return to water to breed.

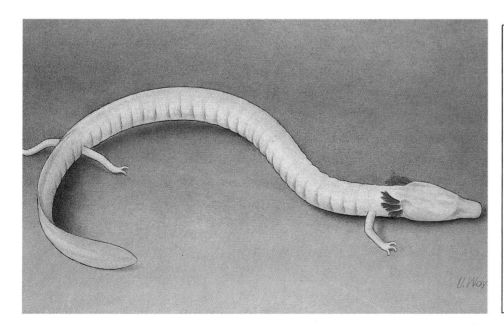

PROFILE

Length: *30 cm (12 in)*.
Weight: *26 g (almost 1.0 oz)*.
Distribution: *Yugoslavia, northern Italy.*
Habitat: *Underground caverns, streams, rivers.*
Breeding: *Internal fertilisation; sometimes gives birth to live young, but usually lays up to 40 eggs which take about 4 months to develop.*
Diet: *Being an agile swimmer, it easily catches small worms, crustacea and fish.*
Longevity: *Up to 15 years in captivity.*
Notes: *Olms are becoming increasingly rare because of pollution.*

CALIFORNIA NEWT

The amphibian with the deadly nerve poison

The California Newt has the ultimate in defence: its tissues and blood contain a most potent poison but, for some unknown reason, this poison does not affect the newt's own body tissues.

The tailed amphibians (Caudata) number about 360 species and are found in a great variety of habitats around the world. The salamanders and newts are the most common forms and both have a characteristically smooth, moist skin. Newts are the more aquatic forms, while the salamanders are well adapted for life out of water.

All newts are carnivorous and most are highly voracious predators of pond and river life. But although they are successful predators, newts are in turn eaten by a wide variety of animals, including snakes, birds, mammals and even beetles and large spiders. It has become necessary for newts to evolve anti-predatory mechanisms and defensive behaviour.

Many newts and salamanders (as well as other amphibians) have the ability to secrete poisons from numerous poison glands in their skin. In some species this poison is quite mild and either acts as an irritant or simply makes the newt taste unpleasant. In other species of newt, however, the poison is very toxic. The skin, muscles and blood of the California Newt (*Taricha torosa*) contain the highly toxic substance tetrodotoxin. This powerful nerve poison is also found in some other species of animal, such as the Puffer Fish.

The tetrodotoxin found in the California Newt is so powerful that one tiny drop would be sufficient to kill 7000 mice. The poison is contained in the tissues and eggs and does not harm the newt itself, but how the California Newt can protect itself from its own poison is not fully understood. It has been found that these newts are even immune to extremely high concentrations of this poison, concentrations which would very quickly deaden the nerve of a frog or toad.

PROFILE

Length: *6.8–8.8 cm (2.7–3.5 in); tail much longer than the body.*
Weight: *8 g (0.28 oz).*
Distribution: *Southern United States.*
Habitat: *Damp areas among leaf litter on forest floors and permanent water in wooded areas.*
Breeding: *Breeds December–May. Internal fertilisation; eggs, laid on vegetation, hatch into larvae which later metamorphose into adults.*
Diet: *Aquatic insect larvae and other arthropods and worms.*
Longevity: *Growth is very slow; may live for up to 12 years.*
Notes: *When molested, the California Newt throws its head back and the large tail is raised and arched over the whole body. Only some species of garter snakes have a tolerance of the California Newt's poison.*

HOCHSTETTER'S FROG

The most primitive of all anurans

Tail-wagging muscles and a very curious life history are just two of the remarkable characteristics of a small group of frogs found in New Zealand — archaic animal remnants on ancient islands.

The islands of New Zealand are geologically very old and form a country with some remarkable fauna and flora which have been isolated on those islands for many millions of years. The only native amphibians found in New Zealand are three species of frog — all in the same genus *Leiopelma*. One of these is called Hochstetter's Frog (*Leiopelma hochstetteri*), after the Austrian naturalist who visited New Zealand and collected some of these strange frogs in 1858.

Adults of all species of *Leiopelma* possess tail-wagging muscles, although no tail is visible. These muscles and other curious anatomical features would seem to be evidence that these frogs are survivors of a long-ago age when the evolution of frogs was in its infancy. During those ancient times, metamorphosis of tadpole to frog probably resulted in tailed frogs and toads; only during later periods of evolution would the

transformation to tail-less frogs be complete.

Hochstetter's Frogs and their two relatives live near very cold streams where the water temperature is always near 4°C (40°F).

They have a most interesting life history, with no free-swimming tadpole stage. Remarkable as it may seem, the tadpole develops into a tiny froglet while still encapsulated in a jelly-coated egg. The froglet first feeds on the remains of the egg and then later preys on tiny insects and spiders. Its rate of growth is relatively very slow and it does not reach the adult stage until three years after hatching.

The first positive record of a New Zealand native frog was not made until 1852 — during the gold rush. The other two species were not discovered until some time later, and now all three are protected.

PROFILE

Length: *Up to 4.2 cm (1.6 in).*
Weight: *8 g (0.3 oz).*
Distribution: *New Zealand, particularly in the remote parts of North Island.*
Habitat: *Cold mountain streams and damp forests.*
Breeding: *Up to about 8 eggs; development of tadpole and its metamorphosis take place within the egg capsule.*
Diet: *Tiny insects, spiders, millipedes and crustacea.*
Longevity: *Insufficient data.*
Notes: *The only other species of* Leiopelma *is found in northwest North America, evidence that these frogs are survivors of an ancient time when the continents formed great land masses.*

SURINAM TOAD

PROFILE

Length: *12–20 cm (4.8–8 in).*
Weight: *100–160 g (3.5–5.6 oz).*
Distribution: *Brazil and Guianas.*
Habits/habitat: *Strictly aquatic: lives on bottom in lakes, ponds and slow-moving streams.*
Breeding: *Up to 60 eggs.*
Diet: *Invertebrates, including tubifex worms, insect larvae, and small fish as well as debris.*
Longevity: *Insufficient data.*
Notes: *This well-camouflaged toad has long been a favourite aquarium animal. Since 1705 there has been much debate over how the eggs arrived on the toad's back, and whether or not it was the male or female which was the living incubator.*

The amphibian that uses its back as an incubator

A flat body, grotesque broad grin, no tongue, no teeth and tiny eyes may be unusual for a toad, but the breeding habits of the Surinam Toad are the most amazing of all the amphibian world.

Found in Brazil and the Guianas, the Surinam Toad (*Pipa pipa*) has the most amazing breeding behaviour. The skin on the female's flat, broad back swells as the male clasps her legs. The eggs (as many as 100) are fertilised as they emerge and the male then pushes them on to the spongy tissue of the female's back. This takes place during a remarkable series of underwater acrobatics: the toads flip themselves upside down to make it easier for the eggs to be positioned on the back of the female. Each egg sits in a tiny depression and is protected by a lid of tissue. Even more amazing is that the eggs hatch into normal tadpoles, but the tadpoles remain in their incubating chambers until metamorphosis; only when they have changed into toadlets do they then force open the lid and emerge from the chamber. The female toad is a living incubator for as long as two to four months.

For a long time it was a mystery how the tadpoles became enclosed in chambers on the female toad's back. One explanation was that the male actually collected up the eggs and placed them, one at a time, in single small chambers on the female's back.

Surinam Toads are experts in scavenging on the bottom of ponds and lakes. They are flattened in appearance and move along the bottom while their front legs and extended, sensitive fingers push food into a wide gaping mouth. Although they have no teeth and no tongue, their powerful limbs and muscular mouth soon overcome wriggling prey. As this toad lives on the bottom in murky water, its eyes have become tiny and almost useless.

RAIN FROG

The anuran that can't swim

The Rain Frog is quite remarkable in that, although its presence is associated with the onset of rain, it lives in habitats that are dry and well away from water, and it is likely to drown if put into water.

Mention frogs and you immediately think of ponds and wet grassy areas, where, indeed, many species of anurans (the tail-less amphibians, frogs and toads) are found. Some frogs have become adapted to dry conditions, and there are many desert frogs which have specialised mechanisms for preventing loss of body water in dry warm conditions.

The Rain Frog or Common Blaasop (*Breviceps adspersus*) is a very large species of the family of narrow-mouthed burrowing frogs (*Microhylidae*). These frogs are so stout that, although they are able to run or walk, they cannot hop.

Found in dry regions of southern Africa, the Rain Frog spends its entire life underground, except when it ventures forth prior to or during periods of torrential rain. On occasions it has appeared above ground just at the end of a drought, which has led to the strongly held belief that the Rain Frog somehow controls the rain.

Rain Frogs, unlike most other species of frogs, do not have to return to water to breed. They lay their eggs in moist sand or soil beneath logs or in specially prepared, smooth-walled burrows, at 30–45 cm (12–18 in) below the surface. They have powerful limbs and spade-like projections on their hindfeet for burrowing. Mating takes place beneath the ground and the eggs are laid in small clumps of jelly within the burrow. The tadpoles never leave the eggs and, in a remarkable fashion, development takes place in the eggs until metamorphosis is complete.

It has been found that Rain Frogs are not able to swim and can easily drown if dropped into water. They escape by inflating their body and floating to safety.

PROFILE

Length: *5.5 cm (2.2 in), male much smaller than female.*
Weight: *5 g (0.17 oz).*
Distribution: *Parts of southern Africa.*
Habitat: *Scrubland, coastal sand dunes, deserts.*
Breeding: *Lays 20–40 eggs in smooth-walled burrow on land; tadpoles develop in the egg.*
Diet: *Subterranean insects, especially termites; earthworms.*
Longevity: *Insufficient data.*
Notes: *Inflating itself to look like a hard round ball (hence the name Blaasop, literally 'blown up') is this frog's one means of defence, but it also produces droplets of a white sticky irritant from its skin.*

HAIRY FROG

PROFILE

Length: *10 cm (4 in).*
Weight: *80 g (2.8 oz).*
Distribution: *Cameroons, West Africa.*
Habitat: *Fast-flowing streams.*
Breeding: *Spawns in fast-flowing water and the eggs are stuck to the underside of rocks.*
Diet: *Small invertebrates, particularly snails; possibly also small mammals.*
Longevity: *4–5 years.*
Notes: *Unlike in most other frogs, the male is larger than the female.*

The anuran that fails to live up to its name

One of the greatest biological mysteries is the so-called Hairy Frog, which does not have hairs and which has been given the most inappropriate name.

The Hairy Frog (*Astylosternus robustus*) is found in streams running through the great forests of the Cameroons of West Africa. Little is known about this species of frog and indeed it is not at all easy to find. The males have very remarkable cutaneous growths of hair-like filaments on the flanks and sides, which are particularly noticeable during the breeding season. Many suggestions have been made as to the function of these filaments: as sensory organs, defence organs, attachments for eggs, poison outlets and camouflage.

On cursory examination, these filaments may have a hair-like appearance, but they are certainly not hairs. They are about 1 cm (less than 0.5 in) long, and are in fact vascular papillae or tiny 'accessory gills' that are used, together with the lungs and the skin, for respiration. Although frogs do have a lung, their skin is well supplied with blood vessels and therefore it can be used for gas exchange. But why the Hairy Frog should have 'accessory gills' is a mystery, because it lives in fast-flowing streams where the water is highly oxygenated.

Hairy Frogs are often seen clinging to wet slippery rocks around waterfalls. To do this they have specially modified fingers and toes which have claws bent sharply downwards for gripping cracks and rough rock surfaces. These claws can be an effective defence against predators, as anybody who has handled these little frogs will know. Croaking and grunting in defence, the Hairy Frog can use its claws to draw blood on a man's finger.

Hairy Frogs are very agile predators. They feed on snails and they possibly attack and eat very small mammals.

SOUTH AFRICAN SHARP-NOSED FROG

The little fellow with a big kick

The South African Sharp-nosed Frog may not be the largest frog in the world, but its long limbs can propel its streamlined, stocky body over far greater distances than any other known species of frog can do.

A few frogs are strictly aquatic, some only walk, but most of the 2510 species are capable of leaps and bounds.

Although all frogs have a similar body shape (no neck, no tail, a squat-shaped body and well-developed limbs), there is tremendous variation in jumping performance. This variation exists both between species and between individuals of the same species. Even one individual will vary greatly in its jumping performance, and there can also be variation in the length of successive jumps.

The larger individuals of any one species can jump farther than small ones. In terms of jumping ability (jumping distance divided by body length, however, the young frogs jump proportionally farther than do adults.

It is not the largest species that have the longest jumps. In one detailed study of the jumping performance of 82 species of frogs from all around the world, the species with the longest jump—of 227 cm (91 in)—was only 5 cm (2 in) long. This leap falls far short of the recorded jumps for the South African Sharp-nosed Frog (*Ptychadena oxyrhynchus*). In three jumps, this active, elusive and long-legged species covered 967.5 cm (32 ft), about 160 times its own body length. This was witnessed by several people, including a zoologist. There is a further, unconfirmed, report that this species made a single leap of over 457 cm (15 ft).

After the Sharp-nosed Frog has propelled itself into the air by its strong, long limbs, it is possible that its long, pointed nose may decrease wind resistance and so increase jumping ability.

PROFILE

Length: *Male 5.5 cm (2.2 in), female 6.6 cm (2.6 in).*
Weight: *Averages about 30 g (1 oz).*
Distribution: *Low-altitude areas of central and southern Africa.*
Habits/habitat: *Grass verges of ponds and streams; not seen during the day and gathers at night.*
Breeding: *Begins to spawn shortly after start of the rainy season.*
Diet: *Mainly insects, but also other small invertebrates.*
Longevity: *Probably 4–5 years.*
Notes: *Breeding as it does in small ponds (sometimes temporary pools) in grass savanna, this small frog needs the longest leaps to escape from the many predators. Unlike the spawn of other grass frogs, the spawn of this species floats on the water surface, then later sinks, where it attaches itself to vegetation.*

GOLDEN ARROW-POISON FROG

The most deadly of all amphibians

Secretions from the skin of Golden Arrow-poison Frogs have for centuries been used by South American Indians as a deadly and effective poison which, when used on arrow tips, can kill large prey in seconds.

The Dendrobatids (arrow-poison frogs) are small, highly coloured frogs which live only in Central and South America. Many amphibians have skin glands which produce a mild irritant, but the skin glands of Dendrobatid frogs produce an incredibly powerful poison: the skin secretions from one species are the most powerful known animal venom and just 0.00001 g (0.0000004 oz) is enough to kill a person. The poison from only one Golden Arrow-poison Frog (*Dendrobates auratus*) is sufficient for use on up to 40 arrows.

It was the Indians of Central and South America who long ago developed a skilful but somewhat unpleasant method of extracting and applying the poison. The little frogs are killed by piercing them with a long, thin stick and then the poison is extracted by gently heating them over a fire; small droplets of the poison appear as the body of the frog becomes warm. The arrows are then dipped into a fermented form of the secretion and dried.

The secretion from the Golden Arrow-poison Frog can quickly and easily result in muscular paralysis, so this poison has been of particular value to the Indians hunting small mammals high in the forest canopy.

Arrow-poison frogs, although very small, are most highly and beautifully coloured. Most have contrasting colours such as yellow and black or iridescent green and black. It is these bright colours that act as a warning to would-be predators.

Although not much study has been carried out on the Dendrobatids, the frogs are known to have remarkable breeding habits. The female produces six eggs which are then cared for by the male, who later carries the tadpoles on his back to a place of safety.

PROFILE

Length: *4 cm (1.6 in).*
Weight: *10 g (0.3 oz).*
Distribution: *Central and South America.*
Habitat: *Moist tropical and temperate forests.*
Breeding: *6 eggs, cared for by the male.*
Diet: *Very small insects and other tiny invertebrates.*
Longevity: *Short lifespan, 2–3 years.*
Notes: *Closely related to the Golden Arrow-poison Frog is a Cuban frog* Sminthillus limbatus—*the smallest frog in the world, measuring only 8–12 mm (less than 0.5 in) and laying only 1 egg at a time.*

TREE FROGS

Acrobatic clowns of the amphibian world

The most conspicuous feature of the many species of tree frogs found throughout the world is the adhesive discs on their hands and toes, but there is more to being a tree frog than just modified toes.

There are about 500 species of tree frogs found throughout the world apart from Antarctica. Tree frogs range in size from a giant species in the West Indies (*Hyla vasta*), with an average length of 9 cm (3.6 in), to the tiny Least Tree Frog (*Hyla ocularis*) of the southern United States, with a maximum length of just 1.5 cm (0.6 in).

The Common European Tree Frog (*Hyla arborea*) has a very wide range, including the south of England where it was introduced earlier this century. It is medium-sized, up to about 5 cm (2 in), with very long limbs relative to the body size. It would be easy prey for many predators were it not for its nocturnal activity and the bright, shiny green colour of its skin, which gives excellent camouflage during the day.

Tree frogs are extremely agile and climb very extensively, sometimes far off the ground. They can cling to the most delicate of twigs, walk along narrow branches and leap among stems and branches like an acrobatic clown. The little Cricket Frog (*Acris gryllus*), a North American tree frog only 3 cm (1.2 in) long, can jump up to 35 times its own length and can also leap at about the same speed as a person walking.

The disc-like adhesive pads enable these frogs to cling to branches and leaves, but the long thin toes can also be used to grab a branch or a twig as they leap about catching insects. Active mainly at night, they have a very keen eyesight and spend much of their time hunting for food. Some species have partially webbed hindfeet, and it is these which help the frogs to glide from branch to branch.

PROFILE

Length: *Adult European Tree Frog up to 5 cm (2 in).*

Weight: *European Tree Frog 18 g (0.6 oz).*

Distribution: *European Tree Frog is found in most of Europe except northern regions.*

Habitat: *Well-vegetated areas near water or swamps and bogs, damp meadows and woodland edges.*

Breeding: *During early summer, spawn produced in foam clusters about the size of a walnut.*

Diet: *Mostly night-flying insects, but also other invertebrates.*

Longevity: *6 years.*

Notes: *Breeding chorus is extremely loud and from a distance it sounds like quacking ducks.*

DARWIN'S FROG

Froglets that breed inside the father's vocal sacs

Discovered in the Argentine by Charles Darwin during the famous voyage of the Beagle, the little Darwin's Frog has a most remarkable method of looking after its young: the minute newly hatched tadpoles are taken into the male's vocal sac.

Frogs and toads are a most successful group of animals, living in a wide variety of habitats ranging from deserts to the trees of tropical rainforests. What is even more notable is the variation in reproduction and development among the 3500 species. Many produce large masses of spawn which is then left to the fate of nature. Some species of frog lay only a few eggs and then protect them from predators; the extent of protection ranges from looking over them to actually carrying the eggs around, loosely attached to the body or in pouches on the frog's back.

The most remarkable form of parental care among frogs is that of mouth-brooding. Two species of mouth-brooding frogs are known from South America, one of these being the famous Darwin's Frog (*Rhinoderma darwinii*),

a small, slender frog and the sole member of the family Rhinodermatidae. Each female produces 20–40 eggs on land which are then guarded by the male for up to 20 days, until hatching commences. Just as the tadpoles are hatching, the male frog gathers them up (about 10–15 at a time) with his tongue and slides them into his relatively immense vocal sacs, where they develop. Each tadpole is nourished by its own individual egg yolk sac.

When only about 1 cm (0.4 in) long, the miniature tadpoles have lost most of their tail. They then leave the male's vocal sacs and continue with normal development.

This remarkable mouth-brooding is matched only by the Australian frog *Rheobatrachus silus*, in which the female takes the tadpoles not into the

vocal sac, but into the stomach, where the process from egg to tadpole to froglet takes place.

PROFILE

Length: *2.6 cm (just over 1 in).*
Weight: *Less than 2 g (0.07 oz).*
Distribution: *Chile and the southern Argentine.*
Habitat: *Shallow, cool streams in moist temperate forests.*
Breeding: *20–40 eggs, taken up by the male for development in the enlarged vocal sac.*
Diet: *Tiny insects and small worms.*
Longevity: *Insufficient data.*
Notes: *Darwin's Frog is unmistakable, as it has a narrow, pointed, false nose.*

PARADOXICAL FROG

The giant that turns into a dwarf

Most frogs metamorphose from small tadpoles into larger froglets, but for some unknown reason the aptly named Paradoxical Frog starts life as a gigantic tadpole, many times larger than the adult frog, and later shrinks when it changes to a frog.

The Pseudidae family of frogs includes several groups of highly aquatic species that inhabit the South American continent. They have no close relatives in the amphibian world and they have proved very difficult to study because, although they are often heard, they are rarely seen.

The most puzzling species is the Paradoxical Frog (*Pseudis paradoxus*), which has the most disproportionate size between tadpole and adult. So different is the size, with the frog being much smaller than the tadpole, that scientists for many years could not believe that the tadpole or larva stage and the adult frog belonged to the same species. The tadpoles grow to a length of 16.8 cm (almost 7 in) and some have even reached the astonishing length of 25 cm (10 in).

These giant tadpoles have a rounded body, large eyes and a high dorsal fin. By contrast, the adult frog is a tiny 5.6 cm (2.2 in) in length or even less. This phenomenon is very rare; it involves not only the whole animal becoming smaller in size, but the vital organs such as heart and gut also seem to shrink. No one knows why this strange reduction in size occurs and no one has been able to suggest what advantage it could be to the Paradoxical Frog.

Paradoxical Frogs are excellent swimmers and spend much of their time in water. If frightened, they can suddenly dive and stir up the muddy bottom of the marsh or pond. A peculiar feature of their toes is that each has an extra joint. Such long toes are a particular advantage for stirring up the muddy bottom, where they can hide or find

small insect larvae which constitutes their food.

PROFILE

Length: *Frog up to 5.6 cm (2.2 in); tadpole 16.8 cm (6.7 in).*
Weight: *30 g (1 oz).*
Distribution: *Amazon and Trinidad.*
Habitat: *Permanent marshes alongside great rivers or major lagoons.*
Breeding: *Eggs laid in a frothy mass among aquatic plants.*
Diet: *Insect larvae and other small invertebrates.*
Longevity: *Insufficient data.*
Notes: *The local inhabitants catch the tadpoles and eat them as a great delicacy.*

INSECTS AND ARACHNIDS

Insects and arachnids (spiders, scorpions and mites) are the most successful animals on earth. They were among the first land-dwelling animals over 400 million years ago. Not only are they the oldest land animals but also the most abundant and widespread. Except for the polar regions they are found everywhere, often in huge numbers.

As competitors with Man they are ferocious, and their powers of rapid multiplication make them almost impossible to exterminate. In spite of Man's battle with them, it is probable that we could not have existed without them! Their numerous activities provide benefits for us, even if they also create problems. They pollinate flowers, producing not only fruit and seed but also honey from the bees. Insects are also responsible for helping in the control of weeds and in the removal of dead animals. What would a warm summer's day be without the hum of bees and the activities of brightly coloured butterflies?

Insects and arachnids have many characters in common, but also several fundamental differences. They have an external skeleton, and their bodies are made up of a number of segments. The two groups have different ways of getting air into the body for respiration. Most insects have a network of tracheoles (narrow tubes running through the body and opening to the outside through spiracles). Many arachnids have cavities that contain gills which, from their resemblance to the pages of a book, are called lung-books. The insect body is divided into three main divisions—head, thorax and abdomen—while most arachnids have the head and thorax combined (cephalothorax). Arachnids also lack the compound eyes found in many adult insects, having simple ocelli. Many insects have antennae, long 'feelers' which are covered with microscopic sense organs; arachnids have two short, paired structures called pedipalps. Generally insects have three pairs of legs, while the arachnids have four pairs. Any small arthropod with wings is an insect; no arachnids have wings, but not all insects have them either.

SPRINGTAILS

The insects with the built-in 'pogo-stick'

The majority of springtails have a built-in 'pogo-stick' at the tip of the abdomen and its use gives the group their name.

Unquestionably, springtails (order Collembola) are the oldest group of six-legged animals. Although popularly considered insects, they are now regarded as a separate group. The oldest known springtail has been found in rocks at Rhynie, Scotland, which are known to be over 400 million years old.

Although all springtails are wingless, they are among the most widespread and abundant creatures and occur world-wide. They live in plant debris, under bark and in a wide variety of habitats — even on the surface of glaciers. Their abundance in meadowlands and litter has been quoted as 2000 specimens in 1 litre (60 cu. in) of soil! They can be found on the surface of water, where they move freely around, held up by the surface tension. Some springtails live on the surface of seashore rocks and pools

and are regularly submerged by high tides. Most species are harmless and assist in the breakdown of plant debris, but a few, such as the 'Lucerne Flea', are crop pests.

The Glacier Springtail or Snow Flea is active at low temperatures. It can move around and jump even when the temperature is below freezing point, when most other insects would be inactive or killed. Most springtails multiply rapidly under suitable conditions; this can result in huge numbers suddenly appearing, even on the surface of snow!

Springtails use their spring as an escape mechanism. They have a modified appendage at the tip of the abdomen which is folded back under the body. This appendage (the furcula) is usually forked at the tip and engages on a catch under the third abdominal seg-

ment. Muscles in the body produce tension and the furcula suddenly breaks free of the catch, projecting the springtail into the air.

PROFILE

Size: *Body length 1–5 mm (0.04–10.2 in).*
Distribution: *Worldwide.*
Food: *Fungal hyphae, plants, algae, pollen, leaf litter.*
Habits/habitat: *Soil-dwelling, in leaf litter, under bark; also on surface of ponds, rockpools, glaciers and snow.*
Notes: *Very abundant: turn over any old flowerpot or log left untouched on the ground and underneath you will see tiny white springtails jumping like fleas.*

DRAGONFLIES

The insects with six legs that cannot walk

The larger dragonflies use their legs in flight to catch insects but, although they use the legs for perching, they cannot really walk on them.

The damselflies (sub-order Zygoptera), which are smaller dragonflies (sub-order Anisoptera), are able to use their legs to move up plant stems when they perch, but the large dragonflies can hardly move on the ground. This is due to the shape of their thorax and the position of their legs, which point forward. The legs form a basket in which insects are caught in flight and then transferred to the jaws.

Dragonflies are a very ancient group. Giant dragonfly-like insects with wingspans of 75 cm (30 in) were flying over 300 million years ago, and true dragonflies were flying well over 200 million years ago. The large dragonflies hold their wings at right angles to the body and cannot fold them. The largest living dragonfly, from South America, has a wingspan of around 19 cm (7.5 in).

Dragonflies are useful and totally harmless insects. One of their names, 'horse-stinger', is a misnomer since they neither sting nor bite mammals. They feed on flying insects and are therefore useful to Man. Dragonfly larvae are aquatic, and are popularly known as freshwater sharks. They are voracious predators, catching aquatic insects, small fish and tadpoles.

Mating of dragonflies and damselflies is unlike that of other insects. The males of the larger species grasp the females behind the head and curl their bodies around, forming a 'wheel' of the two insects. They may even fly in this mating wheel position.

The dragonflies' forewings and hindwings beat alternately, not together as in most insects. This gives them even more flight control and they can hover, move backwards or dart forwards at high speed.

Mating Gomphus plagiatus, *USA.*

PROFILE

Size: *Largest dragonfly has wingspan of 19 cm (7.5 in); large* Anax *species have 100-mm (3.9-in) span. Damselflies usually smaller.*

Distribution: *Worldwide; most numerous in the tropics, usually near fresh water.*

Habits/habitat: *Rarely found far from water except on migration. Larvae aquatic, except one species in Hawaii whose larvae are terrestrial.*

Diet: *Adults feed on flying insects; aquatic larvae prey on other aquatic insects, small fish and tadpoles.*

Notes: *Many species are territorial and will chase other dragonflies away.*

COCKROACHES

One of the earth's greatest survivors

Cockroaches have been on our planet for over 300 million years; they were abundant in the swamp forests which later turned into coal, and 3500 species still exist today.

In the layers of earth around coal there are countless numbers of fossilised cockroaches. These were often larger than present-day cockroaches, but there were also many small ones which lived in the dense swamp forests of the Carboniferous period. This was a time when flowering plants, dinosaurs, birds and Man were many millions of years in the future. Pterodactyls developed and became extinct, as did the dinosaurs; the continents threw up great mountain ranges, and great upheavals separated the Americas from Europe; ice ages came and went; but throughout all this vast time cockroaches were common insects. They lived on rotting vegetation; they could fly; their flattened shape allowed them to slip through narrow gaps, as Man later discovered when they started appearing in his buildings. In short, they had arrived at a successful

structural plan early in evolution and, apart from diversifying and expanding into even more habitats, remain relatively unchanged.

Cockroaches are able to eat an incredible variety of foods, and also many other items such as boot polish, book bindings and even human toenails! Their gut contains protozoa, simple unicellular animals which break down these 'foods'. They are indiscriminate scavengers and their habit of going from rubbish dumps and suchlike to human habitations makes them potential disease-carriers.

Modern cockroaches (family Blattidae) lay their eggs in purse-like capsules. The tiny cockroaches on hatching are like wingless miniatures of their parents, and take ten months to a year to become mature and develop wings. There are about 3500 species of cockroach known today. Theirs is really a long-running success story!

PROFILE

Size: *Tropical species over 50 mm (1.97 in). Cosmopolitan household pests:* Blatta orientalis *25 mm (0.98 in);* B. germanica *16 mm (0.63 in);* Periplaneta americana *38 mm (1.50 in).*

Distribution: *Worldwide.*

Habits/habitat: *Rapid runners, usually nocturnal; some can fly. A few cosmopolitan species associated with Man; especially common in rotting vegetation.*

Diet: *Scavengers, many species able to live on any organic remains.*

Notes: *These are household pests, which spoil more food than they eat.*

PRAYING MANTISES

PROFILE

Size: *Varies according to species.
Mantis religiosa: female 65 mm
(2.6 in), male smaller.*
Distribution: *Most abundant in
tropics and subtropics; several
species in southern Europe.*
Habits/habitat: *Often sit motionless.
Live in a wide variety of habitats.*
Diet: *Insects. Some of the larger
species catch small lizards.*
Notes: *The male's sex drive is such
that mating will continue even after
he has had his head bitten off. The
female gets a mate and a meal in
one!*

Holy terrors

To the female mantis the male is just another meal, and he has to be very careful when approaching or she will seize and eat him.

There are many species of praying mantis (family Mantidae) in the warmer parts of the world. Their apt name comes from their habit of sitting motionless with their 'arms' outstretched in supplication, but they are really after food and indeed are sometimes called 'preying mantids' from the way they catch it. Their front legs are specially modified for grasping prey, usually other insects, and then carrying them up to their strong jaws. These legs are like the blades of a penknife, snapping back to catch their prey.

Mantids sit quietly, waiting for an unsuspecting insect to land near. Sometimes the insect does not see the mantis and walks into the trap; at other times the mantis stalks its prey stealthily and then suddenly grabs it.

Because of their need to be camouflaged, mantids are frequently green or green and brown to match the plants they sit on. Some even take the colours of the plant's flowers, and an unsuspecting insect may not notice until too late that one of the pink petals on a pink flower is a deadly trap. Sitting still,

the mantids themselves are liable to be eaten by birds. Although their camouflage helps conceal them, a few species have taken the deception further. On each forewing they have two rounded patches, usually with lighter centres, which resemble eyes and are called

eyespots. A predator coming near the mantis is suddenly confronted with two 'eyes' which, especially if the mantis spreads its wings a little, make the predator think it is being confronted by a large animal. This is usually enough to frighten away small mammals and birds.

DESERT LOCUST

The world's most destructive insect

One of the biblical plagues, this big grasshopper has been an affliction to Man ever since he started to grow crops.

Locusts are found on most continents, but the Desert Locust (*Schistocerca gregaria*) is a particular pest of Central and North Africa. It also ranges over the Middle East, India and Pakistan and is probably the single most destructive insect in the world.

These locusts have a real Jekyll and Hyde character. For many generations they live relatively solitary lives and behave like most other large grasshoppers. Their eggs hatch into miniature adults, but without wings or fully developed reproductive organs, which feed on plants, grow and moult, and eventually become adult. This is the solitary phase, which is harmless.

Under certain conditions, however, for example when the land is flooded and many locusts have laid their eggs in a small area of ground, the newly hatched hoppers change their behaviour, start congregating and move off in groups. They are darker than during the solitary phase and so warm up more and become more active, and their wings become longer. This is the gregarious or swarming phase, when they can become devastating pests.

If these groups meet others, they join together until there is a vast swarm eating everything in its path. This is terrible enough, but these immature locusts are still flightless at this stage. This is the time when they can be sprayed with some hope of saving the crops. As their numbers increase, they become more active. Finally the wings develop. Huge aerial swarms form which may eventually travel over thousands of miles, totally devastating the crops wherever they land.

Eventually the swarm breaks up, perhaps through weather changes, and the next lot of eggs may not produce another gregarious-phase locust.

PROFILE

Size: *Male 45–55 mm (1.77–2.17 in) long, female 50–60 mm (1.97–2.36 in).*

Distribution: *Africa, Middle East, Pakistan, North India.*

Habits/habitat: *Solitary phase lives like an ordinary grasshopper; gregarious one in swarms.*

Food: *Living plants.*

Notes: *A few Desert Locusts fly to Europe in most years, and some may reach northern Europe including Britain. They are not a pest outside the tropics and subtropics.*

GIANT WETA

The world's most formidable cricket

With a length of 10 cm (4 in) and spiny hindlegs twice as long, this ugly giant cricket can easily inflict a nasty wound on anybody who picks it up.

There is no doubt that the Giant Weta (*Deinacridia heteracantha*) is not an insect one would readily pick up! It is harmless, but it looks, and is, very fearsome and spiny. The mask-like head and spiny appearance does not endear it to us. It lives in trees where it is remarkably well camouflaged and can be quite difficult to see despite its size. The females are larger than the males and have long, sword-like ovipositors for egg-laying; they may lay up to 600 eggs.

The Giant Weta has long featured in Maori mythology as the feared Weta-punga, 'the Ugly Thing'. It has formidable jaws with which it chews fleshy leaves, but it is omnivorous and will eat any insect it manages to catch. Its huge, strongly spiny hindlegs can be moved up and down to make a distinctive rasping

sound. The powerful jaws would certainly give anybody bold enough to pick it up a sharp nip, but the hindlegs, as it struggled, would be more likely to inflict damage. The spines will certainly scratch a person, not particularly painfully but the scratch may become infected.

There are several species of weta in New Zealand. Some of them live in caves, while other ground-living ones are called 'invertebrate mice'. Wetas are an ancient group: fossils are known from over 180 million years ago. The Giant Wetas formerly occurred on the mainland of New Zealand, but are now confined to a few offshore islands. Several species of weta, including the Giant Weta, are classed as vulnerable (to extinction) in the *Insect Red Data Book* and are now protected species.

PROFILE

Size: *Up to 10 cm (4 in) long (including ovipositor) and 18 mm (0.7 in) wide; hindlegs up to 20 cm (8 in) long.*
Weight: *47–70 g (1.7–2.8 oz).*
Distribution: *New Zealand.*
Habits/habitat: *Nocturnal; usually solitary. Giant Wetas are arboreal. Some weta species live in caves, others on ground among rocks.*
Food: *Leaves and insects.*
Notes: *The Giant Weta is now rare and is protected by law, but its survival is threatened by rats accidentally introduced into New Zealand.*

TERMITES

Size: *Workers from 3.5 mm (0.14 in); queen (Macrotermes) 14 cm (5.5 in) long, 35 mm (1.4 in) wide. European species 5–10 mm (0.2– 0.39 in).*

Distribution: *Tropics and subtropics; into southern Europe as far north as Bordeaux.*

Habits/habitat: *Colonial; different 'castes' do different jobs for the colony. Most live in grasslands.*

Food: *Plants, wood. Gut contains symbiotic organisms which break down wood to more digestible sub- stances.*

Notes: *Not related to ants, despite alternative name of 'white ants'. Not all build mounds. Dry-wood termites live on trees and often attack the wood in buildings or burrow into furniture.*

Master builders of the insect world

To build their intricate nests, worker termites painstakingly put each grain of soil in place and cement it with saliva; the final building, a masterpiece of construction, will house millions of termites.

The huge nests of termites (order Isop- tera) which tower over the landscape in the tropics and subtropics may be 30 m (100 ft) or more in diameter, and each species constructs nests with a particular shape. Some of the African species build narrow towers over 8 m (26 ft) high. In *Macrotermes* species these tow- ers constitute the cooling system for an elaborate nest whose intricate structure, fungus gardens and foodstores are all the result of the co-operation of the social termites within the nest. In each colony, which may eventually contain millions of individuals, there is division of labour. The queen is the 'egg-laying machine', and in some species may grow to 14 cm (5.5 in) long and 35 mm (1.4 in) wide. The most numerous ones are the workers. These have powerful jaws but are wingless; their jobs are nest- building, maintenance and finding food for the colony. Less numerous, but conspicuous, are the soldier termites, whose sole duty is guarding the nest. Different species have different types of soldiers: some have a large head with a snout from which they produce a sticky substance which disables attackers; others, with large heads and huge jaws, rush in to attack anything that tries to get into the nest. Some termites even have soldiers which, when the nest is invaded by ants, block off the tunnels by swelling up and then literally exploding, covering the attacker with all the guts of the soldier termite!

The termite nest is riddled with tun- nels, with the queen living in the central chamber. At certain times, more fe- males and males are produced and these are winged. At dusk they leave the nest in thousands, like a fluttering mass of snowflakes. Eventually, after the mating flight, a female will found another termite colony.

PERIODIC CICADA

Seventeen years growing up, but only four weeks as an adult

Of this insect's 17 years of life, only the last four weeks are spent above ground as an adult, the rest of the time being spent in the young stage under ground.

The Periodic Cicada (*Magicicada septemdecim*) gets its alternative name, Seventeen-Year Cicada, from the length of its life cycle. For an insect, the Periodic Cicada is very long-lived. In the southern United States the cycle from egg to adult takes 13 years, while in more northerly parts the whole life cycle takes 17 years.

Cicadas have sucking mouthparts with a short proboscis which they stick into plants to suck the juices. The nymphs, living underground, feed on the roots of trees. The adult cicada makes a slit in a twig and inserts its eggs with a sword-like ovipositor. The nymphs hatch, get to the ground and then dig down with their spade-like front legs. They feed underground,

growing slowly. At times quite large numbers emerge together, and because of their local abundance they are sometimes wrongly called 'locusts'. Before emerging from the ground, the nymphs make little tubes or chimneys of earth in which the final transformation from nymph to adult is achieved.

Like all cicadas, the adult Periodic Cicada makes a loud noise and many of them together in chorus can be deafening. The sound is made by rapid movement of a membrane or 'tymbal' which may oscillate up to 500 times a second. Behind this membrane is a resonating chamber which amplifies the sound. Usually it is the male which makes the sound. Each species of cicada has its own frequency or rhythm and this is

recognised by the females of the species, who are attracted to the singing males.

PROFILE

Size: *Body length 26 mm (1 in), wing-span 76 mm (2.9 in).*
Distribution: *North America.*
Habitat: *Woodlands.*
Diet: *Plant sap sucked with short rostrum (proboscis) in adult and young stages.*
Notes: *Usually only males sing. Other species of cicada occur in southern Europe, and one is found very locally in Britain in the New Forest, Hampshire.*

GREENFLY

Rapid breeders which can ruin our crops

Capable of producing young without mating, greenfly in huge numbers can destroy plants and transmit diseases from one plant to another.

Greenfly or aphids (family Aphidae) are some of the commonest insects that affect not only our garden and crop plants but also those in greenhouses; even indoor plants can be affected. They feed by inserting their elongate mouthparts into the plant and sucking the plant juices. By this method the greenfly not only helps to drain the plant's vitality but also transmits viruses from one plant to another. Their rate of reproduction is prodigious, and for much of the year the young nymphs are born asexually — by parthenogenesis or 'virgin birth'. Only at the onset of less favourable conditions does mating occur.

There are many different species, but not all green; some, such as the aphid pest of beans, are black (blackflies). Many species have a complicated life cycle, with two different host plants. In the autumn the winged male and female aphids are produced, and after mating, the female lays her eggs. These hatch in the following spring into wingless nymphs which soon grow into adults, still without wings; once fully grown, each one starts to produce young by parthenogenesis. These young stages, which are like small editions of the mother aphid, grow rapidly and produce yet more young. The result is a huge population rapidly built up of many wingless aphids. Among them are some winged ones. These fly to another host plant and in turn produce many more aphids. This potential for rapid increase means that one female in a season can produce many millions of offspring.

Fortunately, many of the aphids fall prey to birds, green lacewings, ladybirds and other valuable predators. Although they affect our crops, many species attack plants we consider weeds so, while they do a lot of harm, some of them may be beneficial.

Aphids produce a sweet liquid called honeydew. This is much sought after by ants, which can be seen attending aphids on plants.

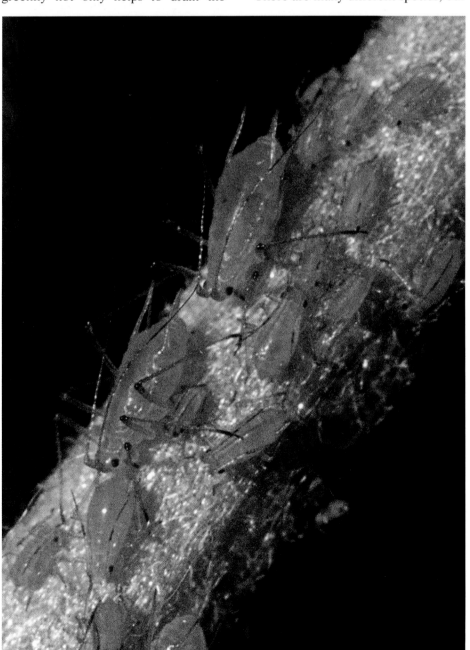

PROFILE

Size: *Majority 2–3 mm (0.08–1.12 in) long, some a little larger.*

Distribution: *Worldwide.*

Habits/habitat: *Found in most situations, both in temperate zones and in the tropics. In temperate zones a pest in greenhouses and on ornamental plants.*

Food: *All feed on plants, sucking the sap.*

Notes: *Transmission of viruses by aphids is a serious problem. Damage on plants frequently causes the curling and distortion of leaves.*

FROGHOPPERS

Philaenus spumarius

Blowing bubbles for its own protection

By blowing bubbles from the end of its body, the young froghopper produces a blanket of foam in which it hides from predators.

Froghoppers or spittlebugs (family Cercopidae) are also known as cuckoo-spit insects. In late spring and summer small patches of foam appear mysteriously on many plants. Since it seemed to appear when the Cuckoo returned to Europe, people thought that it was Cuckoo spit. If the foam is gently blown away a small, usually greenish, insect will be revealed. If you watch carefully, you will see small bubbles begin to appear from the end of its body; gradually the insect covers itself with foam and then stays well hidden under this unlikely blanket.

The insect is the young stage (nymph) of a froghopper, a rather inconspicuous insect when adult. Its name comes from the sudden leap it makes to escape. Froghoppers all feed on plant sap.

Although we can blow the foam off the insect, it is generally unaffected by wind or even heavy rain. Apart from concealing the insect, it also helps to protect the nymph against desiccation. The foam is produced from water which the froghopper nymph takes in from the plant as it feeds. This water is mixed with a slightly viscous substance from glands in the abdomen and then blown out to produce the froth. Many nymphs in a meadow can produce a prodigious amount of foam which can soak the clothes of a person walking through. Some species in the tropics produce large quantities of liquid which drip off the trees in a continuous patter like rain.

Unlike the rather sluggish nymph, the adult is a very active insect but it does not produce foam. While it can walk among the vegetation, when disturbed it produces the characteristic leap. Although the majority of spittlebugs do little damage there are a few species which can damage plants of economic importance.

PROFILE

Size: *Small: e.g.* Propsapia bicinta *(USA) 8–12 mm (0.31–0.47 in);* Philaenus spumarius *(Europe) 5–7 mm (0.20–0.28 in).*

Distribution: *Worldwide.*

Habits/habitat: *Wide variety of habitats, often common in pasturelands. Some are exclusively tree feeders.*

Food: *Sap from grasses, herbaceous plants, shrubs and trees.*

Notes: *In spite of the protective froth, the nymphs are still vulnerable to some parasitic and predatory insects.*

BOMBARDIER BEETLES

The insects that manufacture their own bombs

Bombardier beetle, Australia.

Many insects protect themselves from attack by being distasteful or producing an unpleasant smell if threatened, but these remarkable beetles have developed a kind of chemical warfare: they shoot a offensive liquid at their tormentor.

Bombardier beetles (*Brachinus* species) belong to a group of ground beetles (family Carabidae) most of which are predatory. They are found worldwide and vary in length up to 5 cm (2 in). European species, such as *Brachinus crepitans,* occur in drier places, often in groups under stones, and are sometimes very common. Many species of *Brachinus* are carnivorous and feed on other insects but, although they are strongly built and have well-developed jaws, they still need protection against larger animals.

All the many different species of bombardier beetles have similar defence techniques. When they are attacked, they release chemicals into a specially strengthened chamber in the abdomen.

The chemicals are a hydroquinone and hydrogen peroxide with an enzyme acting as a catalyst. Decomposition of the hydrogen peroxide occurs, and this releases oxygen which produces pressure in the chamber. This pressure shoots out the corrosive hydroquinone with explosive force from a gland near the anus. All this happens in a fraction of a second.

In some beetles the spray is released with an audible pop. The bird or reptile that has seized the beetle quickly releases it or spits it out as it receives a sudden shot of the corrosive mixture. In many cases, the jet of liquid released turns into a fine gas cloud, which certainly has a deterring effect on aggressors. Bombardier beetles, with

their effective gas guns, should be almost invincible.

PROFILE

Size: *Up to 5 cm (2 in) long;* Brachinus crepitans, *7–10 mm (0.27–0.39 in),* B. explodens *4–6.5 mm (0.16–0.26 in).*

Distribution: *Worldwide;* B. crepitans *and* B. explodens *European.*

Habits/habitat: *Varied;* B.crepitans *in chalky areas.*

Diet: *Predatory on smaller insects.*

Notes: *There are in excess of 15,000 species of Carabid beetles in the world. Many of them are predatory on other insects in both larval and adult stages.*

SEXTON BEETLES

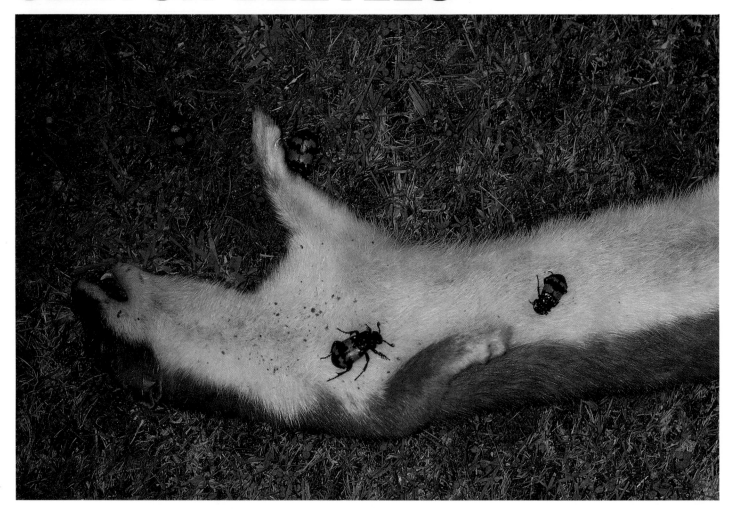

Nature's undertakers

By burying the carcases of small mammals, these beetles effectively 'clean up' the countryside.

Sexton beetles (*Necrophorus* species) belong to a group of insects popularly called 'burying beetles'. They are one of a large number of animals — birds, mammals and insects — which act as scavengers in Nature, clearing up the dead bodies of animals. While the vultures feed on the bodies where they find them and ants carry off parts of dead insects to their hills, the sexton beetles tidily bury the bodies of mice, shrews and voles.

Like flies, sexton beetles have a very acute sense of smell and soon detect the corpse. The first beetles to arrive may well drive off other beetles, although usually they work in pairs, one of each sex. Their aim is to bury the animal as quickly as possible to stop other carrion feeders from getting at it and to keep it

as food for their larvae. Using their jaws and spiny legs, they remove soil from beneath the corpse, scrabbling away until the body sinks down; they may even cut off the corpse's limbs if it makes it easier to bury.

Gradually, and with great determination, they get the corpse deeper and deeper into the ground while all the time they are compacting it. The whole process of burying and compacting the body may take three to ten hours depending on the type of soil. When the body is completely buried, the female excavates a brood chamber and there she lays her eggs. When these hatch, she feeds the larvae on regurgitated food until they are large enough to start feeding on the buried carrion for themselves. They pupate underground, even-

tually emerging as adult beetles to carry on the hunt for carrion for the next generation.

PROFILE

Size: N. vespillo *12–22 mm (0.47–0.79 in) long;* N. humator *15–28 mm (0.59–1.10 in) long;* N. germanicus *25–35 mm (0.98–1.38 in) long.*

Distribution: *Worldwide.*

Habitat: *Woodlands, pastures.*

Food: *Carrion.*

Notes: N. germanicus *has a black body and is often found on corpses of larger animals, while* N. vepilloides *and* N. vespillo *are red and black species, the latter seeking out smaller mammals such as mice.*

RED-BROWN CLICK BEETLE

The standing 'jack-knife' jumper which skips out of danger

If it falls on its back, this beetle is able to flick itself into the air, turn over and land on its feet.

The Red-brown Click Beetle (*Athous haemorrhoidalis*) is also known as 'Skip-jack' from its habit of suddenly jerking up into the air. There are many species of click beetles which are capable of jumping in this odd way. It is when they are doing this that they produce the click sound from which they get their name.

The ingenious mechanism which makes them 'jack-knife' and produces the click is a small peg on the underside of the thorax which, when the beetle arches itself, clicks suddenly into a cavity, causing the insect to thrust itself against the ground. Experiments on *Athous* have shown that, for the beetle to throw itself into the air from a prone position, it takes a lot of effort, as it has to overcome the pull of gravity. These experiments showed that the click mechanism can result in 400 times the force of gravity (400G) being exerted at the onset of the click. The result of this sudden action is to throw the insect up to 30 cm (1 ft) into the air.

Click beetles are common; there are over 10,000 species in the world, and they are a worldwide group. They are often associated with rotting wood or pasturelands. Their larvae, popularly known as wireworms, can destroy the roots of crops and at times are serious pests. These wireworms burrow into roots of cereals and other crops. Many of the adults feed on pollen, while others eat leaves.

Click beetles belong to one of the two firefly families (Elateridae), and a few of them have luminescent structures on the underside of the abdomen.

PROFILE

Size: *10–20 mm (0.39–0.79 in).*
Distribution: *Europe, including Britain.*
Habitat: *Pasture and grasslands.*
Diet: *Larvae (wireworms) feed on roots; adults feed on pollen and nectar.*
Notes: *Some click beetles spend up to 6 years as larvae in the soil.*

FIREFLIES

The insects that use a torch to find their mate

In the tropics whole trees are covered with these beetles, which at night start flashing in time with one another.

Fireflies (species of the genera *Photinus, Photurus* and *Pyrophorus*) and glow-worms (*Lampyris*) are rather nondescript beetles. Nondescript, that is, by day. As dusk falls, tiny spots of light flicker on like myriads of tiny candles. This synchronous flashing of fireflies is a spectacular sight.

Fireflies of the genus *Pyrophorus* occur in many parts of America, but are particularly common in the tropics and subtropics. The females make the brightest light, but in some species even the eggs and pupae may glow. The flickers of light are a means of communication — a sort of insect morse code. Each species has a specific signal: the flashes produced by one female will attract the male only of the same species. The light is produced by the actions of enzymes mixing with a chemical, which then glows. The whole insect does not glow; often it is just the tip of the underside of the abdomen.

Our light bulbs get hot to the touch, which means they are wasting energy. The firefly has a cold, very efficient type of illumination. It has been estimated that 40 *Pyrophorus* are equal to one candle power, while it would need 6000 glow-worms for the same amount of light.

The light is used mainly to bring the sexes together, but a few species have put it to more deadly use. Some female fireflies imitate the signals of the female of another firefly species to attract its males, which they then eat.

Firefly lanterns with huge numbers of fireflies kept in them have been used as light both in the Far East and in the West Indies.

PROFILE

Size: *Varies according to species: e.g. Pyrophorus divergens (USA) 25–45 mm (0.98–1.77 in); Photinus pyralis (USA) 12–15 mm (0.47–0.59 in); Photurus versicolor (USA) 11–15 mm (0.43–0.59 in).*

Distribution: *Worldwide.*

Habitat: *Meadowland, often in damper places; light woodlands and tropical forests.*

Diet: *Larvae prey on slugs and snails. Some of the adults feed on pollen but many do not feed in the adult stage, living instead on reserves built up during the larval stage.*

Notes: *Many of the females are wingless. Although the individual amounts of light produced are small, they are of a wavelength to which human eyes are particularly sensitive.*

GOLIATH BEETLE

A veritable tank of the insect world

There are many large beetles and other insects, like some of the stick-insects, which are much longer, but none has the bulk and weight of the Goliath Beetle, which is built like a tank.

The massive and ponderous Goliath Beetle (*Goliathus meleagris*) has the largest bulk of any living insect. The largest size an insect can achieve is limited by its physiology. Insects breathe by a series of spiracles in their side, with tracheoles running from these through which the air passes. The air is carried to the internal organs along the tracheoles, and it is the rate of diffusion of the air along these that ultimately limits the size of the insect. Every organ in the body must have a supply of oxygen and, although the tracheal system is wonderfully efficient for animals the size of insects, they cannot get any larger with this method of respiration.

Goliath Beetles live in the Congo rainforests, where they lay their eggs in rotting wood. The grubs feed in the rotting wood, eventually growing very large. In the Ituri region of the Congo forests, these grubs are sought after by the Pygmies, who consider them to be a delicacy.

The adult beetles climb trees and, although they usually move slowly, they are capable of surprisingly quick movements at times. Once the beetle gets its legs anchored around a small branch, the branch is more likely to break off than the beetle is to release hold, so tenacious is their grip.

Male Goliath Beetles have a horn at the front which they use in fighting. Each male tries to get the horn under its opponent and throw it on its back.

PROFILE

Length: *Up to 15 cm (5.9 in), female smaller than male.*
Weight: *70–100 g (2.5–3.5 oz).*
Distribution: *Africa.*
Habits/habitat: *Slow-moving tree-climbers in rainforests.*
Diet: *Adults feed on tree sap and fruit, larvae on rotting wood.*
Notes: *There are several large species of beetle related to this giant.*

JEWEL BEETLES

The Methuselahs of the insect world

The life history of these beetles can last for several decades, and one took over 40 years to develop from a larva into a full-grown adult — when it finally emerged from a piece of furniture.

We tend to think of insects as ephemeral creatures. What we overlook is that the adult, flying stage, usually more obvious, is only the end of a long sequence in the life history, from egg, through the immature feeding stages, to the final adult insect. Some butterflies take a year to complete their whole life cycle, while other insects take only a matter of weeks.

The prize for the longest life history in the insect world goes to the jewel beetles (family Bupestridae) whose larvae feed exclusively on wood, which has a low nutritive value. The eggs of these beetles are laid under the bark of the living tree, and the young larvae tunnel into the tree, feeding on the wood. If the tree is felled and then cut into planks, the tunnelling larvae which survive will continue living and feeding inside the plank, even though the wood itself is no longer living. If this wood is then exported and perhaps made into furniture, the larva, providing it is undamaged, goes on burrowing and feeding inside the piece of furniture. Many years later when the larva is fully grown, it will pupate, remaining for a while in the pupal stage before the adult beetle finally emerges — to the surprise and horror of the owner of the piece of furniture! Beetles have emerged from furniture over 20 years after it was made, but the longest-lived must be a jewel beetle which emerged over 40 years after the furniture was bought.

The European Jewel or Splendour Beetle (*Buprestis splendens*) is a metallic green. Some of its tropical relatives are used in jewellery, where their lustrous colours are popular.

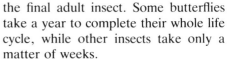

PROFILE

Size: *Length varies from 20 mm to 80 mm (0.79–3.15 in).*

Distribution: *Family worldwide;* Buprestis splendens *Europe.*

Habits/habitat: *Woodlands. Larvae burrow in living trees.*

Diet: *Usually wood, including decaying wood.*

Notes: *In some European countries, these beetles are protected by law against collection.*

FREGATE ISLAND BEETLE

A uniquely isolated beetle threatened by modern tourism

Found only on one small island, 2.5 square km (less than 1 square mile) in area, in the Indian Ocean, this strange beetle's once safe habitat is now in danger from tourist development.

When the original specimens of this beetle (*Polposipus herculeanus*) were sent to Europe, there was a mix-up in labelling them, and for years it was believed that the beetle lived in India or Mauritius. It is now known to be found only on Fregate Island in the Seychelles group.

This beetle is flightless and the elytra (hardened wing cases) are fused along the midline. The elytra are very tough, and the beetle has been described as 'almost uncrushable'. It is well adapted to drier conditions. Its fused elytra form a tough cover which helps to prevent moisture loss from the abdomen.

With little human activity on the island the beetle was considered to be fairly common in 1970. Recently there has been rather more human activity,

and Fregate Island, which could previously be reached only by a long boat trip from the main Seychelles islands, now has a small airstrip. This has resulted in more visitors, and these are already threatening the habitat of this unique beetle. If it dies out there is no question of reintroducing specimens from elsewhere; there is just nothing quite like this species and even its relationships are uncertain. Why it has evolved apparently in isolation is a mystery.

The larva is believed to feed under the bark of a tree, *Pterocarpus indicus*, which was introduced to Fregate Island in the 19th century so that the beetle's original host on the island is not known. The larvae probably eat decaying wood, while the adults may also feed on

decaying wood or on the fungi associated with it.

PROFILE

Size: *25–30 mm (0.98–1.18 in).*
Distribution: *Fregate Island, Seychelles, Indian Ocean.*
Habits/habitat: *Flightless. Lives under bark of* Pterocarpus indicus *tree.*
Diet: *Larvae probably eat rotting wood; adult food unknown, possibly rotting wood or fungus.*
Notes: *There seems little doubt that if the island is developed more, or predators, such as rats, are accidentally introduced, this beetle will become extinct.*

MONARCH

PROFILE

Size: *Wingspan 75–100 mm (3.0–3.9 in).*

Distribution: *North America, including Canada; South America, roughly north of the River Amazon; many Pacific islands, New Zealand, eastern Australia.*

Habits/habitat: *Migratory; in North America migrates to California and Mexico to spend the winter.*

Diet: *Caterpillars feed on milkweed (Asclepia), adults feed freely on nectar.*

Notes: *Colonies of Monarchs are now established in Madeira and the Canary Islands. Those Monarchs which occur in Europe have been blown off course during migration.*

The world's most poisonous butterfly

This is a magnificent butterfly as it flaps along, but appearances are deceptive, for it is poison on the wing.

A large, relatively slow-flying butterfly is an obvious target for a hungry bird, and yet the Monarch or Milkweed Butterfly (*Danaus plezippus*), which flaps along conspicuously, is left alone. It makes no attempt to hide itself — in fact it positively advertises itself! Even its large juicy caterpillar is conspicuous, but is not molested by most predators. The secret of its success is its poisonous flesh. If a bird pecks the butterfly or caterpillar, it soon realises that it is distasteful; if it swallowed the caterpillar, or the butterfly, it would soon be violently sick. The bird would not touch another like it, soon learning that these conspicuous creatures are not for eating.

The poisons in the insect are derived from the plants on which the caterpillars feed. These are species of milkweed (Asclepiadaceae), which are themselves poisonous to most animals, but not to the caterpillars of the Monarch! Monarchs are able to render the cardenolides in the plant harmless to themselves and eat the leaves without any ill effect. The poisons, however, are still toxic to anything that eats the caterpil-

lar. This poison is passed on by the caterpillar through the pupa to the adult; although the adult feeds on nectar, it is still protected by the poisons from the plant on which the caterpillar fed.

Monarchs are famous for their remarkable migration across North Amer-

ica to California and Mexico, where they spend the winter. In the following spring they fly back north, breeding on the way, and a new generation flies as far north as Canada. In most years one or two Monarchs are even seen in Europe, and in some years quite a number get there.

QUEEN ALEXANDRA BIRDWING BUTTERFLY

The giant butterfly that is flown like a kite

Small children in New Guinea tether living birdwing butterflies with strands of plant fibre and fly them like toy kites.

There are many beautiful butterflies, but few are more spectacular in size and colours than birdwing butterflies. One of the most colourful of these is the gleaming male of the Queen Alexandra's Birdwing (*Ornithoptera alexandrae*). The female is rather drab by comparison. Birdwing butterflies are found throughout Malaysia, Indonesia, Papua and into northern Australia. They are the most highly prized butterflies for collectors. In the early days collectors hunted birdwings with guns! They used dust shot to bring them down, and the first known specimens of Queen Alexandra's Birdwing were captured in this way. Their value is clearly reflected in their sale price. A single birdwing butterfly was sold at auction in 1966 in Paris for over 10,000 francs.

The Queen Alexandra's Birdwing is now rare in New Guinea. Since 1966, the species has been protected by law and it is illegal to collect it without a permit, but unfortunately that has not prevented destruction of its habitat, the forests, which are being cut down as land is needed for farming.

An attempt is being made to protect the birdwing butterflies, while also satisfying the collectors and providing an income for the local farmers. The farmers are being encouraged to plant the foodplant of the birdwing and to rear the butterfly. In this way, the farmer gets an income from 'ranching' the butterflies, pressure is taken off the wild population, and the collectors get their specimens. Through the encouragement of ranching, the butterflies themselves

are awarded a degree of protection. This is a very enlightened practical approach to the conservation of these beautiful butterflies.

PROFILE

Size: *Wingspan 170–280mm (6.7–11.0 in).*
Distribution: *New Guinea.*
Habits/habitat: *Rainforest edges. Generally flies 15–30 m (40–80 ft) above the ground.*
Diet: *Caterpillars feed on* Aristolochiap *plants, adults feed on nectar.*
Notes: *Now protected by law in New Guinea, and it is illegal to trade in specimens without a permit from the country of origin.*

AFRICAN MIGRANT BUTTERFLY

The migration that seems to go on forever

A record fly-past by a vast migrating swarm of this species lasted three months.

Every year there are migrations by the appropriately named African Migrant Butterfly (*Catopsilia florella*), in some years on an enormous scale, although little is known of what triggers the increased numbers of this species. Bird migration is a well-known phenomenon; it is only relatively recently that the idea that insects are also capable of migration was accepted.

Even the common Large White Butterfly (*Pieris brassicae*) of Europe migrates, sometimes in large numbers: it crosses the English Channel, and one swarm was so large that as it crossed a cricket pitch it stopped the game. Many of Europe's butterflies migrate up from the warmer south in spring, while the Monarch Butterfly of America is world-famous for its movements. The record must, however, go to the African Migrant. This was watched by a famous entomologist, who said that the butterflies continued in a steady stream past where he was living: at times there were huge swarms, while at others a steady stream of butterflies but, on the whole, continuous over a three-month period.

Butterflies and other insects can swarm in huge numbers. A common African forest butterfly becomes so numerous in roads through the forest that it has stopped cars. The butterflies get caught on car radiators and the engines boil!

Butterfly (and other insect) migration is a one-way trip. In Europe the migrants which fly up from the south in spring and summer do not fly back in the autumn, and most cannot survive the northern winter. There is some evidence for a small southward migration of some butterflies in autumn.

PROFILE

Size: *Wingspan 50–65mm (2.0–2.6 in).*

Distribution: *Africa, Egypt, India, China, Canary Islands.*

Habitat: *Lives in open bush country, but occurs anywhere within its range on migration.*

Diet: *Caterpillar feeds on* Cassia *(Leguminosae).*

Notes: *Several different colour forms of this species have been described, the commonest being greenish-tinged white (males) and yellowish (females).*

DEATH'S HEAD HAWK MOTH

The world's fastest-flying insect

Many normally slow insects can put on a burst of speed if threatened, but hawk moths have been credited with speeds of nearly 54 km/h (34 mph).

The Death's Head Hawk Moth (*Acherontia atropos*) is found in Europe, Africa and North Asia. Its common name comes from the skull-like pattern on the top of the thorax. This is a large hawk moth, with a powerful flight. It is a migrant to northern Europe, including Britain, but generally does not survive the winter there, fresh migrants coming north each spring. The caterpillar, which can reach a length of 15 cm (6 in), feeds on solanaceous plants including potato. It is generally not abundant in northern Europe, but it sometimes becomes common in Central Europe and can be a pest on potatoes.

Recent studies on the aerodynamics of this moth's flight have shown that it is not a simple up-and-down beat of the wings but a much more complicated process. It involves at least four different wing movements which include a twisting motion of the wings. All these happen too rapidly for the eye to see, but have been detected by high-speed photography. The net result is that the wing obtains the maximum amount of uplift in all its movements.

The Death's Head flies at night during warmer weather, feeding not on nectar like many other hawk moths but on the sap of trees and on honey in bees' nests. It was once a pest (it was formerly known as 'Bee Tyger'), but the hives are now designed to keep it out.

The Death's Head can expel air from its body sharply, producing a mouse-like squeak. This combined with the skull motif on the thorax has made people regard it, quite unjustifiably, as harmful.

PROFILE

Size: *Wingspan 102–140mm (4.0–5.5 in)*.

Distribution: *Europe, Asia, Africa.*

Habits/habitat: *Widespread, sometimes moving in large numbers from North Africa to Europe; migrant to northern Europe, including Britain.*

Diet: *Larvae feed on potato (Solanum), tea-tree (Lycium), deadly nightshade (Atropa) and other solanaceous plants. Adults feed on honey in bees' nests.*

Notes: *Pupa will not hatch without a certain amount of warmth. Huge caterpillars, up to 15 cm (6 in) long, have a large spine on the tail and can be found in potato fields.*

INDIAN MOON MOTH

PROFILE

Size: *Wingspan 80–100 mm (3.1– 3.9 in).*
Distribution: *India, China, Malaysia, Indonesia, Sri Lanka.*
Habitat: *Forests.*
Diet: *Caterpillar feeds on various shrubs, such as species of* Prunus, Malus *and* Pyrus.
Notes: *This is one of the most popular insects for amateurs to breed in captivity, and one of the most attractive.*

The most acute sense of smell in Nature

To detect its mate in the dark, the male Indian Moon Moth has developed such an acute sense of smell that it can detect the scent of a female 5 km (over 3 miles) away.

The Indian Moon Moth (*Actias selene*) is one of many moths which have an acute sense of smell. Smell is a means of communication. Although Man certainly has a sense of smell, even if relatively poorly developed, he does not use this so much as other animals. Imagine how important the sense of smell must be if you are a nocturnal animal.

The male Indian Moon Moth has large antennae which are clearly 'feathery'. On each side of the antennae there are large graduated branches, each covered with long hairs. This greatly increases the surface area over which chemical odours can be detected by minute and sensitive scent-detectors. Moon moths can detect the scent of a female about 5 km (over 3 miles) away, but accurate tests on distance are difficult. The chemoreceptors on the antennae are so sensitive that they can detect a single molecule of the scent.

Detection of a smell is not enough; it is important for the moth to find the

female producing it. The male *Actias* can determine the strength of a scent, and, as it increases, move along in the direction of the source. We could certainly follow a smell, perhaps the smell of our lunch, from, say, the garden into the house if the wind was in the right direction! Moths have to be able to

follow the trail of scent through woodland, ignoring all the other scents present, and to follow it around obstacles, in spite of dispersal of the scent in the air. It is probably true to say that the bloodhound is an amateur scent detector when compared with the male Indian Moon Moth seeking its mate.

POLYPHEMUS MOTH

The most prodigious eater in Nature

The caterpillars of this common North American moth eat so much that they can increase their weight by over 80,000 times in just two days.

Although we think first of the locusts as destroyers of vegetation, caterpillars of different species of moths are equally destructive when abundant. Fortunately they do not have the same swarming habits as locusts, but they do eat more food in relation to their body weight than locusts.

The newly hatched caterpillars of the Polyphemus Moth (*Antheraea polyphemus*) are tiny. They have been weighed, and then a check was kept on their weight as they carried on feeding. They increased their initial body weight over a 48-hour period by over 80,000 times. This must be the all-time record for weight increase!

Caterpillars are simply feeding tubes with strong jaws to assist in this one process; their only other function in life is to survive! What a good thing it is that insects are relatively small creatures. Since there may be many caterpillars feeding on one tree, however, they will quickly defoliate it.

The Polyphemus Moth is widespread in North America. In the northern part of its range there is one brood a year, but in the southern part two broods. Many of the oriental species related to the Polyphemus Moth are important for their silk. This is spun as a cocoon by the caterpillar when it pupates, and it is this silk that is unwound and then spun into silk thread. It is often known as wild silk, to distinguish it from the silk produced by the artificially reared silk moths which belong to a related family (Bombycidae).

PROFILE

Size: *Wingspan 100–128 mm (3.9–5.0 in).*
Distribution: *North America.*
Habits: *Nocturnal.*
Diet: *Caterpillar feeds on a wide variety of broadleaved trees.*
Notes: *Most of the close relatives of this species are found in the Orient, where they have been reared for centuries for their silk.*

RED ANT

Pest-controller extraordinaire

Protected by law, the Red Ant is one of the best insurances against pest problems in pine woods.

The Red Ant (*Formica rufa*) is common in pine woods in Europe. It is sometimes called a fire ant from the burning sensation caused when it bites or squirts an acid on to the skin. It is not related to true fire ants, whose sting is very much more painful. In parts of Europe there are laws protecting its nests from destruction; Germany, for example, has had such laws since 1880. A large Red Ant nest may remove 100,000 insects each day from the surrounding trees, and is particularly useful in destroying some of the caterpillar pests of pines. These ants are particularly attracted to aphids or greenfly, which produce a sweet secretion eaten by the ants.

The nests are made of pine needles and bits of plant and may be 30 m (100 ft) in diameter and 1–2 m (3–6.5 ft) high. They have many underground passages and often covered trackways leading to nearby trees. These enable the foraging ants to reach the trees out of sight of predators.

The ants' nest is very highly organised, with workers, queens and males forming a colony which may reach 100,000 individuals, most of them worker ants. Unlike many ants, Red Ants often have several queens in a colony. The eggs are tended by the workers, and the larvae, when they pupate, are wrapped in a papery cocoon (the 'ant-eggs' of fishkeepers).

Red Ants do not have a sting like some species of ants, but they have powerful jaws and a special gland on the abdomen which produces formic acid. They can forcefully eject this acid up to 30 cm (1 ft), and will use it to deter anything coming near them.

PROFILE

Size: *Queens and males 9–10 mm (0.39 in), workers 5–7 mm (0.2–0.27 in).*
Distribution: *Europe and Asia.*
Habitat: *Coniferous woods.*
Diet: *Insects and other small invertebrates.*
Notes: *On a sunny day in May or June swarms of males and females emerge from the nests like a plume of smoke. Mating takes place between ants from different nests.*

HONEY ANTS

A gastronomic delicacy

The honey provided by this strange source comes in tiny 'bottles' and is eagerly sought after in some parts of the world.

There are a number of species of honey ants belonging to different genera in different parts of the world. *Myrmecocystis* ants (shown here) are found in southern United States and Mexico; ants of the genera *Leptomyrmex, Melophorus* and *Camponotus* are found in Australia and New Guinea. These ants live in colonies. The worker ants forage for food while the queen ant lives in the nest, laying eggs; the eggs hatch into larvae which the workers rear.

At first sight their nest is like that of most other ants found commonly all over the world, but honey ants have a strange method of food storage. The workers collect honeydew from aphids (greenfly) and sap exuding from plants, and bring it home to their nest. This liquid is then fed to particular individuals in the nest. As these particular ants are fed more of the honeydew, instead of excreting the excess they store it in their abdomen. The abdomen swells up and stretches, becoming golden-yellow with the store of honey. These living 'honeypots' cannot move and usually attach themselves to the roof of the nest, hanging down like golden pendants.

As food is needed, particularly if it becomes short outside the nest, the honeypots regurgitate their stored honey, drop by drop, to the workers in the nest. No one knows what happens to these remarkable honeypots once they are emptied—whether the same honeypots are used again or whether they die off.

The nests are raided by Man for these tiny honeypots, which are regarded as a great treat. In Mexico they are sold as a special delicacy.

PROFILE

Size: *Up to 10 mm (0.39 in).*
Distribution: *America, Africa, Australia.*
Habitat: *Mostly dry areas and semi-deserts.*
Diet: *Plants and small insects, but some are fed by the worker ants on liquid honeydew from aphids or tree sap.*
Notes: *Also known as desert or honeypot ants. When consumed as a delicacy, the abdomens of the swollen honeypots are nipped off and eaten.*

ARMY ANTS

Vermin-exterminator at your service

An effective way of getting rid of household pests in the tropics is to let the army ants march through the house.

There are many species of ants called army ants, driver ants or legionary ants, from their habit of moving around in columns. The South American species of *Eciton,* illustrated here, and the African *Dorylus* are both equally feared.

Army ants, like other ants, are organised into workers, soldiers, males and females (generally called queens). They move restlessly around in a column, flanked by the large-jawed soldiers. This column, up to 100 m (110 yds) long and 1–2 m (3–6.5 ft) wide, moves in a seething mass along the floor of the forest or savanna, attacking and eating anything too slow to get out of the way. This includes not only insects but lizards and snakes — and there are many horror stories of tethered horses being reduced to skeletons. There is no doubt they would destroy any mammal that was unable to get out of the way. They have a ferocious bite and swarm over their victim, tearing at the flesh. Male driver ants in Africa are called 'sausage flies'; they are large, with huge jaws and a fat, sausage-shaped abdomen.

Every three or four weeks the army ant queen produces a large number of eggs and the column stops. The worker ants often hook their legs together to form a rough brood chamber to protect the queen and the eggs. When the eggs hatch some of the workers go in search of food for the larvae, while others carry the larvae in their jaws as the column moves off. If they come to a hut they will swarm through it, clearing out all the cockroaches and other household pests: a good method of household pest control if you have a strong nerve and keep out of the way!

PROFILE

Size: *25 mm (1 in), males and queens larger.*
Distribution: *Genus* Dorylus, *often called driver ants, Africa; Genus* Eciton, *South America.*
Diet: *Usually insects, but will attack and eat any animal it can catch.*
Habits: *Sociable, moves almost continuously in swarms.*
Notes: *It is said that if army ants meet a fire they will swarm into it and extinguish it with their bodies, so that the rest of the column can march safely on.*

CAMEL OR SUN SPIDERS

The high-speed hairy desert hunters

Looking like big hairy spiders, these large-jawed arachnids move rapidly over arid ground in search of prey and are described as 'like yellow thistledown blowing in the wind'.

For an animal which is little known to most zoologists it is surprising to find so many popular names for the Solifugida (sometimes spelt Solpugida).

Often called camel or sun spiders, solifugids are typical of desert areas. They are well adapted to the drier parts and do not occur in the oases. They are mostly nocturnal and feed on insects, but will eat lizards, small mammals and birds. They are considered to have the strongest 'jaws' (called chelicerae in arachnids) in relation to their size of any animal. These 'jaws' have small projecting growths which act like pincers. When hunting, camel spiders use their long legs to move rapidly in search of their prey. They have been estimated to move at speeds of 16 km/h (10 mph), stopping suddenly, apparently listening for or—more likely—scenting their prey, before dashing off again at high speed.

Solifugids, although they may look like spiders, actually belong to a different group of animals. They have four pairs of walking legs and a pair of pincer-like chelicerae with which they seize their prey.

There are many travellers' tales about these rather terrifying-looking animals, whose span across the legs can reach 15 cm (6 in). They are not dangerous to Man, although they can give a nasty bite. Breathing tubes or trachea carry the air inside the body; in this, camel spiders are similar to insects, and different from most spiders (which have a different respiratory technique using 'lung-books').

PROFILE

Size: *15–70 mm (0.15–2.76 in), but up to 15 cm (6 in) span across outstretched legs.*

Distribution: *Africa, Orient, America; in Europe only in the south of Spain. Absent from Australia.*

Habits/habitat: *Deserts and very arid areas. Very active, usually nocturnal.*

Diet: *Insects, lizards, small birds and mammals.*

Notes: *There are over 800 species of solifugids in deserts in different parts of the world. They are probably the swiftest terrestrial invertebrates.*

BLACK WIDOW

The spider whose very name creates fear in man

There are a number of spiders called 'black widows', but this American species is the most widespread and feared of the group. The female is the killer, whereas the smaller male cannot inject sufficient venom to kill humans.

Fortunately for us, the Black Widow (*Latrodectus mactans*) is not an aggressive species. In fact, quite the reverse — it tries to avoid Man. The habits of this spider, which tends to keep out of the light, mean that when it gets into houses or sheds it is hidden from us. We come across it unexpectedly and thus it tends to bite us out of fear of being attacked.

The venom injected by the bite of the spider is a neurotoxin. It is said to be 15 times more toxic than that of the rattlesnake in the USA. The bite itself produces extreme pain, and then the toxin spreads around the body, causing muscular contraction, nausea and, if untreated, death. Recent developments of antitoxins to the Black Widow bite will undoubtedly save lives.

These spiders usually live in meadows and pastureland and are not dependent in any way on human activities. In the wild they capture other insects, which they paralyse with their venom before sucking the body fluids out. It is difficult to see why this spider has developed such a toxic venom, which is far greater than is needed for its usual prey or most defensive purposes.

When mating, the smaller male spider bears gifts of food for the female, partly to persuade her not to eat him. If he is not quick enough at moving away after mating, then he will certainly be eaten. Like many other spiders, the Black Widows cause their webs to vibrate rapidly to make themselves more difficult to see in the centre of the pulsating web.

The eggs are generally placed inside a cocoon spun by the female spider.

PROFILE

Size: *25 mm (0.98 in) span across legs, with the largest up to 60 mm (2.36 in) across, and a body 15 mm (0.59 in) long.*

Distribution: Latrodectus mactans *restricted to America. Other species of* Latrodectus *widespread in the warmer parts, Orient, Mediterranean countries, South Africa, Australia.*

Habitat: *Meadowland, pastures.*

Diet: *Insects, captured in its untidy web.*

Notes: *Black Widows have been accidentally introduced to a number of countries by cargo ships; no doubt some get mixed with luggage at airports and may be even more widely transported by plane.*

NEPHILA SPIDERS

Spinners of fishing nets and smothering caps

The webs of these spiders are so strong that they are used not only as fishing nets, but also to suffocate adulterous women.

The spiders of the family Araneidae include the familiar orb-web spiders of the temperate zone as well as the larger species of *Nephila* from the tropics. There are over 60 species of *Nephila* and they are found in several continents. Generally the females are large, web-spinning spiders, while the males are much smaller, frequently living in the same web as the female; in some species, the males are so much smaller than the females that when first collected they were thought to be different species.

We tend to think of spiders' webs as delicate silken threads of gossamer, floating on the autumn air, but species of tropical *Nephila* spin a silk which has tremendous elasticity and the tensile strength of steel. Although they trap mostly insects, they will also catch small birds. The spider poisons its prey with a bite and then drains the fluids from the victim's body. The guy-lines for the webs of these large spiders may be 6 m (19.7 ft) long while the web may be 2 m (6.6 ft) in diameter. There are many stories of horseriders losing their hats when they hit one of these webs, and even quite large birds can get tangled up in the threads.

The strength of the threads is put to good — and to rather horrific — uses. The webs are collected and twisted together between the ends of sticks to make a scoop-like fishing net; this is strong enough even for large fish, which are hurled out of the water by the fisherman. In some parts of the Pacific the webs are used as a punishment: they are forced over the heads of women accused of adultery, with the effect of suffocating the hapless victim.

Nephila claviceps

PROFILE

Size: Nephila maculata: *female, body 5 cm (2 in), span across legs 16 cm (6.3 in); male, body 4 mm (0.16 in).*

Distribution: *Most warmer parts of world, with large species in Australia and the Oriental region.*

Habitat: *Mostly forests.*

Diet: *Mostly insects, but larger species will catch small birds.*

Notes: *Some of the extreme contrasts are found between male and female* Nephila *in which the female may be 1000 times the bulk of the male.*

ACKNOWLEDGMENTS

ILLUSTRATION CREDITS

Agence Nature
J.-P. Ferrero 16 83 107 170 177
J. Gohier 54 80
Reille 182
Delacour 192
Chaumeton-Hellio 41 (lower)
Chaumeton-Boris 157
Chaumeton-Lanceau 156
H. Chaumeton 127 (lower)
 140 141 143 (lower) 152 161 176
 178 (upper) 228 (upper)
Lanceau 110 181 (lower)
Other Agence Nature photos 9 95 158

G. Andersson 40

Ardea
H. & J. Beste 12 14 99 120 129
J.-P. Ferrero 15 27
I. R. Beames 19 48 (upper) 64 128
 228 (lower)
A. Warren 22
J. L. Mason 23 (upper) 114 (lower)
 207 218 227
K. W. Fink 8 (upper) 28 (lower) 43
 46 102 (upper) 115 (lower)
A. Greensmith 30
P. Steyn 32 117 122 233
F. Gohier 34 49 62 63 (lower) 100
 (upper) 167 (upper) 181 (upper)
J. Swedberg 35
P. Morris 37 (upper) 37 (lower) 50 60
 69 101 105 153 162 169 (upper)
 178 (lower) 183 193 (upper)
J. Van Gruisen 48 (lower) 63 (upper)
Å. Lindau 65 (lower)
M. D. England 66 112
C. Haagner 70 (upper)
S. Meyers 72
M. Krishnan 73 (lower)
D. Hudden 84
A. Fatras 87 195 (upper)
R. Bunge 91
S. Roberts 109
C. & J. Knights 110
A. D. Trounson & M. C. Clampett 121
J. S. Dunning 125
W. Weisser 126
R. & V. Taylor 136 163
T. Willock 179 (lower)
A. Weaving 185 (lower)
B. Gibbons 219
Other Ardea photos: 26 (upper)
 26 (lower) 68 73 (upper) 96 104

Bild & Form
L. Molin 10 12 131 133 151 (upper)
 161 200 (lower) 201

S. C. Bisserot 222

British Antartic Survey 56

Bruce Coleman Inc. New York
L. Lee Rue III 10 (upper) 10 (lower)
D. R. Kuhn 18
L. Riley 21 119
L. Ditto 23 31
J. Wormer 36
J. & D. Bartlett 41 (upper) 88 (lower)
G. R. Zahm 113
J. Foott 123

R. E. Gossington 144
A. Blank 193
P. A. Betow 196
J. C. Taylor 217

Bruce Coleman Ltd, London
P. Ward 20
N. R. Lightfoot 38 (upper)
W. Lankinen 38 (lower)
G. Ziesler 53
L. Lee Rue III 65 (upper)
P. Gilligan 77
P. Kahl 106
K. Taylor 116
J. Burton 124 143 (upper)
A. Power 139 (upper)
U. Hirsch 145
J. Foott 151
D. Hughes 167 (lower)
A. J. Mobbs 194
U. Woy 195 (lower)
J. Fennell 197
M. Fogden 205
J. M. Burnley 214
H. Rivarda 220

P. Chapman 114 (upper)

Frank Lane Picture Library
G. Moon 108

Guinness Books
Matthew Hillier 9 13 52 59 66 74-75
 83 98 115 (upper) 127 (upper) 190
Other Guinness photos 42 (lower) 67

Heather Angel Biofotos 131

Jacana
Hladik 25
J.-P. Varin 38 231
Ziesler 92
Maes 118
Vial 173
Other Jacana photos 19 81

Natural History Museum, Los Angeles
 County
J. A. Seigel 134

Natural Science Photos
J. Hobday 29 94 211 (upper)
G. Kinns 45
C. A. Walker 57 93
R. Kemp 58 97 (lower)
C. Watson 70 (lower)
H. Axell 90 169 (lower) 172
F. Greenaway 105 (lower)
C. Williams 175 208 229
P. Boston 184 (upper) 221
C. Mattison 186 198 (lower)
C. Banks 189
D. Brown 191
J. A. Grant 211 (lower) 234
M. Chinery 230
P. H. Ward 213 224 (lower)
P. H. & S. L. Ward 188 224 (upper)
 226 235
Other Natural Science Photos photos 89
 97 212 (lower)

Natureza
L. Löfgren 88 (upper) 94 (upper) 100
 (lower)

Naturfotografernas Bildbyrå
T. Holm 139 (upper)

Oxford Scientific Films
M. Black 199
R. Williams 204
J. A. L. Cooke 232 (upper) 232 (lower)

Klas Paysan 200 (upper)

Photo Research Inc.
T. McHugh 150
Other Photo Research photos 164

J. Pope 223

Sea Mammals Research Unit
A. R. Martin 78 (upper)

Seaphot Ltd.
R. Matthews 42
E. Neal 47
D. Rootes 55 (upper) 55 (lower)
K. Scholey 71
Menuhin 75 155 (upper)
R. Mear 85
J. Hector 86 (upper) 86 (lower)
J. Scott 103
H. Voigtman 132
C. Roessler 135 (upper)
F. Schulke 135 (lower)
K. Lucas 138 142 147 155 (lower) 168
 171 184
R. Salm 146 149 159 (lower)
P. David 148
G. Douwma 159 (upper)
B. Wood 165
C. Read 203
J. & G. Lythgoe 209

Ian F. Spellerberg 179 (upper)

Tony Stone Associates 8 17 44 51 76
 79 174 212

University of Gothenburg
C. Andrén & G. Nilsson 180 187

U. S. Navy, Naval Ocean System Center
 137

G. L. Wood 210

Worldwide Butterflies
R. Godder 225

WWF Photolibrary
J. J. Petter 24
P. K. Andersson 59

INDEX